The Gigantic Book of Teachers' Wisdom

EDITED AND INTRODUCED BY ERIN GRUWELL

FOREWORD BY FRANK McCOURT

Skyhorse Publishing

www.skyhorsepublishing.com

Library of Congress Cataloging-in-Publication Data
The gigantic book of teachers' wisdom / edited and Introduced by Erin
Gruwell ; foreword by Frank McCourt.
    p. cm.
 ISBN-13: 978-1-60239-177-2 (hardcover : alk. paper)
 ISBN-10: 1-60239-177-7 (hardcover : alk. paper)
 1. Education—Quotations, maxims, etc. 2. Teaching—Quotations,
maxims,
etc. I. Gruwell, Erin.

PN6084.E38G544 2007
370—dc22
                                    2007026780
Printed in the United States of America

With special thanks to Marissa Angeletti, Stephanie Gomory, Benjamin
Korman, and Junessa Viloria.

Contents

FOREWORD

Frank McCourt

Teaching, as I've written elsewhere, is the downstairs maid of the professions. Teachers are not consulted when big decisions are being made about education. The decisions are made by politicians—for they know what is good for us. Frequently, there are panel discussions on education on television. There are politicians, people from think tanks, professors of education, bureaucrats. No teachers.

This is when I want to reach for a gun—but I don't, of course. I have to resort to my mouth. I try to be patient while I explain to the rich man that the teacher starting salary in this country is barely above poverty level. He looks doubtful when I ask him if he could support a wife and, at least, one child on a salary way under forty thousand dollars a year.

I'm not too agile when discussing the status of teachers in this country. I know they are underpaid. I know there is little respect for them despite the wonderful things said about them in this terrific book, *The Gigantic Book of Teachers' Wisdom*.

When I talked with the rich man, I hadn't yet read *The Gigantic Book*—if "read" is the right word for what you do with this book. You're not going to sit in your easy chair and actually read it. It's a book for dipping into, a bowl of peanuts (bet you can't read just one!), a literary antipasto. Maybe, when this book is published, I'll send the rich man a copy. He will find a few negative comments about teachers, but they're more than balanced by the high praise of teachers by perceptive men and women down the ages.

Here is God's plenty. Between the opening entry, "Teaching is truth mediated by personality," to the closing "Whatever you are, be a good one," there is a word hoard the likes of which you rarely see between the covers of a book.

I don't know what Phyllis Brooks (1915–1995) means by that opening statement, nor do I know whom she was. The book says she was an actress, and I wonder how she achieved pride of place. It just goes to show that everyone has something to say about teachers and teaching.

This last entry about being a "good one" is attributed to Abraham Lincoln, but it doesn't sound like him. Maybe he was depressed at the time. Maybe the war was going against him. Maybe the remark was made to someone aching for a platitude.

I would direct the rich man to fields of gold where there are nuggets of wisdom. Tolerate me for a moment while I offer choice morsels:

"Everyone who is incapable of learning has taken to teaching." Oscar Wilde (1854–1900).

I am sorry to inform you that Oscar, like myself, was an Irishman, of the Island of Saints and Scholars, and that smartass remark goes hand in hand with another smartass remark by George Bernard Shaw: "Those who can, do; those who can't, teach."

Oscar and George were brilliant men with encyclopedic minds, but about teaching they knew bupkes. (That's a Yiddish word for bugger all.)

But don't worry: a few pages later, Shaw redeems himself. He says, "To me the sole hope of human salvation lies in teaching." Right on, Mr. Shaw, and would you pass the word to Oscar, wherever you are, the two of you exhausting the angels with your witty discourse, the two of you knowing full well you were teachers yourselves.

Jump ahead a few years and you find Lee Iacocca urging everyone to "Apply yourself. Get all the education you can, but then, by God, do something. Don't just stand there, make it happen."

A generation later comes this bullet of common sense from P. J. O'Rourke: "Anyway, no drug, not even alcohol, causes the fundamental ills of society. If we're looking for the source of our troubles, we shouldn't test people for drugs, we should test them for stupidity, ignorance, greed, and love of power."

Back to the world of teaching. Here is Ann Richards (1933–2006), former governor of Texas: "Teaching was the hardest work I had ever done, and it remains the hardest work I have done to date."

Here is one I love from Ignacio Estrada: "If a child can't learn the way we teach, maybe we should teach the way they learn." I don't know who Ignacio Estrada is, but wherever he is I want to blow kisses and pin medals to his wise chest, for his comment sums it up for me.

If only the politicians and the rich would pay attention to Ignacio and teachers would teach the way he suggests. If only the politicians would get off that broken nag called No Child Left Behind and stop testing our children till they're numb and senseless and incapable of even thinking.

Listen to Robert Hutchins (1899–1977): "It must be remembered that the purpose of education is not to fill the minds of students with facts . . . it is to teach them to think, if that is possible, and always to think of themselves."

Mr. Hutchins, Mr. Hutchins, stay where you are. You'd be appalled at what is happening in our schools. We are not encouraging thinking. We are killing young minds. We are engaged in some strange activity called "setting standards." We are sucking the dream out of the classroom. Our teachers are on edge, looking over their shoulders, worried their students won't score high on those insane tests.

The rich man sitting next to me at the party assures me that the salaries of New York teachers are more than adequate. He tells me also how lucky teachers are that they get all that time off. They get all the holidays, he tells me, and they get those long summers. Also, they don't work a full day like other "professionals."

Teachers? When did you last see a teacher on any kind of talk show?

The Gigantic Book of Teacher's Wisdom will, maybe, call attention to the "real" world of teaching. Take your time with it. Keep it by your bed. It wouldn't hurt to read a few lines to your children at bedtime. They might grow up and become teachers.

And wouldn't that rock the country!

Frank McCourt
June 2007

INTRODUCTION

Erin Gruwell

As educators, we share one common goal—to see the growth and progress of our students. But one thing is for sure—there is no greater feeling than to see a student "get it." You know what that's like. It's when things "click" in a young mind. It's when the proverbial lightbulb goes on. It's when you see eyes light up in revelry. It's when you see a student accomplish what he or she once thought was impossible. There's nothing better. It is for this reason that we show up to work each day.

One of the greatest lessons I learned from the Freedom Writers was that in order to be a good teacher, I had to be an even better student. The Freedom Writers had what I like to call a "PhD of the Streets," and I quickly found I had 150 teachers who would help me "get it" on a daily basis! My students became savvy teachers and amazed me each and every day with their personal insight and knowledge.

My students taught me a simple lesson: to teach to a student, and not to a test. They taught me to be open to new theories, practices, and modes of thinking, because each student learns in a different way. Not all students pick up the same lessons at the same speed, learn through the same modalities, or grasp ideas by the same means and methods. What works for one may not work for another. Learning is a process.

To help me in the learning process, I found the usage of quotations in my classroom an extremely powerful tool. Not only were they lessons on diversity of opinion, but they also taught about the world as a whole. Quotations became a vehicle that made it easy to transport a wealth of knowledge to the Freedom Writers. For example, when we met the Holocaust survivor Renée Firestone, she poignantly told my students, "Evil prevails when good people do nothing." We posted Renée's quotation on the chalkboard, and it became a rallying cry for my students. They decided that they would no longer stand idly by and watch injustice unfurl. In a similar vein, they continued to find quotations that encouraged them to become social activists, such as Gandhi's "Be the change you want to see in the world." With the inspiration of such powerful quotations, they were, and continue to be, the most powerful young activists I have ever known.

People interpret quotations differently, but we know that one jewel or that one glimmer of hope when we see it. It stares us straight in the face. Becoming better human beings on all levels was my students' goal, and opening their eyes to leading a more positive way of life was mine. So using powerful quotations from the young diarist Anne Frank, who wrote, "In spite of everything, I truly believe that people are good at heart," became another teachable moment.

My students, like so many others, needed a few words of encouragement and relevance when times got rough to keep them focused on what truly mattered—the success and personal growth of their own lives. Soon my students were incorporating quotations into like "What doesn't kill me will make me stronger" or "If we don't learn from history, we are doomed to repeat it" into their daily lives. Suddenly, the usage of quotations allowed them to articulate their dreams of rising above their circumstances.

Since their graduation from Woodrow Wilson High School in 1998, the Freedom Writers have gone on to bigger and better things. They have set—and stuck to—even loftier goals than before. They have compiled their journal entries to craft a *New York Times* #1 bestselling book, *The Freedom Writers Diary* (1999); won numerous awards for outstanding leadership; and been covered in countless media stories. Ironically, now students and teachers use powerful quotations from their book for inspiration, such as our class motto, "When diverse worlds come together, beauty is inevitable!"

Today, the Freedom Writers are teachers, journalists, filmmakers, and music industry professionals. A few even help run the Freedom Writers Foundation, the nonprofit organization we started to promote acceptance and innovative teaching methods in classrooms across the world. None of this would have been possible without the words of authors, poets, and activists, some of whom are quoted in this book.

In the pages of *The Gigantic Book of Teachers' Wisdom*, you will find pearls of wisdom that encourage creative thinking. The book is a compilation of thought-provoking, inspiring quotations that you will identify with and hopefully pass along to your students through the course of their academic careers. Since the quotations are insightful and poignant,

I suggest you read them aloud in class, write them on the board, or simply hold onto the gems of wisdom that mean the most to you.

My hope is that as you read through *The Gigantic Book of Teachers' Wisdom*, you are continually inspired by the words within its pages, in the same way that the Freedom Writers have inspired me. This book was created for those who "fight the good fight" every day and who revel in seeing their students mature, little by little, into hopeful young adults.

Erin Gruwell

June 2007

CHAPTER ONE

The Teacher

Teaching is truth mediated by personality.

—PHYLLIS BROOKS

⟫—◆—⟪

Teaching is the achievement of shared meaning.

—D. B. GOWIN

⟫—◆—⟪

Teaching is the perpetual end and office of all things. Teaching, instruction is the main design that shines through the sky and earth.

—RALPH WALDO EMERSON

⟫—◆—⟪

Everybody who is incapable of learning has taken to teaching.

—OSCAR WILDE

⟫—◆—⟪

Teaching is not a lost art, but the regard for it is a lost tradition.

—JACQUES BARZUN

⟫—◆—⟪

The whole art of teaching is only the art of awakening the natural curiosity of young minds for the purpose of satisfying it afterwards; and curiosity itself can be vivid and wholesome only in proportion as the mind is contented and happy.

—ANATOLE FRANCE

The difficulty is to try and teach the multitude that something can be true and untrue at the same time.

—ARTHUR SCHOPENHAUER

The most important part of teaching is to teach what it is to know.

—SIMONE WEIL

TEACHING: The earth doesn't move every time, but when it does, what a RUSH!

—CAMERON BEATTY

Teaching is the greatest act of optimism.

—COLLEEN WILCOX

If the student fails to learn, the teacher fails to teach.

—ANONYMOUS

If kids come to educators and teachers from strong, healthy, functioning families, it makes our job easier. If they do not come to us from strong, healthy, functioning families, it makes our job more important.

—BARBARA COLOROSE

Teaching is the only major occupation of man for which we have not yet developed tools that make an average person capable of competence and performance. In teaching we rely on the "naturals," the ones who somehow know how to teach.

—PETER DRUCKER

The art of teaching is the art of assisting discovery.

—MARK VAN DOREN

Teachers are expected to reach unattainable goals with inadequate tools. The miracle is that at times they accomplish this impossible task.

—DR. HAIM GINOTT

I cannot teach anybody anything. I can only make them think.

—SOCRATES

There is none who cannot teach somebody something, and there is none so excellent but he is excelled.

—BALTASAR GRACIÁN

I do not teach. I relate.

—MONTAIGNE

◆

We all need someone who inspires us to do better than we know how.

—ANONYMOUS

◆

In teaching you cannot see the fruit of a day's work. It is invisible and remains so, maybe for twenty years.

—JACQUES BARZUN

◆

Good teachers are costly, but bad teachers cost more.

—BOB TALBERT

◆

It must be remembered that the purpose of education is not to fill
the minds of students with facts . . . it is to teach them to think, if that
is possible, and always to think for themselves.

—ROBERT HUTCHINS

The secret of teaching is to appear to have known all your life what you
learned this afternoon.

—ANONYMOUS

Teaching was the hardest work I had ever done, and it remains
the hardest work I have done to date.

—ANN RICHARDS

In teaching children we must seek insensibly to unite knowledge with
the carrying out of that knowledge into practice.

—IMMANUEL KANT

The work of a teacher—exhausting, complex, idiosyncratic, never twice the same—is at its heart, an intellectual and ethical enterprise. Teaching is the vocation of vocations . . .

—WILLIAM AYRES

Good teaching is one-fourth preparation and three-fourths theater.

—GAIL GODWIN

The whole art of teaching is only the art of awakening the natural curiosity of young minds for the purpose of satisfying it afterwards.

—ANATOLE FRANCE

The important thing is not so much that every child should be taught, as that every child should be given the wish to learn.

—JOHN LUBBOCK

You cannot teach a man anything; you can only help him find it within himself.

—GALILEO GALILEI

To teach is to learn twice.

—JOSEPH JOUBERT

In teaching, it is the method and not the content that is the message . . . the drawing out, not the pumping in.

—ASHLEY MONTAGUE

The object of teaching a child is to enable him to get along without his teacher.

—ELBERT HUBBARD

To me the sole hope of human salvation lies in teaching.

—GEORGE BERNARD SHAW

When teaching, light a fire, don't fill a bucket.

—DAN SNOW

We learn by teaching.

—JAMES HOWELL

Teaching is the profession that teaches all the other professions.

—ANONYMOUS

When you teach your son, you teach your son's son.

—TALMUD RABBINICAL WRITINGS

By learning you will teach, by teaching you will learn.

— LATIN PROVERB

Only a teacher? Thank God I have a calling to the greatest profession of all!

— IVAN WELTON FITZWATER

Teachers can change lives with just the right mix of chalk and challenges.

— JOYCE A. MYERS, FROM HER BOOK *HOW MUCH IS ENOUGH?* (1957)

The temple that teachers built will last while ages roll, for that beautiful unseen temple is the child's eternal soul.

— ST. AMBROSE, CATHOLIC BISHOP OF MILAN

Good teaching must be slow enough so that it is not confusing, and fast enough so that it is not boring.

—SIDNEY J. HARRIS

Effective teaching may be the hardest job there is.

—WILLIAM GLASSER

One of the beauties of teaching is that there is no limit to one's growth as a teacher, just as there is no knowing beforehand how much your students can learn.

—HERBERT KOHL

Teaching is a rigorous act of faith.

—SUSAN OHANIAN, TEACHER

The one exclusive sign of thorough knowledge is the power of teaching.

—ARISTOTLE

Among the many purposes of schooling, four stand out to us as having special moral value: to love and care, to serve, to empower and, of course, to learn.

—ANDY HARGREAVES AND MICHAEL FULLAN, FROM THEIR BOOK *WHAT'S WORTH FIGHTING FOR OUT THERE?* (1998)

Teaching is a calling, not a choice.

—MARY ANN ALEXANDER, COSMETOLOGY TEACHER IN YORKTOWN HEIGHTS, NEW YORK

Unfortunately, teaching is often times like golf. So many bad shots in between the good. And those are the few shots that we need to remember.

—HOWARD NERO, FIFTH-GRADE TEACHER FROM NEW HAVEN, CONNECTICUT

Teaching should be full of ideas instead of stuffed with facts.

—ANONYMOUS

Good teaching is primarily an art, and can neither be defined or standardized. . . . Good teachers are born and made; neither part of the process can be omitted.

—JOEL H. HILDEBRAND, IN AN INTERVIEW CONDUCTED SHORTLY
BEFORE HIS HUNDREDTH BIRTHDAY

Hope and its twin, possibility, best describe the art of teaching.

—CAMILLE BANKS-LEE, ENGLISH TEACHER IN OSSINING,
NEW YORK, 2002

Teaching is an exhausting job. I did not, however, expect to be emotionally exhausted. I suppose the easiest way out of this dilemma would be to make myself emotionally unavailable to my students . . . Not this teacher. This teacher can't help but share in some of those emotional moments. I can't turn off a portion of myself when I walk into the classroom. It's either the whole Mrs. Baer or nothing.

> —ALLISON L. BAER, SIXTH-GRADE TEACHER IN OHIO, AS QUOTED
> IN *WHAT TO EXPECT IN YOUR FIRST YEAR TEACHING* (1998)

Teaching is an instinctual art, mindful of potential, craving of realizations, a pausing, seamless process.

> —A. BARTLETT GIAMATTI, FROM "THE AMERICAN TEACHER,"
> *HARPER'S* (1980)

When the uncapped potential of a student meets the liberating art of a teacher, a miracle unfolds.

> —MARY HATWOOD FUTRELL, DEAN AT GEORGE WASHINGTON
> UNIVERSITY

The basic idea behind teaching is to teach people what they need to know.

> —CARL ROGERS

Teaching is the best way I know of regaining balance in your egocentric outlook on life.

> —BARBARA GASPARIK, CHILD DEVELOPMENT TEACHER IN YORKTOWN HEIGHTS, NEW YORK, 2002

———

Teachers are the last bastion against darkness and ignorance. The intensity of this need was my surprise.

> —JAMES W. MORRIS, FIFTH-GRADE TEACHER FROM GEORGIA, QUOTED IN *WHAT TO EXPECT YOUR FIRST YEAR OF TEACHING* (1998)

———

Teaching is the most inherently hopeful act that I know of.

> —PATRICIA MURPHY, TEACHER FROM OTTAWA, QUOTED IN *WHAT'S WORTH FIGHTING FOR OUT THERE?* (1998)

———

Teachers, I believe, are the most responsible and important members of society because their professional efforts affect the fate of the earth.

> —HELEN CALDICOTT

———

One good teacher in a lifetime may sometimes change a delinquent into a solid citizen.

—PHILIP WYLIE

A teacher affects eternity. He can never tell where his influence stops.

—HENRY ADAMS

My heart is singing for joy this morning. A miracle has happened! The light of understanding has shone upon my little pupil's mind, and behold, all things are changed.

—ANNE SULLIVAN, TUTOR TO HELEN KELLER

In an effective classroom, students should not only know what they are doing, they should also know why and how.

—HARRY WONG, AUTHOR OF *THE FIRST DAYS OF SCHOOL*

I teach, therefore I am.

—ANONYMOUS

Never doubt that a small group of thoughtful, committed citizens can change the world. Indeed, it's the only thing that ever has.

—MARGARET MEAD

Getting things done is not always what is most important. There is value in allowing others to learn, even if the task is not accomplished as quickly, efficiently or effectively.

—R. D. CLYDE

We are commanded to love God with all our minds, as well as with all our hearts, and we commit a great sin if we forbid or prevent that cultivation of the mind in others which would enable them to perform this duty.

—ANGELINA GRIMKE, EARLY ABOLITIONIST AND WOMEN'S RIGHTS ADVOCATE

The task of the modern educator is not to cut down jungles,
but to irrigate deserts.

—C. S. Lewis

Moral education, as I understand it, is not about inculcating obedience
to law or cultivating self-virtue, it is rather about finding within us an
ever-increasing sense of the worth of creation. It is about how we can
develop and deepen our intuitive sense of beauty and creativity.

—Andrew Linzey, animal rights activist

One good schoolmaster is worth a thousand priests.

—Robert Green Ingersoll

We are born weak, we have need of help; we are born destitute
of everything, we stand in need of assistance; we are born stupid, we
have need of understanding. All that we are not possessed of at our birth,
and which we require when we grow up, is bestowed on us by education.

—Jean-Jacques Rousseau

I believe that education is all about being excited about something. Seeing passion and enthusiasm helps push an educational message.

—STEVE IRWIN, THE CROCODILE HUNTER

There are two kinds of teachers: the kind that fill you with so much quail shot that you can't move, and the kind that just gives you a little prod behind and you jump to the skies.

—ROBERT FROST

To teach is to touch lives forever.

—ANONYMOUS

A poor surgeon hurts one person at a time. A poor teacher hurts 130.

—ERNEST L. BOYER

He that is taught only by himself has a fool for a master.

—BEN JONSON

The fact we must remember is that we are educating students for a world that will not be ours but will be theirs. Give them a chance to be heard.

—DR. CARLOS P. ROMULO, FILIPINO DIPLOMAT, POLITICIAN, SOLDIER, JOURNALIST, AND AUTHOR

The first idea that the child must acquire, in order to be actively disciplined, is that of the difference between good and evil; and the task of the educator lies in seeing that the child does not confound good with immobility, and evil with activity.

—MARIA MONTESSORI

I think education is power. I think that being able to communicate with people is power. One of my main goals on the planet is to encourage people to empower themselves.

—OPRAH WINFREY

Teachers who inspire know that teaching is like cultivating a garden, and those who would have nothing to do with thorns must never attempt to gather flowers.

—ANONYMOUS

No one has yet fully realized the wealth of sympathy, kindness, and generosity hidden in the soul of a child. The effort of every true education should be to unlock that treasure.

—EMMA GOLDMAN (1869–1940), A.K.A "RED EMMA," LITHUANIAN-BORN ANARCHIST KNOWN FOR HER WRITINGS AND SPEECHES

I believe that every human soul is teaching something to someone nearly every minute here in mortality.

—M. RUSSELL BALLARD, MORMON LEADER

I touch the future. I teach.

—CHRISTA MCAULIFFE, TEACHER KILLED ON *CHALLENGER* SPACE SHUTTLE

Teacher: The child's third parent.

—HYMAN BERSTON

＊

Teaching kids to count is fine, but teaching them what counts is best.

—BOB TALBERT

＊

Good teaching is more a giving of right questions than a giving
of right answers.

—JOSEF ALBERS

＊

For every one of us that succeeds, it's because there's somebody there
to show you the way out. The light doesn't always necessarily have to be
in your family; for me it was teachers and school.

—OPRAH WINFREY

＊

The empires of the future are the empires of the mind.

—WINSTON CHURCHILL

———◆———

Any genuine teaching will result, if successful, in someone's knowing how to bring about a better condition of things than existed earlier.

—JOHN DEWEY

———◆———

Where there is an open mind there will always be a frontier.

—CHARLES F. KETTERING

———◆———

Give me four years to teach the children and the seed I have sown will never be uprooted.

—VLADIMIR LENIN

———◆———

Only the mind cannot be sent into exile.

  —OVID

Ｉ know but one freedom, and that is the freedom of the mind.

  —ANTOINE DE SAINT-EXUPÉRY

Education . . . is a painful, continual, and difficult work to be done in kindness, by watching, by warning . . . by praise, but above all, by example.

  —JOHN RUSKIN

Men learn while they teach.

  —LUCIUS A. SENECA

I put the relation of a fine teacher to a student just below the relation of a mother to a son.

—THOMAS WOLFE

Life is an exciting business, and most exciting when it is lived for others.

—HELEN KELLER

Blessed is the influence of one true, loving human soul on another.

—GEORGE ELIOT

'Tis education forms the common mind
Just as the twig is bent, the tree's inclined.

—ALEXANDER POPE (1688–1744), FROM HIS COLLECTION OF ESSAYS
MORAL ESSAYS: EPISTLE TO RICHARD BOYLE, EARL OF BURLINGTON

The most important function of education at any level is to develop the personality of the individual and the significance of his life to himself and to others. This is the basic architecture of a life; the rest is ornamentation and decoration of the structure.

—GRAYSON KIRK

Those who educate children are more to be honored than those who produce them; for these only gave them life, those the art of living well.

—ARISTOTLE

Better than a thousand days of diligent study is one day with a great teacher.

—JAPANESE PROVERB

A human being is not attaining his full heights until he is educated.

—HORACE MANN

Events in our classrooms today will prompt world events tomorrow.

—J. LLOYD TRUMP, AS QUOTED IN *THE TEACHER AND THE TAUGHT*
(1963)

———

He then learns that in going down into the secrets of his own mind
he has descended into the secrets of all minds.

—RALPH WALDO EMERSON

———

Education is the jewel casting brilliance into the future.

—MARI EVANS

———

The whole object of education is . . . to develop the mind. The mind
should be a thing that works.

—SHERWOOD ANDERSON

———

The utmost extent of man's knowledge is to know that he knows nothing.

—JOSEPH ADDISON, FROM *ESSAY ON PRIDE* (1794)

He who can, does. He who cannot, teaches.

—GEORGE BERNARD SHAW

Those who can't do, teach. Those who can't teach, teach gym.

—WOODY ALLEN

We make the road, others will make the journey.

—VICTOR HUGO, FROM HIS BOOK *THOUGHTS*, TRANSLATED IN 1907

Teaching gives me a greater sense of my own humanity.

—CAMILLE BANKS-LEE, ENGLISH TEACHER IN OSSINING, NEW YORK, 2002

Behold, I do not give lectures or a little charity
When I give I give myself.

—WALT WHITMAN

None of my other teachers held me up to the same standard as my English teacher, Ms. Tsang. I eventually learned to hold myself up to the same standard.

—MELISSA MACOMBER, THE BANCROFT SCHOOL CLASS OF 1989, 2002

I entered the classroom with the conviction that it was crucial for me and every other student to be an active participant, not a passive consumer . . . education that connects the will to know with the will to become.

—"BELL HOOKS," FROM HER BOOK *TEACHING TO TRANSGRESS* (1994)

I still felt the responsibility twenty-four hours a day! Teaching wasn't only my job, it was fast becoming my lifestyle.

—SCOTT D. NIEMANN, THIRD- AND FOURTH-GRADE TEACHER IN ALASKA, AS QUOTED IN *WHAT TO EXPECT YOUR FIRST YEAR TEACHING* (1998)

In our world of big names, curiously, our true heroes tend to be anonymous. In this life of illusion and quasi-illusion, the person of solid virtues who can be admired for something more substantial than his well-knownness often proves to be the unsung hero: the teacher, the nurse, the mother, the honest cop, the hard worker at lonely, underpaid, unglamorous, unpublicized jobs.

—DANIEL J. BOORSTIN, FROM HIS BOOK *THE IMAGE* (1961)

People snicker, "Those who can't do, teach." But, oh, how right they are. I could never, ever do all I dream of doing. I could never ever be an opera star, a baseball umpire . . . a great lover, a great liar, a trapeze artist, a writer, a dancer . . . or a thousand other aspirations I have had, while having only been given one thin ticket in this lottery of life!

—ESMÉ RAJI CODELL, FROM HER BOOK *EDUCATING ESMÉ* (1999)

Rosie, an autistic child, talks to me now and can say her name. Possibly she could have reached these milestones in another classroom, but it happened in mine. What greater joy can a teacher feel than to witness a child's success?

—MICHELLE L. GRAHAM, FIRST-GRADE TEACHER IN MINNESOTA,
    AS QUOTED IN *WHAT TO EXPECT YOUR FIRST YEAR TEACHING* (1998)

It is written that he who governs well, leads the blind; but that he who teaches, gives them eyes.

—DAVID O. McKAY, MORMON HUMANITARIAN AND EDUCATOR

I don't think we expect enough of students. There are a lot of fabulous young people out there. They just need someone to show them the way.

—RAFE ESQUITH, 1992 DISNEY TEACHER OF THE YEAR AND *PARENT
    MAGAZINE*'S 1997 TEACHER OF THE YEAR, FROM HOBART BOULEVARD
    ELEMENTARY SCHOOL IN LOS ANGELES, CALIFORNIA

Most of us end up with no more than five or six people who remember us. Teachers have thousands of people who remember them for the rest of their lives.

—ANDREW ROONEY

I owe a lot to my teachers and mean to pay them back someday.

—STEPHEN LEACOCK

Jade best describes the art of teaching because it is the symbol of growth. As a teacher you must always find news ways of growing, and you must always strive to find new ways to helping your students grow. Only in growth can the crop be harvested.

—LYLEE STYLE, ENGLISH TEACHER IN YORKTOWN HEIGHTS, NEW YORK, 2002

Thirty-one chances. Thirty-one futures, our futures. It's an almost psychotic feeling, believing that part of their lives belongs to me.

Everything they become, I also become. And everything about me, they helped to create.

—ESMÉ RAJI CODELL, FROM HER BOOK *EDUCATING ESMÉ* (1999)

I am quite sure that in the hereafter she will take me by the hand and lead me to my proper seat.

—BERNARD BARUCH, ON ONE OF HIS EARLY TEACHERS IN *NEWS SUMMARIES* (1955)

It's a vital thing to remember both as creative people and those who have the opportunity to nurture the creativity in others. Creativity requires courage!

—THOMAS KINKADE

An education that does not strive to promote the fullest and most thorough understanding of the world is not worthy of the name.

—GEORGE S. COUNTS, AS QUOTED IN *THE TEACHER AND THE TAUGHT* (1963)

The direction in which education starts a man will determine his future life.

—PLATO

Education is a kind of continuing dialogue, and a dialogue assumes . . . different points of view.

—ROBERT M. HUTCHINS, ON ACADEMIC FREEDOM IN *TIME*

The ability to think straight, some knowledge of the past, some vision of the future, some skill to do useful service, some urge to fit that service into the well-being of the community—these are the most vital things education must try to produce.

—VIRGINIA GILDERSLEEVE, FROM HER BOOK *MANY A GOOD CRUSADE* (1954)

To prepare for complete living is the function which education has to discharge; and the only rational mode of judging of an education course is, to judge in what degree it discharges such function.

—HERBERT SPENCER, FROM HIS ESSAY "ONE EDUCATION" (1859)

The need for imagination, a sense of truth, and a feeling of responsibility—these are the three forces which are the very nerve of education.

—RUDOLF STEINER

Teaching is what teachers expect to do every day. To reach out positively and supportively to twenty-seven youngsters for five hours or so each day in an elementary school classroom is demanding and exhausting. To respond similarly to four to six successive classes of twenty-four or more students each at the secondary level may be impossible.

—JOHN GOODARD, FROM HIS BOOK *A PLACE CALLED SCHOOL* (1984)

Human beings are full of emotion, and the teacher who knows how to use it will have dedicated learners. It means sending dominant signals instead of submissive ones with your eyes, body, and voice.

—LEON LESSINGER

In communities, the best disciplinary strategies are those that teach students citizenship and help students become caring adults. Key are the standards, values, and commitments that makes up a constitution for living together.

—THOMAS J. SERGIOVANNI FROM HIS BOOK *BUILDING COMMUNITY IN SCHOOLS* (1994)

Children are liquid. They shape themselves to fit the form of the container into which they are placed. . . . I am forever indebted to my teachers. They had enough faith to swing the bucket, because they knew that it was in the very nature of the water to remain right there.

—PAULA POLK LILLARD FROM HER BOOK *MONTESSORI TODAY: A COMPREHENSIVE APPROACH TO EDUCATION FROM BIRTH TO ADULTHOOD* (1996)

On a good day, I know it's not every day, we can part the sea
And on a bad day, I know it's not every day, glory beyond our reach.

—CHRIS ROBINSON, FROM HIS POEM "WISER TIME" (1994)

I do not teach children, I give them joy.

—ISADORA DUNCAN

No matter what accomplishments you achieve, somebody helped you.

—ALTHEA GIBSON

The influence of each human being on others in this life is a kind
of immortality.

—WINSTON CHURCHILL

A man who becomes conscious of the responsibility he bears toward a human being who affectionately waits for him, or to an unfinished work, will never be able to throw away his life. He knows the "why" for his existence, and will be able to bear almost any "how."

—VIKTOR FRANKL, AUSTRIAN NEUROLOGIST, PSYCHIATRIST,
AND HOLOCAUST SURVIVOR

If you would thoroughly know anything, teach it to others.

—TRYON EDWARDS

Invest in a human soul. Who knows? It might be a diamond in the rough.

—MARY MCLEOD BETHUNE, EDUCATOR BORN TO FORMER SLAVE

It takes a city to raise a child.

—ADAIR LARA

Children are not born knowing the many opportunities that are theirs for the taking. Someone who does know must tell them.

—RUTH HILL VIGUERS, EDITOR OF *THE HORN BOOK* (1958–1967),
FROM "RUTH HILL VIGUERS"

The best education is not given to students; it is drawn out of them.

—GERALD BELCHER

The moment one gives close attention to anything, even a blade of grass, it becomes a mysterious, awesome, indescribably magnificent world in itself.

—HENRY MILLER

There are two ways of spreading light; to be the candle or the mirror that reflects it.

—EDITH WHARTON

If you have knowledge, let others light their candles in it.

—MARGARET FULLER

At the end of the visit, Diana reviews the events and the learning with the children. She asks the children their favorite event. "The alone walk," they all clamor. Walking all alone along the trail. Each one being brave, courageous. Discovering that they can find their own way.

—LOIS ROBIN, REFERRING TO A SCHOOL OUTING WITH DIANA ALMENDARIZ, A NATIVE AMERICAN CULTURAL INTERPRETER DESCENDED FROM THE NISENAN-MAIDU TRIBE, FROM "A DAY WITH DIANA," *NATIVE CALIFORNIA* (1991)

When I transfer my knowledge, I teach. But when I transfer my beliefs, I indoctrinate.

—ARTHUR C. DANTO, FROM HIS BOOK *ANALYTICAL PHILOSOPHY OF KNOWLEDGE* (1968)

Teaching a solid subject such as English forced me to create a detailed schedule and lesson plan and to get things done efficiently without wasting time. I couldn't just amble into class each day without precise preparation.

—JOHN WOODEN

⊰◈⊱

The great teachings unanimously emphasize that all the peace, wisdom, and joy in the universe are already within us; we don't have to gain, develop, or attain them. We're like a child standing in a beautiful park with his eyes shut tight. We don't need to imagine trees, flowers, deer, birds, and sky; we merely need to open our eyes and realize what is already here, who we really are. As soon as we quit pretending we're small or unholy.

—ANONYMOUS

⊰◈⊱

That in education we should proceed from the simple to the complex, is a truth which has always been to some extent acted upon: not professedly, indeed, nor any means consistently. The mind develops. Like all things that develop it progresses from the homogeneous to the heterogeneous; and a normal training system, being an objective counter-part of this subjective process, must exhibit a like progression.

—HERBERT SPENCER, FROM HIS ESSAY "INTELLECTUAL EDUCATION" (C. 1854)

I have come to believe that a great teacher is a great artist and that there are as few as there are any other great artists. Teaching might even be the greatest of the arts since the medium is the human mind and spirit.

—JOHN STEINBECK

The teacher is just a boat to take the student over the river.

—BUDDHA

Upon our children—how they are taught—rests the fate—or fortune— of tomorrow's world.

—B. C. FORBES, FINANCIAL JOURNALIST, AUTHOR, AND FOUNDER OF *FORBES* MAGAZINE

It is noble to teach oneself; it is still nobler to teach others.

—MARK TWAIN

———◆———

Education is the most powerful weapon which you can use to change the world.

—NELSON MANDELA

———◆———

Everyone and everything around you is your teacher.

—KEN KEYES, JR.

———◆———

I have come to a frightening conclusion. I am the decisive element in the classroom. It is my personal approach that creates the climate. It is my daily mood that makes the weather. As a teacher, I possess tremendous power to make a child's life miserable or joyous.

—HAIM GINOTT

———◆———

The teacher's task is to initiate the learning process and then get out
of the way.

—JOHN WARREN

I am that most fortunate of men for I am eternal. Others live merely
in the world of today; I live in the world of tomorrow. . . . For I am
charged with that most sacred mission—to transmit all that our forebears
lived for, loved for, and died for to the next generation.

—RABBI ZEV SCHOSTAK

The business of teaching is carried forward . . . because some individuals
of extraordinary vitality and strength of personality engage in it and
the fire that helps to guide them kindles the spirits of the young people
whose lives they touch.

—WOODROW WILSON

A wise man knows and will keep his place; but a child is ignorant of his,
and therefore cannot confine himself to it. There are a thousand avenues

through which he will be apt to escape; it belongs to those who have the care of his education, therefore, to prevent him; a task, by the way, which is not very easy.

—JEAN-JACQUES ROUSSEAU

It is one thing to show a man that he is in error, and another to put him in possession of truth.

—JOHN LOCKE

To teach a man how he may learn to grow independently, and for himself, is the greatest service that one man can do another.

—BENJAMIN JOWETT

If you can read this, thank a teacher.

—ANONYMOUS

We cannot hold a torch to light another's path without brightening our own.

—BEN SWEETLAND

The critical factor is not class size but rather the nature of the teaching as it affects learning.

—C. B. NEBLETTE

Education should turn out the pupil with something he knows well and something he can do well.

—ALFRED NORTH WHITEHEAD

From what we get, we can make a living; what we give, however, makes a life.

—ARTHUR ASHE

Far and away the best prize that life offers is the chance to work hard at work worth doing.

—THEODORE ROOSEVELT

The future of the world is in my classroom today, a future with the potential for good or bad.

—IVAN WELTON FITZWATER

Education is helping the child realize his potentialities.

—ERICH FROMM

Education is much more than a matter of imparting the knowledge and skills by which narrow goals are achieved. It is also about opening the child's eyes to the needs and rights of others.

—TENZIN GYATSO, THE FOURTEENTH DALAI LAMA

None of us got where we are solely by pulling ourselves up by our bootstraps. We got here because somebody—a parent, a teacher, an Ivy League crony or a few nuns, bent down and helped us pick up our boots.

—THURGOOD MARSHALL

We make the best contribution in areas where our hearts call us to serve; and often these are areas where we have either a natural talent or interest.

—THOMAS KINKADE

The beautiful compensation of developing favorable self-concepts in students is that the teacher cannot build positive self-concepts in students without building his own.

—WILLIAM PURKEY

The greater part of the people we assign to educate our children we know for certain are not educated. Yet we do not doubt that they can give what they have not received, a thing which cannot be otherwise acquired.

—GIACOMO LEOPARDI

No one has ever taught anything to anybody.

—CARL ROGERS

Teachers are people who start things they never see finished, and for which they never get thanks until it is too late.

—MAX FORMAN

The vanity of teaching doth oft tempt a man to forget that he is a blockhead.

—GEORGE SAVILE, MARQUIS OF HALIFAX (1633–1695), ENGLISH STATESMAN AND ESSAYIST

You don't have to think too hard when you talk to teachers.

    —J. D. SALINGER

One of the true tests of leadership is the ability to recognize a problem before it becomes an emergency.

    —ARNOLD GLASOW

The highest of distinctions is service to others.

    —KING GEORGE VI

A leader is someone who helps improve the lives of other people or improve the system they live under.

    —SAM ERVIN

The first duty of a lecturer—to hand you after an hour's discourse
a nugget of pure truth to wrap up between the pages of your notebooks
and keep on the mantelpiece for ever.

—Virginia Woolf

Forget committees. New, noble, world-changing ideas always come from
one person working alone.

—H. Jackson Brown, Jr., from his book *Life's Little Instruction Book* (2000)

The second most important job in the world, second only to being a good
parent, is being a good teacher.

—S. G. Ellis

I cannot teach you; only help you to explore yourself.

—Bruce Lee

The world does not pay for what a person knows. But it pays for what a person does with what he knows.

—LAURENCE LEE

Great minds are to make others great. Their superiority is to be used, not to break the multitude to intellectual vassalage, not to establish over them a spiritual tyranny, but to rouse them from lethargy, and to aid them to judge for themselves.

—WILLIAM ELLERY CHANNING

Be all that you can be. Find your future—as a teacher.

—MADELINE FUCHS HOLZER, ARTS IN EDUCATION DIRECTOR FOR THE NEW YORK STATE COUNCIL ON THE ARTS

The first condition of education is being able to put someone to wholesome and meaningful work.

—JOHN RUSKIN

Your best teacher is your last mistake.

—RALPH NADER

When the student is ready the teacher will appear.

—LAO-TZU (C. 600 B.C.), KNOWN AS "OLD MASTER," CHINESE
PHILOSOPHER, FOUNDER OF CHINESE TAOISM

He who dares to teach must never cease to learn.

—ANONYMOUS

There's no word in the language I revere more than "teacher." My heart
sings when a kid refers to me as his teacher, and it always has. I've
honored myself and the entire family of man by becoming a teacher.

—PAT CONROY, FROM HIS BOOK *PRINCE OF TIDES* (1986)

We live in a time of such rapid change and growth of knowledge that
only he who is in a fundamental sense a scholar—that is, a person who

continues to learn and inquire—can hope to keep pace, let alone play
the role of guide.

—NATHAN M. PUSEY, FROM HIS BOOK *THE AGE OF THE SCHOLAR* (1963)

My first year has been as disappointing as it was rewarding. . . . I have
lost and found hope, reviewed and revised, and finally concluded that my
presence here is much more important that I had thought it would be.

—CATHERINE MCTAMANEY, HIGH SCHOOL TEACHER FROM TENNESSEE,
AS QUOTED IN *WHAT TO EXPECT YOUR FIRST YEAR TEACHING* (1998)

I have been maturing as a teacher. New experiences bring
new sensitivities and flexibility.

—HOWARD LESTER, FIRST-YEAR TEACHER

Creativity does not exist on a continuum. Rather, there are small groups
of teachers in every school that work in unique systems.

—JIM SCHULZ, 2000 DISNEY TEACHER OF THE YEAR, FROM HELENA,
MONTANA

But the first day of school is our second New Year's. It is our day to make resolutions, to look backward to former lapses and triumphs and to look ahead, usually with a mix of anxiety and hope, to the year to come.

> —MARK EDMUNDON, FROM "SOUL TRAINING," *THE NEW YORK TIMES MAGAZINE* (2002)

Choose a job you love, and you will never have to work a day in your life.

> —CONFUCIUS

Philosophy lies deeper. It is not her office to teach men how to use their hands. The object of her lessons is to form the soul.

> —LUCIUS A. SENECA, FROM HIS BOOK *EPISTULAE AND LUCILIUM* (63 C.E.)

All teachers were to be respected like gods, and God Himself was the greatest of all school superintendents. Long after I had ceased to believe that our teachers could see with the back of their heads, it was still understood by me that they knew everything.

—ALFRED KAZIN, FROM HIS BOOK *A WALKER IN THE CITY* (1951)

I don't know what your destiny will be, but one thing I know: the only ones among you who will be truly happy are those who will have sought and found how to serve.

—ALBERT SCHWEITZER

It is nobler to be good, and it is nobler to teach others to be good—and less trouble!

—MARK TWAIN

I'm not a teacher: only a fellow-traveler of whom you asked the way. I pointed ahead—ahead of myself as well as you.

—GEORGE BERNARD SHAW

There were great frustrations, setbacks, and embarrassing moments, but the pleasure of teaching young people was more than money could buy.

—JOHN WOODEN, FROM HIS BOOK *MY PERSONAL BEST* (2004)

A professor can never better distinguish himself in his work than by encouraging a clever pupil, for the true discoverers are among them, as comets amongst the stars.

—CAROLUS LINNAEUS

True undoubting is the teacher's part, continual undoubting the part of the pupil.

—FRANZ KAFKA

Painter Marc Chagall is my favorite pupil and what I like about him is that after listening attentively to my lessons he takes his paints and brushes and does something absolutely different from what I have told him.

—LEON BAKST

We Teach Success.

—HOFSTRA UNIVERSITY advertising slogan

Any activity becomes creative when the doer cares about doing it right, or doing it better.

—JOHN UPDIKE

A classic lecture, rich in sentiment,
With scraps of thunderous epic lilted out
By violet-hooded Doctors, elegies
And quoted odes, and jewels five-words long,

That on the stretched forefinger of all Time
Sparkle for ever.

—ALFRED LORD TENNYSON, FROM HIS BOOK *THE PRINCESS* (1847)

Few have been taught to any purpose who have not been their own
teachers.

—SIR JOSHUA REYNOLDS

The Lord & the teacher face me. Who should I kneel before? I pay
my obeisance to you, my teacher, since you took me to the Lord.

—SUFI SAINT KABIR, INDIAN MYSTIC

Those who live life for themselves will be stuck with themselves—and
little else.

—THOMAS KINKADE

And just as I've always wanted our players to be a part of the student body, so too have I always wanted our students to be a part of our team. And I think that our students have been that.

—Bobby Knight

The most dangerous leadership myth is that leaders are born—that there is a genetic factor to leadership. This myth asserts that people simply either have certain charismatic qualities or not. That's nonsense; in fact, the opposite is true. Leaders are made rather than born.

—Warren G. Bennis

There is nothing training cannot do. Nothing is above its reach. It can turn bad morals to good; it can destroy bad principles and recreate good ones; it can lift men to angel-ship.

—Mark Twain

No matter what your product is, you are ultimately in the education business. Your customers need to be constantly educated about the many advantages of doing business with you, trained to use your products more effectively, and taught how to make never-ending improvement in their lives.

—ROBERT G. ALLEN

Every truth has four corners: as a teacher I give you one corner, and it is for you to find the other three.

—CONFUCIUS

CHAPTER TWO

The Philosophy Behind Good Teaching

What the teacher is, is more important than what he teaches.

—KARL A. MENNINGER

The teacher as a person is more important than the teacher as a technician. What he is has more effect than anything he does.

—JACK CANFIELD

Wherever there are beginners and experts, old and young, there is some kind of learning going on, some kind of teaching. We are all pupils and we are all teachers.

—GILBERT HIGHET

It's what you learn after you know it all that counts.

—EARL WEAVER

Who dares to teach, must never cease to learn.

—John Cotton Dana

—————

What is important is to keep learning, to enjoy challenge, and to tolerate ambiguity. In the end there are no certain answers.

—Martina Horner

—————

Instruction begins when you, the teacher, learn from the learner; put yourself in his place so that you may understand ... what he learns and the way he understands it.

—Søren Kierkegaard

—————

Acquire new knowledge whilst thinking over the old, and you may become a teacher of others.

—Confucius

—————

The teacher who is indeed wise
Does not bid you to enter the house of his wisdom
But rather leads you to the threshold of your mind.

—KAHLIL GIBRAN, FROM HIS BOOK *THE PROPHET* (1923)

The best teacher is the one who suggests rather than dogmatizes, and inspires his listener with the wish to teach himself.

—EDWARD BULWER-LYTTON

The mediocre teacher tells. The good teacher explains. The superior teacher demonstrates. The great teacher inspires.

—WILLIAM ARTHUR WARD

Patience is the key to paradise.

—ARMENIAN PROVERB

Patience is the companion of wisdom.

—ST. AUGUSTINE

Have a heart that never hardens, and a temper that never fires, and a touch that never hurts.

—CHARLES DICKENS

Many of us carry memories of an influential teacher who may scarcely know we existed, yet who said something at just the right time in our lives to snap a whole world into focus.

—LAURENT A. DALOZ

One looks back with appreciation to the brilliant teachers, but with gratitude to those who touched our human feeling. The curriculum is so much necessary raw material, but warmth is the vital element for the growing plant and for the soul of the child.

—CARL JUNG

They may forget what you said but they will never forget how you made them feel.

—ANONYMOUS

Your heart is slightly bigger than the average human heart, but that's because you're a teacher.

—AARON BACALL

You can pay people to teach, but you can't pay them to care.

—MARVA COLLINS, FROM HER BOOK *MAKING A DIFFERENCE IN THE CLASSROOM* (1992)

A word of encouragement during a failure is worth more than an hour of praise after success.

—ANONYMOUS

To waken interest and kindle enthusiasm is the sure way to teach easily and successfully.

—TYRON EDWARDS

No man can be a good teacher unless he has feelings of warm affection toward his pupils and a genuine desire to impart to them what he himself believes to be of value.

—BERTRAND RUSSELL

A word as to the education of the heart. We don't believe that this can be imparted through books; it can only be imparted through the loving touch of the teacher.

—César Chávez

Teachers believe they have a gift for giving; it drives them with the same irrepressible drive that drives others to create a work of art or a marker or a building.

—A. Bartlett Giamatti

Too often we underestimate the power of a touch, a smile, a kind word, a listening ear, and honest compliment, or the smallest act of caring, all of which have the potential to turn a life around.

—Dr. Leo Buscaglia

The close observer soon discovers that the teacher's task is not to implant facts but to place the subject to be learned in front of the learner and, through sympathy, emotion, imagination, and patience, to awaken in the learner the restless drive for answers and insights which enlarge the personal life and give it meaning.

—Nathan M. Pusey

A teacher who is attempting to teach, without inspiring the pupil with a desire to learn, is hammering on a cold iron.

—Horace Mann

The task of the excellent teacher is to stimulate "apparently ordinary" people to unusual effort. The tough problem is not in identifying winners: it is in making winners out of ordinary people.

—K. Patricia Cross

The test of a good teacher is not how many questions he can ask his pupils that they will answer readily, but how many questions he inspires them to ask him which he finds it hard to answer.

—ALICE WELLINGTON ROLLINS

Teaching is not a profession; it's a passion.

—ANONYMOUS

No one should teach who is not in love with teaching.

—MARGARET E. SANGSTER

The gift of teaching is a peculiar talent, and implies a need and a craving in the teacher himself.

—JOHN JAY CHAPMAN

There is no real teacher who in practice does not believe in the existence of the soul, or in a magic that acts on it through speech.

—ALLAN BLOOM

Conviction is worthless unless it is converted to conduct.

—THOMAS CARLYLE

A good teacher is a master of simplification and an enemy of simplism.

—LOUIS A. BERMAN

To know how to suggest is the great art of teaching. To attain it we must be able to guess what will interest; we must learn to read the childish soul as we might a piece of music. Then, by simply changing the key, we keep up the attraction and vary the song.

—HENRI-FRÉDÉRIC AMIEL, FROM HIS MEMOIR *JOURNAL IN TIME* (1864)

Setting an example is not the main means of influencing another, it is the only means.

—ALBERT EINSTEIN

Example is the school of mankind, and they will learn at no other.

—EDMUND BURKE

Children have more need of models than critics.

—JOSEPH JOUBERT

Those who trust us educate us.

—GEORGE ELIOT

The secret of education is respecting the pupil.

—RALPH WALDO EMERSON

Love them enough to risk their not liking you. Children must know that there are consequences to be suffered when they are not nice.

—CAROL AVILA, TEACHER FROM RHODE ISLAND AND 1995 PRESIDENTIAL AWARD WINNER FOR EXCELLENCE IN SCIENCE TEACHING

Patience is the greatest of all virtues.

—DIONYSIUS CATO

Beware the fury of a patient man.

—JOHN DRYDEN

Patience, that blending of moral courage with physical timidity.

—THOMAS HARDY

Lack o' pep is often mistaken for patience.

—KIN HUBBARD

Patience is necessary, and one cannot reap immediately where one has sown.

—SØREN KIERKEGAARD

You have to have a lot of patience to learn patience.

—STANISLAW J. LEC

Patience, the beggar's virtue.

> —PHILIP MASSINGER, FROM HIS BOOK *A NEW WAY TO PAY OLD DEBTS* (1631)

Nothing comes of so many things, if you have patience.

> —JOYCE CAROL OATES

Patience and Diligence, like Faith, move Mountains.

> —WILLIAM PENN, FROM HIS BOOK *SOME FRUITS OF SOLITUDE* (1693)

All's well in the end, if you've only the patience to wait.

> —FRANÇOIS RABELAIS, FROM HIS BOOK *GARGANTUA AND PANTAGRUE* (1532–1552)

It is very strange … that the years teach us patience; that the shorter our time, the greater our capacity for waiting.

—ELIZABETH TAYLOR

Patience doesn't always help, but impatience never does.

—RUSSIAN PROVERB

A good teacher is one who helps you become who you feel yourself to be. A good teacher is also one who says something that you won't understand until 10 years later.

—JULIUS LESTER

The teacher is one who made two ideas grow where only one grew before.

—ELBERT HUBBARD

The true teacher defends his pupils against his own personal influence. He inspires self-distrust. He guides their eyes from himself to the spirit that quickens him. He will have no disciple.

—AMOS BRONSON ALCOTT

That is the difference between good teachers and great teachers: good teachers make the best of a pupil's means; great teachers foresee a pupil's ends.

—MARIA CALLAS

Effective teachers seek feedback and consensus on their decisions and make sure that students understand.

—LINDA SHALAWAY

A wise teacher makes learning a joy.

—ANONYMOUS

The most effective teacher will always be biased, for the chief force in teaching is confidence and enthusiasm.

—JOYCE CARY

An understanding heart is everything in a teacher, and cannot be esteemed highly enough.

—CARL JUNG

The best teacher is one who suggests rather than dogmatizes, and inspires his listener with the wish to teach himself.

—ANONYMOUS

He that teaches us anything which we knew not before is undoubtedly to be reverenced as a master.

—SAMUEL JOHNSON

A good teacher is like a candle—it consumes itself to light the way for others.

—ANONYMOUS

⬗

A great teacher is one who possesses information, intelligence, and the instincts to know how to present what he knows.

—SOCRATES

⬗

The gift of a great teacher is creating an awareness of greatness in others.

—GRETA K. NAGEL, FROM HER BOOK *THE TAO OF TEACHING* (1998)

⬗

A good teacher is one who can understand those who are not very good at explaining, and explain to those who are not very good at understanding.

—DWIGHT D. EISENHOWER

⬗

Inspired teachers . . . cannot be ordered by the gross from the factory. They must be discovered one by one, and brought home from the woods and swamps like orchids. They must be placed in a conservatory, not in a carpenter shop; and they must be honored and trusted.

—JOHN JAY CHAPMAN

Have you ever really had a teacher? One who saw you as a raw but precious thing, a jewel that, with wisdom, could be polished to a proud shine?

—MITCH ALBOM, FROM HIS BOOK *TUESDAYS WITH MORRIE* (1997)

A good teacher is never done with their preparation—grading, evaluations, planning—because they are always trying to reinvent, improve, and inspire.

—DR. DAVID CARLSON

Endeavor first, to broaden your children's sympathies and, by satisfying their daily needs, to bring love and kindness into such unceasing contact with their impressions and their activity, that these sentiments may be engrafted in their hearts.

—JOHANN HEINRICH PESTALOZZI

There are a number of teachers I wouldn't mind buying a drink, but precious few I'd like to sit and talk with while they drink it.

—GREG MacGILPIN, TEACHER'S COLLEGE OF COLUMBIA UNIVERSITY

Experienced teachers . . . are an invaluable resource to the first-year teachers who are willing to admit that they have much to learn.

—ROBERT GRESS, TEACHER FROM LEXINGTON, KENTUCKY

Compassionate teachers fill a void left by working parents who aren't able to devote enough attention to their children. A good education consists of much more than useful facts and marketable skills.

—CHARLES PLATT

You can't stop a teacher when they want to do something. They just *do* it.

—J. D. SALINGER, FROM HIS BOOK *THE CATCHER IN THE RYE* (1951)

I was still learning when I taught my last class.

—CLAUDE M. FUESS

A great teacher never strives to explain his vision. He simply invites you to stand beside him and see for yourself.

—REVEREND E. INMAN

There is humane aggression in being a great teacher, as well as genuine love.

> —MARK EDMUNDSON, FROM "SOUL TRAINING," *THE NEW YORK TIMES MAGAZINE* (2002)

To be a teacher in the right sense is to be a learner. I am not a teacher, only a fellow student.

> —SØREN KIERKEGAARD

Good teachers must primarily be enthusiasts—like writers, painters, and priests, they must have a sense of vocation—a deep-rooted unsentimental desire to do good.

> —NOËL COWARD

A teacher is one who makes himself progressively unnecessary.

> —THOMAS CARRUTHERS

I like a teacher who gives you something to take home to think about besides homework.

—LILY TOMLIN

A professor is one who talks in someone else's sleep.

—ANONYMOUS

Good teachers are those who know how little they know. Bad teachers are those who think they know more than they don't know.

—R. VERDI

The most extraordinary thing about a really good teacher is that he or she transcends accepted educational methods. Such methods are designed to help average teachers approximate the performance of good teachers.

—MARGARET MEAD

Good teachers empathize with kids, respect them, and believe that each one has something special that can be built upon.

—ANN LIEBERMAN

If ever there can be a cause worthy to be upheld by all toil or sacrifice that the human heart can endure, it is the cause of education.

—HORACE MANN

What greater or better gift can we offer the republic than to teach and instruct our youth?

—MARCUS T. CICERO

A good teacher must be able to put himself in the place of those who find learning hard.

—ELIPHAS LEVI, FRENCH OCCULTIST

Teachers teach because they care. Teaching young people is what they do best. It requires long hours, patience, and care.

—HORACE MANN

We think of the effective teachers we have had over the years with a sense of recognition, but those who have touched our humanity we remember with a deep sense of gratitude.

—ANONYMOUS

Joe Rinaldi changed his teaching style to meet the student's learning needs. He never got frustrated when you didn't "get it." Instead, he changed the way he explained it.

—DEBBIE SABATO, FOURTH-GRADE TEACHER IN DENVER, COLORADO

I love to feel proud: proud of a child who learns the English language, proud of a child who makes the perfect M, proud of a child who acts like a friend and can be a model for the class, proud of a child who learns his or her line for the school play.

—KAREN GUARDINO, KINDERGARTEN TEACHER IN SCARSDALE,
 NEW YORK

———⇒◆⇐———

Fifteen years after I sat on the big cozy rug in her kindergarten classroom, Ms. Cerbone remembered my name, the bows I used to wear in my hair, the dresses that my mom made for me. Each time we ran into each other, she would recall the memories with a smile. She never forgot.

—KIM WALKLEY BUCKLEY, BEDFORD HILLS ELEMENTARY SCHOOL
 CLASS OF 1981

———⇒◆⇐———

Each of Dr. Dominquez's classes were intense and draining, but worthwhile. He was the one teacher I could go to for advice and trust that I would get an honest answer.

—SUZIE DEROBERTS, HARVARD UNIVERSITY CLASS OF 1996

———⇒◆⇐———

The best teachers teach from the heart, not from the book.

—ANONYMOUS

⟨—◆—⟩

I still cannot get used to how much my heart soars with every student's success, and how a piece of my heart is plucked away when any student slips away.

—DELISSA L. MAI, NINTH-GRADE TEACHER IN WYOMING, AS QUOTED IN
WHAT TO EXPECT IN YOUR FIRST YEAR OF TEACHING (1998)

⟨—◆—⟩

Before I grew out of my shell, Ms. Sartor knew how shy I was. She wouldn't make me speak in front of the other students. Later, though, she would ask me questions, one-on-one.

—WENDY JACKSON, WESTON ELEMENTARY SCHOOL CLASS OF 1981

⟨—◆—⟩

Professor Rimmerman would bleed red ink all over your paper. You still might eke out a B, but he would definitely let you know what to work on next time around.

—Marvin T. Lao, Hobart College class of 1994

Ms. Kennedy taught me to love writing. Every story came back with a smiley face at the top of the page.

—John McEdelman, Bedford Village Elementary School class of 1981

Ms. Tulin was funny, laid back, kind of funky. She allowed you to be a teenager but also demanded respect and order in the classroom. We learned about the Holocaust, survival in the wilderness, ourselves … and she was wonderful at facilitating all of this.

—Carrie Peck, Fox Lane Middle School class of 1985

I determined that there should not be a minute in the day when my children should not be aware of my face and my lips that my heart was theirs, that their happiness was my happiness, and their pleasures my pleasures.

> —JOHANN HEINRICH PESTALOZZI, AS QUOTED IN *THE TEACHER AND THE TAUGHT* (1963)

———◆———

Mr. Shanley's kindness put me at ease and gave me confidence to learn. It's hard to absorb information when your brain is congested with doubt, and his encouragement helped me to relax and, in turn, to excel academically. He's the one I will remember because he's the one who seemed to care.

> —MEREDITH MCWADE, FOX LANE HIGH SCHOOL CLASS OF 1989

———◆———

Ms. Lambert gave us quizzes every day, not just as a way of dipsticking our understanding but as a means of evaluating her own clarity in teaching. I've never been so prepared for a class in my life.

> —SUZIE DEROBERTS, FOX LANE HIGH SCHOOL CLASS OF 1992

———◆———

Mr. Ehrhard was so interesting that you absolutely wanted to share in everything he cared about. He was the physics teacher who recommended *The Catcher in the Rye* and we all read it, of our own free will.

—ALICIA SOLÍS, WESTON HIGH SCHOOL CLASS OF 1990

—————

I must have talked a great deal because Martha used to say again and again, "You remember you said this, you said that …" She remembered everything I said, and all my life I've had the feeling that what I think and what I say are worth remembering. She gave me that.

—ERIC HOFFER, ON MARTHA BAUER, THE WOMAN WHO RAISED HIM AFTER HIS MOTHER DIED, FROM "PROFILES: THE CREATIVE SITUATION," THE *NEW YORKER* (1967)

—————

Teachers who really value their emotional bonds to students are willing to experiment with alternative structures that make these bonds stronger.

—ANDY HARGREAVES AND MICHAEL FULLAN, FROM THEIR BOOK *WHAT'S WORTH FIGHTING FOR OUT THERE?* (1998)

—————

Gladly would he learn and gladly teach.

—Geoffrey Chaucer, on the Clerk in *The Canterbury Tales*

The ultimate leader is one who is willing to develop people to the point that they eventually surpass him or her in knowledge and ability.

—Fred A. Manske, Jr.

A good coach will make his players see what they can be rather than what they are.

—Ara Paraseghian

The test of a good coach is that when they leave, others will carry on successfully.

—Anonymous

Outstanding leaders go out of their way to boost the self-esteem of their personnel. If people believe in themselves, it's amazing what they can accomplish.

—SAM WALTON

The boss drives people; the leader coaches them. . . . The boss inspires fear; the leader inspires enthusiasm. The boss says "I"; the leader says "WE." The boss fixes the blame for the breakdown; the leader fixes the breakdown. The boss says, "GO"; the leader says, "Let's GO!"

—H. GORDON SELFRIDGE

It is the greatest achievement of a teacher to enable his students to surpass him.

—JOHN KEMENY

Terry Culleton made that impact on me. "If you want a future in writing, I think you've got it," he wrote on one paper. "If you're willing to try."

—KEITH DIXON, GEORGE SCHOOL CLASS OF 1989

The man who can make hard things easy is the educator.

—RALPH WALDO EMERSON

I asked a student one day why he thought he was doing so much better than last year. He gave whole new meaning to my orientation. "It's because I like myself now when I'm with you," he said.

—ANONYMOUS TEACHER, AS QUOTED BY EVERETT SHOSTROM IN MAN, THE MANIPULATOR (1968)

CHAPTER THREE

Words from the Wise

Do not train children to learning by force and harshness; but direct them to it by what amuses their minds, so that you may be better able to discover with accuracy the peculiar bent of the genius of each.

—PLATO

Education should be gentle and stern, not cold and lax.

—JOSEPH JOUBERT

As a teacher I feel I have a moral obligation to help the children in my classroom grow toward becoming full human beings and to feel successful. Teaching cognitive skills is not enough.

—JEAN MEDICK

Don't set your wit against a child.

—JONATHAN SWIFT

No use to shout at them to pay attention. If the situations, the materials, the problems before the child do not interest him, his attention will slip off to what does interest him, and no amount of exhortation or threats will bring him back.

—HENRY HOLT

People's behavior makes sense if you think about it in terms of their goals, needs, and motives.

—THOMAS MANN

If I compliment them, I mean it. If I don't think they are doing a good job, I lay it on the line. I demand respect from them and I give them respect, and I think they are important.

—LENNI ABEL, ART TEACHER AND 2000 DISNEY TEACHER OF THE YEAR, FROM THE BRONX, NEW YORK

I let the kids know exactly what I expect. I praise them when they meet those expectations and point it out to them when they don't.

—Ron Clark, fifth-grade teacher and 2000 Disney Teacher of the Year, from Harlem, New York

The more you prepare outside of class, the less you perspire in class. The less you perspire in class, the more you inspire the class.

—Ho Boon Tiong

If a child can't learn the way we teach, maybe we should teach the way they learn.

—Ignacio Estrada

A teacher should have maximal authority, and minimal power.

—Thomas Szasz

Don't try to fix the students, fix ourselves first. The good teacher makes the poor student good and the good student superior. When our students fail, we, as teachers, too, have failed.

—MARVA COLLINS, FROM HER BOOK *MAKING A DIFFERENCE IN THE CLASSROOM* (1992)

Treat the students the way you would want to be treated.

—ANONYMOUS

Teachers should guide without dictating, and participate without dominating.

—C. B. NEBLETTE

Remember that you are a teacher; you are helping people, making them feel safer, taking them from fear to love, from ignorance to knowledge.

—STUART WILDE

A schoolmaster should have an atmosphere of awe, and walk wonderingly, as if he was amazed at being himself.

—WALTER BAGEHOT

If the teacher is not respected and the student not cared for, confusion will arise, however clever one is.

—LAO-TZU

All kids need is a little help, a little hope, and somebody who believes in them.

—EARVIN "MAGIC" JOHNSON

Nothing you do for children is ever wasted.

—GARRISON KEILLOR

A teacher ought, therefore, to be as agreeable as possible, that remedies, which are rough in their nature, may be rendered soothing by gentleness of hand; he ought to praise some parts of his pupils' performances, tolerate some, and to alter others, giving his reasons why the alterations are made.

—QUINTILIAN

Learning must never be imposed as a Task, nor made a Trouble to them. There may be Dice and Playthings with the Letters on them to teach Children the Alphabet by playing; and twenty other Ways may be found, suitable to their particular Tempers, to make this kind of Learning a Sport to them.

—JOHN LOCKE, FROM HIS BOOK *SOME THOUGHTS CONCERNING EDUCATION AND OF THE CONDUCT OF THE UNDERSTANDING* (1693)

One of the most important things a teacher can do is to send the pupil home in the afternoon liking himself just a little better than when he came in that morning.

—ERNEST MELBY, COMMUNITY EDUCATOR ADVOCATE

You can't teach people everything they need to know. The best you can do is position them where they can find what they need to know when they need to know it.

—SEYMOUR PAPERT

Never tell a young person that something cannot be done. God may have been waiting for centuries for somebody ignorant enough of the impossibility to do that thing.

—DR. J. A. HOLMES

The finest gift you can give anyone is encouragement. Yet, almost no one gets the encouragement they need to grow to their full potential. If everyone received the encouragement they need to grow, the genius in most everyone would blossom and the world would produce abundance beyond our wildest dreams.

—SIDNEY MADWED

Never tell people how to do things. Tell them what to do and they will surprise you with their ingenuity.

—GEORGE PATTON

Teaching high school, in addition to knowing one's subject matter thoroughly and being able to convey it to others, requires the grit of a long-distance runner, the stamina of a boxer going fifteen rounds, the temperament of a juggler, and the street smarts of a three-card Monte dealer.

—PROFESSOR LARRY CUBAN

We think it's about little techniques and tricks, but techniques only take you so far. We need teachers who care about kids, who care about what they teach, and who can communicate with kids.

—PARKER J. PALMER, FROM HIS BOOK *THE COURAGE TO TEACH* (1997)

Whatever you want to teach, be brief.

—HORACE

It would be a great advantage to some schoolmasters if they would steal two hours a day from their pupils, and give their own minds the benefit of the robbery.

—J. F. BOYSE

Every leader needs to remember that a healthy respect for authority takes time to develop. It's like building trust. You don't instantly have trust, it has to be earned.

—MIKE KRZYZEWSKI, COLLEGE BASKETBALL COACH

The job of an educator is to teach students to see the vitality in themselves.

—JOSEPH CAMPBELL

Life is amazing: and the teacher had better prepare himself to be a medium for that amazement.

—EDWARD BLISHEN

Learn in order to teach and to practice.

—TALMUD RABBINICAL WRITINGS

Instruction begins when you, the teacher, learn from the learner; put yourself in his place so that you may understand . . . what he learns and the way he understands it.

—SØREN KIERKEGAARD

Acquire new knowledge whilst thinking over the old, and you may become a teacher of others.

—CONFUCIUS

Patience is the key to paradise.

—ARMENIAN PROVERB

Patience is the companion of wisdom.

—ST. AUGUSTINE

A teacher's purpose is not to create students in his own image, but to develop students who can create their own image.

—ANONYMOUS

Creative minds have always been known to survive any kind of bad training.

—ANNA FREUD

A teacher who is attempting to teach, without inspiring the pupil with a desire to learn, is hammering on a cold iron.

—HORACE MANN

Give the pupils something to do, not something to learn; and the doing is of such a nature as to demand thinking; learning naturally results.

—JOHN DEWEY

Merely to stuff the child with a lot of information, making him pass examinations, is the most unintelligent form of education.

—JIDDU KRISHNAMURTI

Spoon feeding in the long run teaches us nothing but the shape of the spoon.

—*THE OBSERVER*, "SAYINGS OF THE WEEK," OCTOBER 7, 1951

Seek help. Always question us veteran teachers and we will find the answers together.

—Carol Avila, teacher from Rhode Island and 1995 Presidential Award winner for Excellence in Science Teaching

The teacher's task is not to implant facts but to place the subject to be learned in front of the learner and, through sympathy, emotion, imagination, and patience, to awaken in the learner the restless drive for answers and insights which enlarge the personal life and give it meaning.

—Nathan M. Pusey

"Aliveness" in the teacher must pass over to "aliveness" in the children.

—Rudolf Steiner

If in any manner we can stimulate the higher form of knowing, new passages are opened for us into nature; the mind flows into and through things hardest and highest and metamorphosis is possible.

—RALPH WALDO EMERSON

Three things give the student the possibility of surpassing his teacher: ask a lot of questions, remember the answers, teach.

—JAN AMOS COMÉNIUS

Teachers must regard every imperfection in the pupil's comprehension not as a defect but as a deficit in his or her own instruction, and endeavor to develop the ability to discover a new method of teaching.

—LEO TOLSTOY

If you become a teacher, by your pupils you'll be taught.

—OSCAR HAMMERSTEIN II

There is nothing more unequal than the equal treatment of unequal people.

—THOMAS JEFFERSON

———⟫◆⟪———

Mentoring is all about people—it's about caring, about relationships and sensitivity. As it becomes increasingly in vogue it is becoming too formulated—concerned with performance metrics, critical success factors, investment and spending. It'll be a disaster.

—RENÉ CARAYOL, BUSINESS GURU

———⟫◆⟪———

You teach best what you most need to learn.

—RICHARD BACH

———⟫◆⟪———

The lecturer should give the audience full reason to believe that all his powers have been exerted for their pleasure and instruction.

—MICHAEL FARADAY

———⟫◆⟪———

Theories and goals of education don't matter a whit if you do not consider your students to be human beings.

—LOU ANN WALKER

When love and skill work together, expect a masterpiece.

—JOHN RUSKIN

A man should first direct himself in the way he should go. Only then should he instruct others.

—BUDDHA

Everything should be made as simple as possible, but not simpler.

—ALBERT EINSTEIN

To arrive at the simple is difficult.

—RASHID ELISHA

Being entirely honest with oneself is a good exercise.

—SIGMUND FREUD

The way to gain a good reputation is to endeavor to be what you desire to appear.

—SOCRATES

These children taught me a very simple but often overlooked principle. Believe in a child's power to succeed and they will succeed.

—MAGGIE KEYSER, 1999 DISNEY TEACHER OF THE YEAR, FROM LAFAYETTE ELEMENTARY SCHOOL

The teaching goes on.

—MITCH ALBOM, FROM HIS BOOK *TUESDAYS WITH MORRIE* (1997)

Sometimes the last thing learners need is for their preferred learning style to be affirmed. Agreeing to let people learn only in a way that feels comfortable and familiar can restrict seriously their chance for development.

—STEPHEN BROOKFIELD

I was always prepared for success, but that means that I have to be prepared for failure, too.

—SHEL SILVERSTEIN

One of the least discussed ways of carrying a student through a hard unit of material is to challenge him with a change to exercise his full powers, so that he may discover the pleasure of full and effective functioning.

—JEROME S. BRUNER, AS QUOTED IN *THE TEACHER AND THE TAUGHT* (1963)

We must beware of what I will call "inert ideas" that is to say, ideas that are merely received into the mind without being utilized or tested or thrown into fresh combinations.

—ALFRED NORTH WHITEHEAD, FROM HIS BOOK *AIMS OF EDUCATION AND OTHER ESSAYS* (1967)

Our highest endeavor must be to develop free human beings, who are able of themselves to impart purpose and direction to their lives.

—RUDOLF STEINER

Only that which does not teach, which does not cry out, which does not persuade, which does not condescend, which does not explain, is irresistible.

—W. B. YEATS

The mind, like the body, cannot assimilate beyond a certain rate; and if you ply it with facts faster than it can assimilate them, they are soon rejected again: instead of being built into the intellectual fabric, they fall out of recollection after the passing of the examination for which they were got up.

—HERBERT SPENCER

As teachers, we must constantly try to improve schools and we must keep working at changing and experimenting and trying until we have developed ways of teaching every child.

—ALBERT SHANKER

Teaching consists of causing people to go into situations from which they cannot escape, except by thinking. Do not handicap your children by making their lives easy.

—ROBERT HEINLEIN, FROM HIS BOOK *THE NOTEBOOKS OF LAZARUS LONG* (1973)

You need to have a plan of sorts, but don't become consumed by it. Winds change.

—JOSEPH EHRHARD, PHYSICS TEACHER FROM WESTON, CONNECTICUT

Teachers who get "burned out" are not the ones who are constantly learning, which can be exhilarating, but those who feel they must stay in control and ahead of the students at all times.

—FRANK SMITH

Few things help an individual more than to place responsibility upon him, and to let him know that you trust him.

—BOOKER T. WASHINGTON

When angry, count to ten, before you speak; if very angry, an hundred.

—THOMAS JEFFERSON, IN A LETTER TO THOMAS JEFFERSON SMITH (1825)

The benefits gained from learning how to manage conflict constructively far outweigh the costs of learning time lost by students being upset and angry.

—THOMAS J. SERGIOVANNI, FROM HIS BOOK *BUILDING COMMUNITY IN SCHOOLS* (1994)

When I taught in public high school for three years I always ate lunch with a different group of students whether they were in my class or not, until I got to know most of them. The teachers thought I was idiotic, but they didn't realize that it actually made it easier for me to teach, that before I could effectively discipline students, I had to earn their friendship and respect.

—MARVA COLLINS, FROM HER BOOK *MAKING A DIFFERENCE IN THE CLASSROOM* (1992)

You can preach at them: that is a hook without a worm; you can order them to volunteer: that is dishonest; you can call upon them: you are needed, and that approach will hardly ever fail.

—KURT HAHN, AS QUOTED IN *RECLAIMING YOUTH AT RISK: OUR HOPE FOR THE FUTURE* (1990)

Children may forget what you say, but they'll never forget how you make them feel.

—PARKER J. PALMER

I have never reprimanded a boy in the evening—darkness and a troubled mind are a poor combination.

—FRANK L. BOYDEN

I have one rule—attention. They give me theirs and I give them mine.

—SISTER EVANGELIST, ON TEACHING HIGH SCHOOL STUDENTS,
AS QUOTED IN *THE GAZETTE* (1980)

It takes time to persuade men to do even what is for their own good.

—THOMAS JEFFERSON, IN A LETTER TO REVEREND CHARLES CLAY
(1790)

No trace of slavery ought to mix with the studies of the freeborn man . . .
No study, pursued under compulsion, remains rooted in the memory.

—PLATO

Love is at the root of all healthy discipline.

> —FRED ROGERS, FROM HIS BOOK *MISTER ROGERS TALKS WITH PARENTS* (1983)

Sometimes parents require new teachers to earn their trust. They view us as experimenting with their kid. If you show them you really care, then they are supportive.

> —MIKE BENEVENTO, TEACHER FROM UPPER SADDLE RIVER, NEW JERSEY, AS QUOTED IN *SURVIVAL GUIDE FOR NEW TEACHERS* (2000)

We must accept finite disappointment, but we must never lose infinite hope.

> —MARTIN LUTHER KING, JR.

Strength does not come from physical capacity. It comes from an indomitable will.

> —MAHATMA GANDHI

Before you can inspire with emotion, you must be swamped with it yourself. Before you can move their tears, your own must flow. To convince them, you must yourself believe.

—WINSTON CHURCHILL

Be kind whenever possible . . . It is always possible.

—TENZIN GYATSO, THE FOURTEENTH DALAI LAMA

There will be stumbling blocks or stepping stones; it all depends on how we use them.

—ANONYMOUS

An atmosphere of trust, love, and humor can nourish extraordinary human capacity.

—MARILYN FERGUSON, FROM HER BOOK *THE AQUARIAN CONSPIRACY* (1987)

Children love repetition, but not when it's overdone. They will lose interest if you progress too slowly, and if you go too quickly the materials will be beyond their comprehension.

—Elizabeth G. Hainstock, from her book *Teaching Montessori in the Home* (1968)

If people do not try very hard to understand what a child says, he may come to feel that most of the time there is not much point in saying anything.

—John Holt, from his book *How Children Learn* (1967)

One great Reason why many Children abandon themselves wholly to silly sports and trifle away all their time insipidly is because they have found their Curiosity baulk'd and their Enquiries neglected. But had they been treated with more Kindness and Respect and their Questions answered, as they should, to their Satisfaction, I doubt not but they would have taken more Pleasure in Learning and improving their Knowledge.

—John Locke, from his book *Some Thoughts Concerning Education and of the Conduct of the Understanding* (1693)

Allow time for your child to complete each activity that she begins.

—TERRY MALLOY, FROM HIS BOOK *MONTESSORI AND YOUR CHILD: A PRIMER FOR PARENTS* (1974)

The lines which are set for him for his imitation in writing should not contain useless sentences, but such as convey some moral instruction. The remembrance of such admonitions will attend him to old age, and will be of use even for the formation of his character.

—QUINTILIAN

If a child is reading aloud to you and comes to a word she doesn't understand, don't immediately ask her to sound it out. Instead, say, "What makes sense here?" Then the child has to think about how that word fits in with what she's been reading.

—MASHA KABAKOW RUDMAN, UNIVERSITY OF MASSACHUSETTS EDUCATOR, AS QUOTED IN "IMPROVED READING BEGINS AT HOME, WHERE A CHILD CAN SEE HOW READING FITS IN WITH OTHER ACTIVITIES," THE *NEW YORK TIMES* (1992)

I like to have a thing suggested rather than told in full. When every detail is given, the mind rests satisfied and the imagination loses the desire to use its own wings.

—THOMAS BAILEY ALDRICH

Be all that you can be. Find your future—as a teacher.

—MADELINE FUCHS HOLZER, ARTS IN EDUCATION DIRECTOR FOR THE NEW YORK STATE COUNCIL ON THE ARTS

I wish I could persuade every teacher to be proud of his occupation—not conceited or pompous, but proud. People who introduce themselves with the shamed remark that they are "just teachers," give me despair in my heart.

—WILLIAM GARR

You can't direct the wind but you can adjust the sails.

—ANONYMOUS

If you want to make good use of your time, you've got to know what's most important and then give it all you've got.

—LEE IACOCCA, AMERICAN INDUSTRIALIST AND FORMER HEAD OF CHRYSLER

You must first know what people need, and then invest yourself where you are most needed.

—RUSSELL H. CONWELL, AMERICAN BAPTIST MINISTER, LAWYER, WRITER, ORATOR, AND FOUNDER OF TEMPLE UNIVERSITY

I always prefer to believe the best of everybody; it saves so much trouble.

—RUDYARD KIPLING

Attitudes are more important than facts.

—KARL A. MENNINGER

One of the best ways to persuade others is with your ears—by listening to them.

—Dean Rusk, former U.S. Secretary of State

I can but think that the world would be better and brighter if our teachers would dwell on the duty of happiness as well as the happiness of duty; for we ought to be as bright and genial as we can, if only because to be cheerful ourselves is a most effectual contribution to the happiness of others.

—John Lubbock

A compliment is verbal sunshine.

—Robert Orben, American magician and comedy writer

The purpose of education is to make the choices clear to people, not to make the choices for people.

—Peter McWilliams, writer and cannabis activist

You need to be aware of what others are doing, applaud their efforts, acknowledge their successes, and encourage them in their pursuits. When we all help one another, everybody wins.

—JIM STOVALL

We must have the courage to examine everything, discuss everything, and even to teach everything.

—CONDORCET, MATHEMATICIAN AND EARLY POLITICAL SCIENTIST

All students can learn and succeed, but not in the same day, in the same way.

—WILLIAM G. SPADY

Education should be the process of helping everyone to discover his uniqueness, to teach him how to develop that uniqueness, and then to show him how to share it because that's the only reason for having anything.

—DR. LEO BUSCAGLIA

We should never pretend to know what we don't know, we should not feel ashamed to ask and learn from people below, and we should listen carefully to the views of the cadres at the lowest levels. Be a pupil before you become a teacher; learn from the cadres at the lower levels before you issue orders.

—MAO TSE-TUNG

You teach a little by what you say. You teach the most by what you are.

—HENRIETTA MEARS

Interest can produce learning on a scale compared to fear as a nuclear explosion to a firecracker.

—STANLEY KUBRICK

One of the great strengths of caring as an ethos is that it does not assume that all students should be treated by some impartial standards of fairness. Some students need more attention than others.

—Nel Noddings, from her book *Caring: A Feminist Perspective* (1984)

Do not appear so scholarly, I pray you. Humanize your talk, and speak to be understood. Do you think a Greek name gives more weight to your reasons?

—Molière

If you are truly serious about preparing your child for the future, don't teach him to subtract—teach him to deduct.

—Fran Lebowitz, from her book *Social Studies* (1981)

You cannot teach a man anything; you can only help him find it within himself.

—Galileo Galilei

Kind words can be short and easy to speak, but their echoes are endless.

—MOTHER TERESA

When discipline was required, I tried to dole it out in a manner that was firm but fair, with no emotionalism or anger attached. Anger prevents proper thinking and makes you vulnerable.

—JOHN WOODEN, FROM HIS BOOK *MY PERSONAL BEST* (2004)

Practice is the best of all instructors.

—PUBLILIUS SYRUS

Children have real understanding only of that which they invent themselves, and each time that we try to teach them too quickly, we keep them from reinventing it themselves.

—JEAN PIAGET

Not many of you should become teachers, my brothers and sisters, for you know that we who teach will be judged with greater strictness.

—JAMES 3:1

Are we influencing student's self-concept in positive or negative ways? . . . How can a person feel liked unless somebody likes him? How can a person feel wanted unless somebody wants him? . . . And how can a person feel that he is capable unless he has some success?

—ARTHUR COMBS

It is no matter what you teach them first, any more than what leg you shall put into your breeches first. You may stand disputing which is best to put in first, but in the mean time your breech is bare.

—SAMUEL JOHNSON

The most prominent requisite to a lecturer, though perhaps not really the most important, is a good delivery; . . . I am sorry to say that the generality of mankind cannot accompany us one short hour unless the path is strewn with flowers.

—MICHAEL FARADAY, AS QUOTED IN *ADVICE TO A LECTURER* (1960)

There is no such whetstone, to sharpen a good wit and encourage a will to learning, as is praise.

—ROGER ASCHAM

A pupil from whom nothing is ever demanded which he cannot do, never does all he can.

—JOHN STUART MILL, FROM HIS 1873 AUTOBIOGRAPHY

Let people realize clearly that every time they threaten someone or humiliate or hurt unnecessarily or dominate or reject another human being, they become forces for the creation of psychopathology, even if these be small forces. Let them recognize that every man who is kind, helpful . . . and warm, is a psychotherapeutic force.

—ABRAHAM MASLOW

You can't wipe away tears with notebook paper.

—CHARLES SCHULZ

Too much rigidity on the part of teachers should be followed by a brisk spirit of insubordination on the part of the taught.

—AGNES REPPLIER

When inspiration does not come to me, I go half way to meet it.

—SIGMUND FREUD

He who wishes to teach us a truth should not tell it to us, but simply suggest it with a brief gesture, a gesture which starts an ideal trajectory in the air along which we glide until we find ourselves at the feet of the new truth.

—JOSE ORTEGA Y GASSET

It is easier for a teacher to command than to teach.

—JOHN LOCKE

Pick battles big enough to matter, small enough to win.

—JONATHAN KOZOL, NONFICTION WRITER, EDUCATOR, AND ACTIVIST, FROM HIS BOOK *ON BEING A TEACHER (1994)*

Perhaps the most important single cause of a person's success or failure educationally has to do with the question of what he believes about himself.

—ARTHUR COMBS

In nature there are neither rewards nor punishments—there are consequences.

—ROBERT GREEN INGERSOLL

What a teacher doesn't say is a telling part of what a student hears.

—MAURICE NATANSON

A leader knows what's best to do; a manager knows merely how best to do it.

—KENNETH ADELMAN

You cannot manage men into battle. You manage things; you lead people.

—GRACE MURRAY HOPPER, NAVAL OFFICER AND PIONEER IN COMPUTER PROGRAMMING

No person can be a great leader unless he takes genuine joy in the successes of those under him.

—W. A. NANCE

You get the best effort from others not by lighting a fire beneath them, but by building a fire within.

—BOB NELSON

The key to successful leadership today is influence, not authority.

—KENNETH BLANCHARD

The speed of the leader determines the rate of the pack.

—WAYNE LUKAS

Teachers who inspire realize there will always be rocks in the road ahead of us.

—ANONYMOUS

<hr>

The man who follows a crowd will never be followed by a crowd.

—S. DONNELL

<hr>

I found out that if you are going to win games, you had better be ready to adapt.

—SCOTTY BOWMAN, HOCKEY COACH

<hr>

There are 86,400 seconds in a day. It's up to you to decide what to do with them.

—JIM VALVANO

<hr>

Coaches have to watch for what they don't want to see and listen to what they don't want to hear.

—JOHN MADDEN

The first task of a leader is to keep hope alive.

—JOE BATTEN

I don't know any other way to lead but by example.

—DON SHULA

Setting a goal is not the main thing. It is deciding how you will go about achieving it and staying with that plan.

—KNUTE ROCKNE

Leadership is a matter of having people look at you and gain confidence, seeing how you react. If you're in control, they're in control.

—PAT RILEY

I believe managing is like holding a dove in your hand. If you hold it too tightly you kill it, but if you hold it too loosely, you lose it.

—TOMMY LASORDA

I do not believe in the gifted. If the students have *ganas* [Spanish for desire], I can make them do it.

—JAIME ESCALANTE, MATH TEACHER AND BASIS FOR THE FILM
STAND AND DELIVER (1988)

My philosophy of learning, like my blood type, is be positive. Keeping student attitudes positive is vital to their success in learning.

—DAVID PLEACHER

A "no" uttered from deepest conviction is better and greater than a "yes" merely uttered to please, or what is worse, to avoid trouble.

—MAHATMA GANDHI

You don't have to teach people to be human. You need to teach them how to stop being inhuman.

—ELDRIDGE CLEAVER

If those about him will talk to him often about the Stories he has read and hear him tell them, it will, besides other Advantages, add Encouragement and Delight to his Reading, when he find there is some Use and Pleasure in it.

—JOHN LOCKE, FROM HIS BOOK *SOME THOUGHTS CONCERNING EDUCATION AND OF THE CONDUCT OF THE UNDERSTANDING* (1693)

Look up and not down; look forward and not back; look out and not in; and lend a hand.

—E. E. HALE

Impatience never commanded success.

—EDWIN H. CHAPIN

———◆———

What gives light must endure burning.

—VIKTOR FRANKL

———◆———

You have to have confidence in your ability, and then be tough enough to follow through.

—ROSALYNN CARTER

———◆———

You cannot have a learning organization without a shared vision. . . . A shared vision provides a compass to keep learning on course when stress develops.

—PETER SENGE, AUTHOR OF *THE DANCE OF CHANGE* (1999)

———◆———

I am sure it is one's duty as a teacher to try to show boys that no opinions, no tastes, no emotions are worth much unless they are one's own. I suffered acutely as a boy from the lack of being shown this.

—A. C. BENSON

The secret to productive goal setting is in establishing clearly defined goals, writing them down and then focusing on them several times a day with words, pictures, and emotions as if we've already achieved them.

—DENIS WAITLEY

The work can wait while you show the child the rainbow, but the rainbow won't wait while you do the work.

—PATRICIA CLAFFORD

It is not so much what is poured into the student, but what is planted that really counts.

—ANONYMOUS

The powers of students sometimes sink under too great severity in correction . . . while they fear everything, they cease to attempt anything.

—QUINTILIAN

Let the no! once pronounced, be as a brazen wall, against which when a child hath some few times exhausted his strength without making any impression, he will never attempt to overthrown again.

—JEAN-JACQUES ROUSSEAU

You can't hold a man down without staying down with him.

—BOOKER T. WASHINGTON

A decline in the extrinsic payoff requires a compensating improvement in the intrinsic satisfaction of learning if students are to be motivated.

—HENRY M. LEVIN

There is no such thing as a weird human being. It's just that some people require more understanding than others do.

—TOM ROBBINS, FROM HIS BOOK *ANOTHER ROADSIDE ATTRACTION* (1971)

No act of kindness, no matter how small, is ever wasted.

—AESOP

Work 'em hard, play 'em hard, feed 'em up to the nines and send 'em to bed so tired that they are asleep before their heads are on the pillow.

—FRANK L. BOYDEN, AS QUOTED IN *NEWS SUMMARIES* (1954)

Fun is a good thing, but only when it spoils nothing better.

—GEORGE SANTAYANA, FROM HIS BOOK *THE SENSE OF BEAUTY* (1896)

Do not use compulsion, but let early education be rather a sort of amusement.

—Plato

Those acquirements crammed by force into the mind of children simply clog and stifle intelligence. In order that knowledge be properly digested, it must be swallowed with a good appetite.

—Anatole France

Accustom your children constantly to this; if a thing happened at one window and they, when relating it, say that it happened at another do not let it pass, but instantly check them; you do not know where deviation from truth will end.

—Samuel Johnson

Your child is mainly interested in the process of doing things; he is not very concerned with the end results.

—TERRY MALLOY, FROM HIS BOOK *MONTESSORI AND YOUR CHILD: A PRIMER FOR PARENTS* (1974)

Most teachers waste their time by asking questions which are intended to discover what a pupil does not know whereas the true art of questioning has for its purpose to discover what the pupil knows or is capable of knowing.

—ALBERT EINSTEIN

Develop a built-in bullshit detector.

—ERNEST HEMINGWAY

Praise, like gold and diamonds, owes its value only to its scarcity.

—SAMUEL JOHNSON

Do not on any account attempt to write on both sides of the paper at once.

—W. C. STELLAR AND R. J. YEATMAN, FROM THEIR BOOK *1066 AND ALL THAT* (1930)

Erect no artificial walls that might limit potential, stifle creativity, or shackle innovation.

—MIKE KRZYZEWSKI

To suggest is to create—to describe is to destroy.

—ROBERT DOISNEAU

Language is a living, kicking, growing, flitting, evolving reality, and the teacher should spontaneously reflect its vibrant and protean qualities.

—JOHN A. RASSIAS, AS QUOTED IN *QUOTE* (1974)

It is not every question that deserves an answer.

—PUBLIUS SYRUS

It is not every question that deserves an answer.

Ask a silly question and you'll get a silly answer.

—AMERICAN PROVERB

If you don't like the question that's asked, answer some other question.

—HOWARD BAKER

The simplest questions are the hardest to answer.

—NORTHROP FRYE

A question not to be asked is a question not to be answered.

—ROBERT SOUTHEY, FROM HIS BOOK *THE DOCTOR* (1812)

No answer is also an answer.

—DANISH PROVERB

———◆———

There's no good answer to a stupid question.

—RUSSIAN PROVERB

———◆———

Almost all important questions are important precisely because they are not susceptible to quantitative answer.

—ARTHUR SCHLESINGER, JR.

———◆———

CHAPTER FOUR

Those We Teach and Those Who Raise Them

I have found the best way to give advice to your children is to find out what they want and then advise them to do it.

—HARRY S. TRUMAN

There are only two lasting bequests we can hope to give our children. One is roots; the other, wings.

—HODDING CARTER

Where did we ever get the crazy idea that in order to make children do better, first we have to make them feel worse? Think of the last time you felt humiliated or treated unfairly. Did you feel like cooperating or doing better?

—JANE NELSON

You can understand and relate to most people better if you look at them— no matter how old or impressive they may be—as if they are children.

—LEO ROSTEN

When I approach a child, he inspires in me two sentiments; tenderness for what he is, and respect for what he may become.

—LOUIS PASTEUR

If we don't stand up for children, then we don't stand for much.

—MARIAN WRIGHT EDELMAN

If a child is to keep alive his inborn sense of wonder, he needs the companionship of at least one adult who can share it, rediscovering with him the joy, excitement, and mystery of the world we live in.

—RACHEL CARSON

To value his own good opinion, a child has to feel that he is a worthwhile person. He has to have confidence in himself as an individual.

—SIDONIE GRUENBERG

A young child is, indeed, a true scientist, just one big question mark. What? Why? How? I never cease to marvel at the recurring miracle of growth, to be fascinated by the mystery and wonder of this brave enthusiasm.

—VICTORIA WAGNER

A characteristic of the normal child is he doesn't act that way very often.

—ANONYMOUS

Kids: they dance before they learn there is anything that isn't music.

—WILLIAM STAFFORD

Children are one-third of our population and all of our future.

—SELECT PANEL FOR THE PROMOTION OF CHILD HEALTH, 1981

Even when freshly washed and relieved of all obvious confections, children tend to be sticky.

—FRAN LEBOWITZ

━━◆◆◆━━

If our American way of life fails the child, it fails us all.

—PEARL S. BUCK, AUTHOR OF *THE JOY OF CHILDREN* (1964)

━━◆◆◆━━

Every child comes with the message that God is not yet discouraged of man.

—RABINDRANATH TAGORE

━━◆◆◆━━

Children make you want to start life over.

—MUHAMMAD ALI

━━◆◆◆━━

Youth is a perpetual intoxication; it is a fever of the mind.

—François Duc de la Rochefoucauld

Children find everything in nothing; men find nothing in everything.

—Giacomo Leopardi

Women gather together to wear silly hats, eat dainty food, and forget how unresponsive their husbands are. Men gather to talk sports, eat heavy food, and forget how demanding their wives are. Only where children gather is there any real chance of fun.

—Mignon McLaughlin, from her book *The Neurotic's Notebook* (1960)

The real menace in dealing with a five-year-old is that in no time at all you begin to sound like a five-year-old.

—Joan Kerr, from her book *Please Don't Eat the Daisies* (1957)

Children are contemptuous, haughty, irritable, envious, sneaky, selfish, lazy, flighty, timid, liars, and hypocrites, quick to laugh and cry, extreme in expressing joy and sorrow, especially about trifles, they'll do anything to avoid pain but they enjoy inflicting it: little men already.

—JEAN DE LA BRUYÈRE, FROM HIS BOOK *LES CARACTÈRES* (1688)

There are no seven wonders of the world in the eyes of a child. There are seven million.

—WALT STREIGHTIFF

If I had influence with the good fairy who is supposed to preside over the christening of all children, I should ask that her gift to each child in the world be a sense of wonder so indestructible that it would last throughout life.

—RACHEL CARSON

You can learn many things from children. How much patience you have, for instance.

—FRANKLIN P. ADAMS, AMERICAN JOURNALIST

Never raise your hands to your kids. It leaves your groin unprotected.

—RED BUTTONS

The young always have the same problem—how to rebel and conform at the same time. They have now solved this by defying their parents and copying one another.

—QUENTIN CRISP

Little children, headache; big children, heartache.

—ITALIAN PROVERB

Heredity is what sets the parents of a teenager wondering about each other.

> —LAURENCE J. PETER

Don't laugh at a youth for his affectations; he is only trying on one face after another to find a face of his own.

> —LOGAN PEARSALL SMITH, FROM "AGE AND DEATH," *AFTERTHOUGHTS* (1931)

If you want to recapture your youth, just cut off his allowance.

> —AL BERNSTEIN

Perhaps one way of coping with the population explosion would be to give every potential parent some experience in driving a school bus.

> —FRANKLIN P. JONES

When buying a used car, punch the buttons on the radio. If all the stations are rock and roll, there's a good chance the transmission is shot.

—Larry Lujack

Too many of today's children have straight teeth and crooked morals.

—Anonymous

Adolescence: A stage between infancy and adultery.

—Ambrose Bierce, from his book *The Devil's Dictionary* (1911)

The best substitute for experience is being sixteen.

—Raymond Duncan

The teenager seems to have replaced the Communist as the appropriate target for public controversy and foreboding.

—EDGAR FRIEDENBERG

The invention of the teenager was a mistake. Once you identify a period of life in which people get to stay out late but don't have to pay taxes— naturally, no one wants to live any other way.

—JUDITH MARTIN

There's nothing wrong with the younger generation that becoming taxpayers won't cure.

—DAN BENNETT

Teenagers complain there's nothing to do, then stay out all night doing it.

—BOB PHILLIPS

Telling a teenager the facts of life is like giving a fish a bath.

—ARNOLD GLASOW

I have seen my kid struggle into the kitchen in the morning with outfits that need only one accessory: an empty gin bottle.

—ERMA BOMBECK

You don't have to suffer to be a poet. Adolescence is enough suffering for anyone.

—JOHN CIARDI, AS QUOTED IN *THE SIMMONS REVIEW* (FALL 1962)

A boy becomes an adult three years before his parents think he does, and about two years after he thinks he does.

—LEWIS B. HERSHEY, AS QUOTED IN *NEWS SUMMARIES* (DECEMBER 31, 1951)

How strange that the young should always think the world is against them—when in fact that is the only time it is for them.

    —MIGNON MCLAUGHLIN, FROM HER BOOK *THE NEUROTIC'S NOTEBOOK* (1960)

At fourteen you don't need sickness or death for tragedy.

    —JESSAMYN WEST

It is hard to convince a high-school student that he will encounter a lot of problems more difficult than those of algebra and geometry.

    —EDGAR W. HOWE

Adolescents are not monsters. They are just people trying to learn how to make it among the adults in the world, who are probably not so sure themselves.

    —VIRGINIA SATIR, FROM HER BOOK *NEW PEOPLEMAKING* (1988)

The troubles of adolescence eventually all go away—it's just like a really long, bad cold.

—Dawn Ruelas

I never expected to see the day when girls would get sunburned in the places they do now.

—Will Rogers

My adolescence progressed normally: enough misery to keep the death wish my usual state, an occasional high to keep me from actually taking the gas-pipe.

—Faye Moskowitz

When I was a teenager, I read a lot of Poe.

—Dario Argento

It's things like the Phil Spector records. On one level they were rebellion, on another level they were keeping the teenager in his place.

—LESTER BANGS

Your modern teenager is not about to listen to advice from an old person, defined as a person who remembers when there was no Velcro.

—DAVE BARRY

Until the rise of American advertising, it never occurred to anyone anywhere in the world that the teenager was a captive in a hostile world of adults.

—GORE VIDAL

First he wrought, and afterwards he taught.

—GEOFFREY CHAUCER

A child can ask questions that a wise man cannot answer.

—ANONYMOUS

Juvenile appraisals of other juveniles make up in clarity what they lack in charity.

—EDGAR FRIEDENBERG

Children are the true connoisseurs. What's precious to them has no price—only value.

—BEL KAUFMAN

A torn jacket is soon mended; but hard words bruise the heart of a child.

—HENRY WADSWORTH LONGFELLOW

I had a great feeling of relief when I began to understand that a youngster needs more than just subject matter. Oh, I know mathematics well, and I teach it well. I used to think that that was all I needed to do. Now I teach children, not math. I accept the fact that I can only succeed partially with some of them.

—ANONYMOUS TEACHER, AS QUOTED BY EVERETT SHOSTROM IN *MAN, THE MANIPULATOR (1968)*

Perhaps a child who is fussed over gets a feeling of destiny, he thinks he is in the world for something important and it gives him drive and confidence.

—BENJAMIN SPOCK

A child should always say what's true, / And speak when he is spoken to, / And behave mannerly at table: At least as far as he is able.

—ROBERT LOUIS STEVENSON

Life's aspirations come in the guise of children.

—RABINDRANATH TAGORE

It is true that a child is always hungry all over; but he is also curious all over, and his curiosity is excited about as early as his hunger.

—CHARLES DUDLEY WARNER

All young people want to kick up their heels and defy convention; most of them would prefer to do it at a not too heavy cost.

—ELMER DAVIS

The average teenager still has all the faults his parents outgrew.

—ANONYMOUS

Those who love the young best stay young longest.

—EDGAR FRIEDENBERG

Children need invitations the way flowers need sunshine. When they are treated with indifference, they are likely to become indifferent to themselves and to school.

—WILLIAM PURKEY

———⋙◆⋘———

A child does not thrive on what he is prevented from doing, but what he actually does.

—MARCELENE COX, IN *LADIES' HOME JOURNAL* (1945)

———⋙◆⋘———

When teachers have a low expectation level for their children's learning, the children seldom exceed that expectation. This is the self-fulfilling prophecy.

—JOHN NIEMEYER

———⋙◆⋘———

What a shame it is that children are constantly being ranked and evaluated. What a shame it is that superior achievement of one child tends to debase the achievement of another.

—Morris Rosenberg, from his book *Society and the Adolescent Self-Image* (1965)

The denunciation of the young is a necessary part of the hygiene of older people, and greatly assists in the circulation of the blood.

—Logan Pearsall Smith

Train up a child in the way he should go: and when he is old, he will not depart from it.

—Proverbs 22:6

A child is owed the greatest respect; if you ever have something disgraceful in mind, don't ignore your son's tender years.

—Juvenal

It should be noted that children at play are not playing about; their games should be seen as their most serious-minded activity.

—MONTAIGNE, FROM *ESSAIS* (1580)

At first the infant,
Mewling and puking in the nurse's arms.
And then the whining schoolboy with his satchel,
And shining morning face creeping like snail
Unwilling to school.

—WILLIAM SHAKESPEARE, FROM *AS YOU LIKE IT*

Men are generally more careful of the breed of their horses and dogs than their children.

—WILLIAM PENN, FROM HIS BOOK *SOME FRUITS OF SOLITUDE* (1693)

Alas, regardless of their doom,
The little victims play!

No sense have they of ills to come.
Nor care beyond to-day.

—THOMAS GRAY, FROM HIS POEM "ODE ON A DISTANT PROSPECT OF ETON COLLEGE" (1747)

The Child is father of the Man;
And I could with my days to be
Bound each to each by natural piety.

—WILLIAM WORDSWORTH, FROM HIS POEM "MY HEART LEAPS UP WHEN I BEHOLD" (1807)

A child's a plaything for an hour.

—CHARLES LAMB, FROM HIS POEM "PARENTAL RECOLLECTIONS" (1809)

The place is very well and quiet and the children only scream in a low voice.

—LORD BYRON, IN A LETTER TO HIS WIFE, 1813

You are a human boy, my young friend. A human boy. O glorious to be a human boy! . . . O running stream of sparkling joy to be a soaring human boy!

—CHARLES DICKENS, FROM HIS BOOK *BLEAK HOUSE* (1853)

Go practice if you please
With men and women: leave a child alone
For Christ's particular love's sake!

—ROBERT BROWNING, FROM HIS BOOK *THE RING AND THE BOOK* (1868–1869)

You will find as the children grow up that as a rule children are a bitter disappointment—their greatest object being to do precisely what their parents do not wish and have anxiously tried to prevent.

—QUEEN VICTORIA, IN A LETTER TO THE CROWN PRINCESS OF PRUSSIA, 1876

Children are given us to discourage our better emotions.

—SAKI (H. H. MUNRO)

━━◆━━

There is no end to the violations committed by children on children, quietly talking alone.

—ELIZABETH BOWEN, FROM HER BOOK *THE HOUSE IN PARIS* (1935)

━━◆━━

Childhood is Last Chance Gulch for happiness. After that, you know too much.

—TOM STOPPARD, FROM HIS BOOK *WHERE ARE THEY NOW?* (1973)

━━◆━━

Our schools are improving. It's our childhoods that are not.

—KEITH GEIGER, IN THE *NEW YORK TIMES* (JULY 5, 1991)

━━◆━━

With the birth of each child, you lose two novels.

    —CANDIA McWILLIAMS, IN *THE GUARDIAN* (MAY 5, 1993)

Allowing children to be free of child-rearing did not, after all, produce a generation of happy, carefree, uncomplicated, altruistic, and creative people. The experiment seems to suggest that a great deal of what we think of as "human nature" in the best sense—compassion, fairness, conscience—is, in fact, taught.

    —JUDITH MARTIN, AS QUOTED IN HER BOOK *MISS MANNERS RESCUES CIVILIZATION* (1996)

Young people are thoughtless as a rule.

    —HOMER

It is an illusion that youth is happy, an illusion of those who have lost it.

    —W. SOMERSET MAUGHAM

As a result of all his education, from everything he hears and sees around him, the child absorbs such a lot of lies and foolish nonsense, mixed in with essential truths, that the first duty of the adolescent who wants to be a healthy man is to disgorge it all.

—ROMAIN ROLLAND

We cannot always build the future for our youth, but we can build our youth for the future.

—FRANKLIN DELANO ROOSEVELT

When you see a problem child, look for a problem parent.

—ANONYMOUS

Spare the rod and spoil the child.

—ENGLISH PROVERB

Those who love their children don't think of the rod.

—GREEK PROVERB

———◆———

There is a brilliant child locked inside every student.

—MARVA COLLINS

———◆———

We must teach our children to dream with their eyes open.

—HARRY EDWARDS

———◆———

It is the responsibility of every adult . . . to make sure that children hear what we have learned from the lessons of life and to hear over and over that we love them and that they are not alone.

—MARIAN WRIGHT EDELMAN

———◆———

A hundred years from now it will not matter what my bank account was, the sort of house I lived in, or the kind of car I drove . . . but the world may be different because I was important in the life of a child.

—KATHY DAVIS, FORMER LT. GOVERNOR OF INDIANA

Education is more than filling a child with facts. It starts with posing questions.

—D. T. MAX

Children should be led into the right paths, not by severity, but by persuasion.

—TERENCE

Children require guidance and sympathy far more than instruction.

—ANNE SULLIVAN, TUTOR TO HELEN KELLER

A child educated only at school is an uneducated child.

—GEORGE SANTAYANA

Never have ideas about children, and never have ideas for them.

—GEORGE ORWELL

Teach a child how to think, not what to think.

—SIDNEY SUGARMAN

Never help a child with a task at which he feels he can succeed.

—MARIA MONTESSORI

When you want to teach children to think, you begin by treating them seriously when they are little, giving them responsibilities, talking to them candidly, providing privacy and solitude for them, and making them readers and thinkers of significant thoughts from the beginning. That's if you want to teach them to think.

—BERTRAND RUSSELL

The kids in our classroom are infinitely more significant than the subject matter we teach.

—MELADEE MCCARTY

What we want is to see the child in pursuit of knowledge, and not knowledge in pursuit of the child.

—GEORGE BERNARD SHAW

While we try to teach our children all about life, our children teach us what life is all about.

—ANGELA SCHWINDT

Many things can wait. Children cannot. Today their bones are being formed, their blood is being made, their senses are being developed. To them we cannot say "tomorrow." Their name is today.

—GABRIELA MISTRAL, CHILEAN TEACHER

The Founding Fathers in their wisdom decided that children were an unnatural strain on parents. So they provided jails called schools, equipped with tortures called an education.

—JOHN UPDIKE

The task is simple. We will organize children and teach them in a perfect way the things their fathers and mothers are doing in an imperfect way.

—JOHN D. ROCKEFELLER GENERAL EDUCATION BOARD (1906)

Expecting all children the same age to learn from the same materials is like expecting all children the same age to wear the same size clothing.

—MADELINE HUNTER

A child miseducated is a child lost.

—JOHN F. KENNEDY

Since every effort in our educational life seems to be directed toward making of the child a being foreign to itself, it must of necessity produce individuals foreign to one another, and in everlasting antagonism with each other.

—EMMA GOLDMAN

Children are unpredictable. You never know what inconsistency they're going to catch you in next.

—FRANKLIN P. JONES

A child cannot be taught by anyone who despises him, and a child cannot afford to be fooled.

—JAMES BALDWIN

There is always one moment in childhood when the door opens and lets the future in.

—GRAHAM GREENE, FROM HIS BOOK *THE POWER AND THE GLORY* (1940)

Children's talent to endure stems from their ignorance of alternatives.

—MAYA ANGELOU, FROM HER BOOK *I KNOW WHY THE CAGED BIRD SINGS* (1969)

When a child asks you something, answer him, for goodness' sake. But don't make a production of it. Children are children, but they can spot an evasion quicker than adults, and evasion simply muddles 'em.

—HARPER LEE

Kids today are oriented to immediacy. Theirs is a world of fast foods, fast music, fast cars, fast relationships, and fast gratification. They are not buying our promise for tomorrow because they don't think we can deliver, and they are probably right.

—LeRoy E. Hay, 1983 National Teacher of the Year

Children and adults alike share needs to be safe and secure; to belong and to be loved; to experience self-esteem through achievement, mastery, recognition, and respect; to be autonomous; and to experience self-actualization by pursuing one's inner abilities and finding intrinsic meaning and satisfaction in what one does.

—Thomas J. Sergiovanni, from his book *Building Community in Schools* (1994)

Young people need much more to be demanded of them. They need to be needed, they need to give, they need opportunities to show love, courage, sacrifice. They need to be part of a cause that it's larger then the sum of their individual appetites. They need to believe in something.

—Thomas Sobol, in his closing address to the Summer Law Institute at Columbia University, 2000

I had learned to respect the intelligence, integrity, creativity, and capacity for deep thought and hard work latent somewhere in every child; they had learned that I differed from them only in years and experience, and that as I, an ordinary human being, loved and respect them, I expected payment in kind.

—SYBIL MARSHALL, ON EIGHTEEN YEARS AS TEACHER IN A ONE-ROOM SCHOOL IN ENGLAND, FROM HER BOOK *AN EXPERIMENT IN EDUCATION* (1963)

Teenagers go to college to be with their boyfriends and girlfriends; they go because they can't think of anything else to do; they go because their parents want them to and sometimes because their parents don't want them to; they go to find themselves, or to find a husband, or to get away from home, and sometimes even to find out about the world in which they live.

—HAROLD HOWE II, AS QUOTED IN *NEWSWEEK* (1976)

Chaperons don't enforce morality; they force immorality to be discreet.

—JUDITH MARTIN

I see the mind of the five-year-old as a volcano with two vents: destructiveness and creativeness.

—SYLVIA ASHTON-WARNER, FROM HER BOOK *TEACHER* (1963)

Genius, when young, is divine.

—BENJAMIN DISRAELI, FROM HIS BOOK *CONINGSBY; OR, THE NEW GENERATION* (1884)

No one can keep a secret better than a child.

—VICTOR HUGO, FROM *LES MISÉRABLES* (1862)

So long as little children are allowed to suffer, there is no true love in this world.

—ISADORA DUNCAN, AS QUOTED IN *THIS QUARTER* (1929)

I long to remain a child, and I am still one in many respects.

—JEAN-JACQUES ROUSSEAU, FROM *CONFESSIONS, BOOK FOUR* (1782)

Such, such were the joys
When we all, girls and boys
In our youth time were seen
On the Echoing Green

—WILLIAM BLAKE, FROM HIS BOOK *SONGS OF INNOCENCE* (1789)

Children are likely to live up to what you believe of them.

—CLAUDIA ALTA TAYLOR "LADY BIRD" JOHNSON

What you teach your children is what you really believe in.

—CATHY WARNER WEATHERFORD

A child who constantly hears "don't," "be careful," "stop" will eventually be overtaken by schoolmates, business associates, and rival suitors.

—MARCELENE COX

A child's attitude towards everything is an artist's attitude.

—WILLA CATHER, FROM HER BOOK *THE SONG OF THE LARK* (1932)

Every child is an artist. The problem is how to remain an artist once he grows up.

—PABLO PICASSO

If you want your children to keep their feet on the ground, put some responsibility on their shoulders.

—ABIGAIL VAN BUREN ("DEAR ABBY")

It is difficult to give children a sense of security unless you have it yourself. If you have it, they catch it from you.

—Dr. William C. Menninger

It is frightening to think that you make your children merely by being yourself.

—Simone de Beauvoir, from her book *Les Belles Images*

Never allow your child to call you by your first name. He hasn't known you long enough.

—Fran Lebowitz, from her book *Social Studies* (1981)

Children seldom misquote you. In fact, they usually repeat word for word what you shouldn't have said.

—Anonymous

Never do for a child what he is capable of doing for himself.

> —ELIZABETH HAINSTOCK, FROM HER BOOK *TEACHING MONTESSORI IN THE HOME* (1968)

If we continually try to force a child to do what he is afraid to do, he will become more timid, and will use his brains and energy, not to explore the unknown, but to find ways to avoid the pressures we put on him.

> —JOHN HOLT (1923–1985), FROM HIS BOOK *HOW CHILDREN LEARN* (1967)

At every step the child should be allowed to meet the real experiences of life; the thorns should never be plucked from his roses.

> —ELLEN KEY, FROM HER BOOK *THE CENTURY OF THE CHILD*

To nourish children and raise them against the odds is in any time, any place, more valuable than to fix bolts in cars or design nuclear weapons.

> —MARILYN FRENCH

A child is a curly, dimpled lunatic.

—RALPH WALDO EMERSON

Children always take the line of most persistence.

—MARCELENE COX, IN *LADIES' HOME JOURNAL* (1945)

Children are natural Zen masters; their world is brand new in each and every moment.

—JOHN BRADSHAW

Children are the living messages we send to a time we will not see.

—JOHN W. WHITEHEAD, FROM HIS BOOK *THE STEALING OF AMERICA* (1983)

Children have two visions, the inner and the outer. Of the two the inner vision is brighter.

—SYLVIA ASHTON-WARNER

To talk to a child, to fascinate him, is much more difficult than to win an electoral victory. But is it much more rewarding.

—COLETTE, FRENCH AUTHOR

Children who are not spoken to by . . . responsive adults will not learn to speak properly. Children who are not answered will stop asking questions. They will become incurious. And children who are not told stories and who are not read to will have few reasons for wanting to learn.

—GAIL HALEY, IN HER CALDECOTT MEDAL ACCEPTANCE SPEECH, 1971.

Little people (i.e., babies) should be encouraged always to tell whatever they hear particularly striking to some brother, sister, or servant, immediately before the impression is erased by the intervention of newer occurrences.

—SAMUEL JOHNSON

Children do not extract meaning from what they hear others saying; they try, instead, to relate what has been said to what is going on.

—JUDITH NEWMAN, FROM HER BOOK *WHOLE LANGUAGE: THEORY IN USE* (1984)

It is not a child's hearing of the word, but its accompanying intonation that is understood.

—JEAN-JACQUES ROUSSEAU, FROM HIS BOOK *EMILE; OR, TREATISE ON EDUCATION* (1762)

When I was a kid they didn't call it dyslexia. They called it, you know, you were slow, or you were retarded, or whatever. What you can never change is the effect that the words "dumb" and "stupid" have on young people.

—WHOOPI GOLDBERG

How children feel and interact is as important to their competence and success as how well they think . . . Thinking and feeling go hand in hand. It's not to say that thinking is less important, just not more important.

—DR. JACK SHONKOFF, BRANDEIS UNIVERSITY

Love your children with all your hearts, love them enough to discipline them before it is too late . . . Praise them for important things, even if you have to stretch them a bit. Praise them a lot. They live on it like bread and butter and they need it more than bread and butter.

—LAVINA CHRISTENSEN FUGAL, ON BEING NAMED MOTHER OF THE YEAR (1955)

The child learns about the world first of all by playing with it.

—ALAN HOWARD

Education commences at the mother's knee, and every word spoken within the hearing of little children tends towards the formation of character.

—HOSEA BALLOU

The potential possibilities of any child are the most intriguing and stimulating in all creation.

—RAY L. WILBUR

They come to me without any inkling of what talent and power of perception they have . . . and very rarely has anyone ever bothered to credit their insight.

—LENNI ABEL, ART TEACHER AND 2000 DISNEY TEACHER OF THE YEAR, FROM THE BRONX, NEW YORK

We worry about what a child will be tomorrow, yet we forget that he or she is someone today.

—STACIA TAUSCHER

Child, give me your hand that I may walk in the light of your faith in me.

—HANNAH KAHN

To be alienated is to lack a sense of belonging, to feel cut off from family, friends, school, or work—the four worlds of childhood.

—URIE BRONFENBRENNER, AS QUOTED IN THE *PHI DELTA KAPPAN* (1986)

A cynical young person is almost the saddest sight to see, because it means that he or she has gone from knowing nothing to believing in nothing.

—MAYA ANGELOU

Spring, spring is here at last
And now, and now
We can run through the grass
We can jump
We can sing
We can hug and kiss
A little black bug
Oh Spring, oh Spring is here at last!

—MELISSA BROOKS KELLY, A NINE-YEAR-OLD IN *WEE WISDOM* (1978)

In the end, it's not what you do for your children but what you've taught them to do for themselves.

—ANN LANDERS

That best academy, a mother's knee.

—JAMES RUSSELL LOWELL, AMERICAN ROMANTIC WRITER

If a child lives with approval, he learns to like himself.

—DOROTHY LAW NOLTE

The adult works to perfect his environment, whereas the child works to perfect himself, using the environment as a means. . . . The child is a being in a constant state of transformation.

—E. M. STANDING, FROM HER BOOK *MARIA MONTESSORI: HER LIFE AND WORK* (1957)

Likely as not, the child you can do the least with will do the most to make you proud.

—MIGNON MCLAUGHLIN, FROM HER BOOK *THE SECOND NEUROTIC'S NOTEBOOK* (1966)

Play gives children a chance to practice what they are learning. . . . They have to play with what they know to be true in order to find out more, and then they can use what they learn in new forms of play.

—FRED ROGERS

Tiny children want to learn to the degree that they are unable to distinguish learning from fun. They keep this attitude until we adults convince them that learning is not fun.

—GLENN DOMAN, FROM HIS BOOK *HOW TO TEACH YOUR BABY TO READ: THE GENTLE REVOLUTION* (1964)

A Child must learn early to believe that she is somebody worthwhile, and that she can do many praiseworthy things.

—BENJAMIN MAYS

The young do not know enough to be prudent, and therefore they attempt the impossible—and achieve it, generation after generation.

—PEARL S. BUCK, AUTHOR OF *THE JOY OF CHILDREN* (1964)

When childhood dies, its corpses are called adults and they enter society, one of the politer names of hell. That is why we dread children, even if we love them, they show us the state of our decay.

—BRIAN ALDISS

Children need love, especially when they do not deserve it.

—HAROLD S. HULBERT

Parents of young children should realize that few people, and maybe no one, will find their children as enchanting as they do.

—BARBARA WALTERS, FROM HER BOOK *HOW TO TALK WITH PRACTICALLY ANYBODY ABOUT PRACTICALLY ANYTHING* (1970)

Don't worry that children never listen to you. Worry that they are always watching you.

—ROBERT FULGHUM, ESSAYIST AND AUTHOR OF *ALL I REALLY NEED TO KNOW I LEARNED IN KINDERGARTEN* (1988)

The most deadly of all sins is the mutilation of a child's spirit.

—ERIK ERIKSON

When I was young there was no respect for the young, and now that I am old there is no respect for the old. I missed out coming and going.

—J. B. PRIESTLEY

Childhood shows the man, as morning shows the day.

—JOHN MILTON

Two important things to teach a child: to do and to do without.

—MARCELENE COX, IN *LADIES' HOME JOURNAL* (1957)

There must be such a thing as a child with average ability, but you can't find a parent who will admit that it is his child.

—THOMAS BAILEY, FLORIDA STATE SUPERINTENDENT OF SCHOOLS

There are few successful adults who were not first successful children.

—ALEXANDER CHASE

The world is not given to you by your parents. It is loaned to you by your children.

—KENYAN PROVERB

I have faith in young people because I know the strongest emotions which prevail are those of love and caring and belief and tolerance.

—BARBARA JORDAN

The fortune of our lives therefore depends on employing well the short period of our youth.

—THOMAS JEFFERSON, IN A LETTER TO HIS DAUGHTER MARTHA (1787)

Let parents then bequeath to their children not riches, but the spirit of reverence.

—PLATO

———◆———

Adults are obsolete children.

—THEODOR "DR. SEUSS" GEISEL

———◆———

Just think of the tragedy of teaching children not to doubt.

—CLARENCE DARROW

———◆———

Men dress their children's minds as they do their bodies, in the prevailing fashion.

—HERBERT SPENCER

———◆———

The finest aid to adult education is children.

—CHARLES T. JONES AND BOB PHILLIPS, FROM THEIR BOOK *WIT AND WISDOM* (1985)

The surest way to corrupt a youth is to instruct him to hold in higher esteem those who think alike than those who think differently.

—FRIEDRICH NIETZSCHE

Perhaps the most valuable result of all education is the ability to make yourself do the thing you have to do, when it ought to be done, whether you like it or not.

—THOMAS HUXLEY

There is a greater advance from the infant to the speaking child than there is from the schoolboy to a Newton.

—ANONYMOUS, IN E. M. STANDING'S *MARIA MONTESSORI: HER LIFE AND WORK* (1957)

If one throws a stone into a river, it produces a succession of ripples. But most men live without being conscious of a responsibility which extends beyond themselves. And that—I think—is at the root of our misery.

—FRANZ KAFKA

Let such teach others who themselves excel,
And censure freely who have written well.

—ALEXANDER POPE

The young don't know what age is, and the old forget what youth was.

—SEUMAS MACMANUS

Let the potential artist in our children come to life that they may surmount industrial monotonies and pressures.

—BARBARA MORGAN, FIRST NASA EDUCATOR ASTRONAUT AND BACK-UP FOR THE *CHALLENGER* MISSION

In the effort to give good and comforting answers to the young questioners whom we love, we very often arrive at good and comforting answers for ourselves.

—Ruth Goode

———❖———

I think of discipline as the continual everyday process of helping a child learn self-discipline.

—Fred Rogers

———❖———

CHAPTER FIVE

The Philosophy of Learning

We teach what we like to learn and the reason many people go into teaching is vicariously to re-experience the primary joy experienced the first time they learned something they loved.

—STEPHEN BROOKFIELD

You are rewarding a teacher poorly if you remain always a pupil.

—FRIEDRICH NIETZSCHE

Teachers open the door. You enter by yourself.

—CHINESE PROVERB

Learning is not a spectator sport.

—ANONYMOUS

Learning is something students do, NOT something done to students

—ALFIE KOHN

———◆———

A master can tell you what he expects of you. A teacher, though, awakens your own expectations.

—PATRICIA NEAL

———◆———

The greatest sign of success for a teacher . . . is to be able to say, "The children are now working as if I did not exist."

—MARIA MONTESSORI

———◆———

The dream begins with a teacher who believes in you, who tugs and pushes and leads you to the next plateau, sometimes poking you with a sharp stick called "truth."

—DAN RATHER

———◆———

If I am walking with two other men, each of them will serve as my teacher. I will pick out the good points of the one and imitate them, and the bad points of the other and correct them in myself.

—CONFUCIUS

That is what learning is. You suddenly understand something you've understood all your life, but in a new way.

—DORIS LESSING

Learning to teach is a bigger job than universities, schools, experience, or personal disposition alone can accomplish.

—SHARON FEIMAN-NEMSER

Every student can learn, just not on the same day, or the same way.

—GEORGE EVANS

Learning without thought is labor lost; thought without learning is perilous.

—Confucius

———◆———

You can teach a student a lesson for a day; but if you can teach him to learn by creating curiosity, he will continue the learning process as long as he lives.

—Clay P. Bedford

———◆———

Live as if you were to die tomorrow. Learn as if you were to live forever.

—Mahatma Gandhi

———◆———

I am learning all the time. The tombstone will be my diploma.

—Eartha Kitt

———◆———

You learn something every day if you pay attention.

—RAY LEBLOND

<hr />

I have never in my life learned anything from any man who agreed with me.

—DUDLEY FIELD MALONE

<hr />

People learn something every day, and a lot of times it's that what they learned the day before was wrong.

—BILL VAUGHAN, FORMER COLUMNIST FOR THE *KANSAS CITY STAR*

<hr />

The beautiful thing about learning is that no one can take it away from you.

—B. B. KING

<hr />

The most useful piece of learning for the uses of life is to unlearn what is untrue.

—ANTISTHENES

⟹◆⟸

Some people will never learn anything, for this reason, because they understand everything too soon.

—ALEXANDER POPE

⟹◆⟸

Children have to be educated, but they have also to be left to educate themselves.

—ERNEST DIMNET, FROM HIS BOOK *THE ART OF THINKING* (1928)

⟹◆⟸

A single conversation with a wise man is better than ten years of study.

—CHINESE PROVERB

⟹◆⟸

I don't think much of a man who is not wiser today than he was yesterday.

—ABRAHAM LINCOLN

Beware of the man who works hard to learn something, learns it, and finds himself no wiser than before.

—KURT VONNEGUT

Learning is a treasure that will follow its owner everywhere.

—CHINESE PROVERB

I am always ready to learn, although I do not always like being taught.

—WINSTON CHURCHILL

There are many things which we can afford to forget which it is yet well to learn.

—OLIVER WENDELL HOLMES, JR.

—————⊳◆⊲—————

I am defeated, and know it, if I meet any human being from whom I find myself unable to learn anything.

—GEORGE HERBERT PALMER

—————⊳◆⊲—————

I believe that the testing of the student's achievements in order to see if he meets some criterion held by the teacher is directly contrary to the implications of therapy for significant learning.

—CARL ROGERS

—————⊳◆⊲—————

It's what you learn after you know it all that counts.

—HARRY S. TRUMAN

—————⊳◆⊲—————

No matter how one may think himself accomplished, when he sets out to learn a new language, science, or the bicycle, he has entered a new realm as truly as if he were a child newly born into the world.

—FRANCES WILLARD, FROM HER BOOK *HOW I LEARNED TO RIDE THE BICYCLE*

Anyone who stops learning is old, whether at twenty or eighty. Anyone who keeps learning today is young. The greatest thing in life is to keep your mind young.

—HENRY FORD

It is not hard to learn more. What is hard is to unlearn when you discover yourself wrong.

—MARTIN H. FISCHER

You have learned something. That always feels at first as if you had lost something.

—H. G. WELLS (1866–1946)

Every act of conscious learning requires the willingness to suffer an injury to one's self-esteem. That is why young children, before they are aware of their own self-importance, learn so easily; and why older persons, especially if vain or important, cannot learn at all.

—THOMAS SZASZ, FROM HIS BOOK *THE SECOND SIN* (1973)

When there is much desire to learn, there of necessity will be much arguing, much writing, many opinions; for opinion in good men is but knowledge in the making.

—JOHN MILTON, FROM HIS BOOK *AREOPAGITICA* (1644)

It is through suffering that learning comes.

—AESCHYLUS

⟫⟪

The justest division of human learning is that derived from the three different faculties of the soul, the seat of learning; history being relative to the memory, poetry to the imagination, and philosophy to the reason.

—FRANCIS BACON, FROM HIS BOOK *THE ADVANCEMENT OF LEARNING* (1605)

⟫⟪

He that has less Learning than his Capacity is able to manage shall have more Use of it than he that has more than he can master. For no Man can have an active and ready Command of that which is too heavy for him.

—SAMUEL BUTLER, FROM "THOUGHTS ON VARIOUS SUBJECTS," *THE GENUINE REMAINS IN VERSE AND PROSE OF MR. SAMUEL BUTLER, AUTHOR OF* HUDIBRAS (1759)

⟫⟪

Learning makes a man fit Company for himself.

—THOMAS FULLER

⟫⟪

A little learning misleadeth, and a great deal often stupifieth the understanding.

>—MARQUIS OF HALIFAX, FROM "FALSE LEARNING," *POLITICAL, MORAL AND MISCELLANEOUS REFLECTIONS* (1750)

And the same age saw Learning fall, and Rome.

>—ALEXANDER POPE, FROM HIS ESSAY *AN ESSAY ON CRITICISM* (1711)

It is only when we forget all our learning that we begin to know.

>—HENRY DAVID THOREAU, FROM HIS JOURNAL

Learning makes the wise wiser and the foolish more foolish.

>—ENGLISH PROVERB

Learning acquired in youth is inscribed on stone.

—TAMIL PROVERB

We think too much about effective methods of teaching and not enough about effective methods of learning.

—JOHN CAROLUS

Learning teacheth more in one year than experience in twenty, and learning teacheth safely, when experience maketh more miserable than wise. . . . It is costly wisdom that is bought by experience.

—ROGER ASCHAM

Learn from others what to pursue and what to avoid, and let your teachers be the lives of others.

—DIONYSIUS CATO

Learn one thing well first.

—JOHN CLARKE, IN *PROVERBS: ENGLISH AND LATINE* (1639)

In ancient times, men learned with a view to their own improvement. Nowadays, men learn with a view to the approbation of others.

—CONFUCIUS

A primary method of learning is to go from the familiar to the unfamiliar.

—GLENN DOMAN, FROM HIS BOOK *HOW TO TEACH YOUR BABY TO READ: THE GENTLE REVOLUTION* (1964)

What we have learned from others becomes our own by reflection.

—RALPH WALDO EMERSON, IN HIS "BLOTTING BOOK"

You are as who has a private door that leads him to the King's chamber. You have learned nothing rightly that you have not learned so.

—RALPH WALDO EMERSON, FROM HIS JOURNAL

It is impossible for a man to begin to learn what he thinks he knows.

—EPICTETUS, FROM *DISCOURSES* (101 C.E.)

'Tis harder to unlearn than to learn.

—THOMAS FULLER

You learn more from getting your butt kicked than from getting it kissed.

—TOM HANKS

Most learning is not the result of instruction. It is rather the result of unhampered participation in a meaningful setting.

—IVAN ILLICH, FROM HIS BOOK *DESCHOOLING SOCIETY* (1970)

Learn to do good.

—ISAIAH 1:17

Be done with rote learning
And its attendant vexations.

—LAO-TZU

Robert F. Kennedy was one of the few adults, one of the few politicians, who kept learning after they grew up. Most of us just build up our intellectual capital and then live off it.

—FRANK MANKIEWICZ, FROM "OF KENNEDY AND KING," *SAN FRANCISCO SUNDAY EXAMINER & CHRONICLE*, JUNE 6, 1993

To learn is no easy matter and to apply what one has learned is even harder.

—MAO TSE-TUNG

Men are either learned or learning; the rest are blockheads.

—MUHAMMAD

It is right to learn even from one's enemies.

—OVID

Each day grow older, and learn something new.

—SOLON, ONE OF THE SEVEN SAGES OF GREECE

Let us learn on earth those things whose knowledge might continue in heaven.

—St. Paul's School motto, Concord, New Hampshire

———⊰◆⊱———

Before making a practical beginning on the job, the apprentice has had an opportunity to follow some general and summary course of instruction, so as to have a framework ready prepared in which to store the observations he is shortly to make. Furthermore he is able . . . to avail himself of sundry technical courses which he can follow in his leisure hours, so as to coordinate step by step the daily experience he is gathering.

—Hippolyte Adolphe Taine

———⊰◆⊱———

Learn in order to teach and to practice.

—Talmud Rabbinical writings

———⊰◆⊱———

Learn to teach yourself.

—ANONYMOUS

Learn as though you would never be able to master it; hold it as though you would be in fear of losing it.

—CONFUCIUS

It is always the season for the old to learn.

—AESCHYLUS

One may receive the information but miss the teaching.

—JEAN TOOMER

Learning is by nature curiosity.

—PHILO

If you keep your mind sufficiently opened, people will throw a lot of rubbish into it.

—WILLIAM ORTON

I believe that children learn best when given the opportunity to taste, feel, see, hear, manipulate, discover, sing, and dance their way through learning.

—KATY GOLDMAN, TEACHER FROM PINE, ARIZONA, AS QUOTED IN *SURVIVAL GUIDE FOR NEW TEACHERS* (2002)

Only the curious will learn and only the resolute overcome the obstacles of learning. The quest quotient has always excited me more than the intelligence quotient.

—EUGENE S. WILSON, AS QUOTED IN THE *READER'S DIGEST* (1968)

I was taught the way of progress is neither swift nor easy.

—MARIE CURIE

The essence of learning is the ability to manage change by changing yourself.

—ARIE DE GUES, FROM HIS BOOK *THE LIVING COMPANY* (1997)

Even without success, creative persons find joy in a job well done. Learning for its own sake is rewarding.

—MIHALY CSIKSZENTMIHALYI, FROM HIS BOOK *CREATIVITY: FLOW AND THE PSYCHOLOGY OF DISCOVERY AND INVENTION* (1997)

Creative activity could be described as a type of learning process where teacher and pupil are located in the same individual.

—ARTHUR KOESTLER

The wisest mind has something yet to learn.

—GEORGE SANTAYANA

How sustained an episode a learner is willing to undergo depends upon what the person expects to get from his efforts, in the sense of such external things as grades but also in the sense of a gain in understanding.

—JEROME S. BRUNER, AS QUOTED IN *THE TEACHER AND THE TAUGHT* (1963)

Learning is a social process that occurs through interpersonal interaction within a cooperative context. Individuals, working together, construct shared understandings and knowledge.

—DAVID JOHNSON, FROM HIS BOOK *ACTIVE LEARNING: COOPERATION IN THE COLLEGE CLASSROOM* (1991)

Learning is often spoken of as if we were watching the open pages of all the books which we have ever read, and then, when occasion arises, we select the right page to read aloud to the universe.

—ALFRED NORTH WHITEHEAD, AS QUOTED IN *THE TEACHER AND THE TAUGHT* (1963)

Mistakes are the portals of discovery.

—JAMES JOYCE, FROM HIS BOOK *DUBLINERS* (1914)

It is what we think we know already that often prevents us from learning.

—CLAUDE BERNARD

We learn well and fast when we experience the consequences of what we do—and don't do.

—ANONYMOUS

I find that a great part of the information I have was acquired by looking up something and finding something else on the way.

—FRANKLIN P. ADAMS

For many, learning is a spiral, where important themes are visited again and again throughout life, each time at a deeper, more penetrating level.

—JEROLD W. APS, FROM HIS BOOK *TEACHING FROM THE HEART* (1996)

One must learn by doing the thing, for though you think you know it, you have no certainty until you try.

—ARISTOTLE

Anxiety checks learning. An overall feeling of inferiority, a temporary humiliation, a fit of depression, defiance, or anger, a sense of being rejected, and many other emotional disturbances affect the learning process. The reverse is true; a feeling of well-being and of being respected by others stimulates an alert mind, willingness to participate, and an attitude conducive to learning.

—EDNA LeSHAN, FROM HER BOOK *THE CONSPIRACY AGAINST CHILDHOOD* (1967)

In the broadest sense, learning can be defined as a process of progressive change from ignorance to knowledge, from inability to competence, and from indifference to understanding.

—CAMERON FINCHER

Learning proceeds in fits and starts.

—JEROLD W. APS, FROM HIS BOOK *TEACHING FROM THE HEART* (1996)

Learning is always rebellion. . . . Every bit of new truth discovered is revolutionary to what was believed before.

—MARGARET LEE RUNBECK

Most people would say that what I am doing is "learning to play" the cello. But these words carry into our minds the strange idea that there exists two very different processes: One, learning to play the cello; and two, playing the cello. . . . We learn to do something by doing it. There is no other way.

—JOHN HOLT

That's what learning is, after all; not whether we lose the game, but how we lose and how we've changed because to it and what we take away from it that we never had before.

—RICHARD BACH, IN HIS BOOK *THE BRIDGE ACROSS FOREVER* (1984)

I am still learning.

—MICHELANGELO

Learning is an active process. We learn by doing. . . . Only knowledge that is used sticks in your mind.

—DALE CARNEGIE

You must learn day by day, year by year, to broaden your horizon. The more things you love, the more you are interested in, the more you enjoy, the more you are indignant about, the more you have left when anything happens.

—ETHEL BARRYMORE

Learning is a process of preparing to deal with new situations.

—ALVIN TOFFLER

Learning is discovering that something is possible.

—FRITZ PERLS

Whatever is good to know is difficult to learn.

—GREEK PROVERB

One of the weaknesses of our society is that history is still news to most people.

—GRANT FAIRLEY

Learn avidly. Question repeatedly what you have learned. Analyze it carefully. Then put what you have learned into practice intelligently.

—CONFUCIUS

Seeing much, suffering much, and studying much are the three pillars of learning.

—BENJAMIN DISRAELI

The moment you stop learning, you stop leading.

—RICK WARREN

Learning is finding out what you already know, Doing is demonstrating that you know it, Teaching is reminding others that they know it as well as you do. We are all learners, doers, and teachers.

—RICHARD BACH

Learn as much as you can while you are young, since life becomes too busy later.

—Dana Stewart Scott

We learn more by looking for the answer to a question and not finding it than we do from learning the answer itself.

—Lloyd Alexander

Learning is like rowing upstream: not to advance is to drop back.

—Chinese proverb

We learn simply by the exposure of living, and what we learn most natively is the tradition in which we live.

—David P. Gardner

Nothing we learn in this world is ever wasted.

—ELEANOR ROOSEVELT

You don't understand anything until you learn it more than one way.

—MARVIN MINSKY

To learn, you must want to be taught.

—PROVERBS 12:1

Wealth, if you use it, comes to an end; learning, if you can use it, increases.

—SWAHILI PROVERB

What we learn with pleasure we never forget.

—LOUIS MERCIER

As long as you live, keep learning how to live.

—Lucius A. Seneca

———

Try to learn about everything and everything about something.

—Thomas Huxley

———

The illiterate of the twenty-first century will not be those who cannot read and write, but those who cannot learn, unlearn, and relearn.

—Alvin Toffler

———

The man who is too old to learn was probably always too old to learn.

—Henry S. Haskins

———

Learning is what most adults will do for a living in the twenty-first century.

—BOB PERELMAN

Never stop learning; knowledge doubles every fourteen months.

—ANTHONY J. D'ANGELO, FROM HIS BOOK *THE COLLEGE BLUE BOOK* (1995)

I have never met a man so ignorant that I couldn't learn something from him.

—GALILEO GALILEI

Learning is not compulsory . . . neither is survival.

—W. EDWARDS DEMING

Learning is not attained by chance. It must be sought for with ardor and attended to with diligence.

—ABIGAIL ADAMS

All learning begins with the simple phrase, "I don't know."

—ANONYMOUS

Of all the civil rights for which the world has struggled and fought for 5,000 years, the right to learn is undoubtedly the most fundamental.

—W. E. B. DU BOIS

When asked what learning was the most necessary, he said, "Not to unlearn what you have learned!"

—DIOGENES LAERTIUS, BIOGRAPHER OF ANCIENT GREEK PHILOSOPHERS

Learning is never done without errors and defeat.

—VLADIMIR LENIN

He is educated who knows where to find out what he doesn't know.

—GEORG SIMMEL

Try to put into practice what you already know, and in doing so you will in good time discover the hidden things which you now inquire about.

—HENRY VAN DYKE

If a man will begin with certainties, he shall end in doubts; but if he will be content to begin with doubts, he shall end in certainties.

—FRANCIS BACON, FROM HIS BOOK *THE ADVANCEMENT OF LEARNING* (1605)

In completing one discovery we never fail to get an imperfect knowledge of others of which we could have no idea before, so that we cannot solve one doubt without creating several new ones.

—JOSEPH PRIESTLY

Much that passes for education . . . is not education at all but ritual. The fact is that we are being educated when we know it least.

—DAVID P. GARDNER

It is by extending oneself, by exercising some capacity previously unused that you come to a better knowledge of your own potential.

—HAROLD BLOOM, IN *SHORT STORIES AND POEMS FOR EXCEPTIONALLY INTELLIGENT CHILDREN* (2001)

I don't divide the world into the weak and the strong, or the successes and the failures, those who make it or those who don't. I divide the world into learners and non-learners.

—BENJAMIN BARBER

If you study to remember, you will forget, but if you study to understand, you will remember.

—Anonymous

No matter how occupied a man may be, he must snatch at least one hour for study daily.

—The Bratzlaver, in Louis I. Newman's composition, *The Hasidic Anthology* (1934)

The elevation of the mind ought to be the principal end of all our studies.

—Edmund Burke, in his book *A Philosophical Inquiry into the Origin of Our Ideas of the Sublime and the Beautiful* (1756)

Let the great book of the world be your principal study.

—Lord Chesterfield, in a letter to his son (1751)

Study the teachings of the Great Sages of all sects impartially.

—GAMPOPA, TIBETAN RELIGIOUS LEADER

The love of study, a passion which derives fresh vigor from enjoyment, supplies each day, each hour, with a perpetual source of independent and rational pleasure.

—EDWARD GIBBON, IN HIS BOOK *MEMOIRS OF MY LIFE AND WRITINGS* (1869)

Alexander Pope, finding little advantage from external help, resolved thenceforward to direct himself, and at twelve formed a plan of study which he completed with little other incitement than the desire of excellence.

—SAMUEL JOHNSON, FROM "POPE," *LIVES OF ENGLISH POETS* (1781)

Just as eating contrary to the inclination is injurious to the health, so study without desire spoils the memory, and it retains nothing that it takes in.

—LEONARDO DA VINCI

Study in joy and good cheer, in accordance with your intelligence and heart's dictates.

—RASHI

The great business of study is to form a mind adapted and adequate to all times and all occasions; to which all nature is then laid open, and which may be said to possess the key of her inexhaustible riches.

—SIR JOSHUA REYNOLDS, FROM "DISCOURSE ELEVEN," *DISCOURSES ON ART* (1769–1790)

I don't love studying. I hate studying. I like learning. Learning is beautiful.

—NATALIE PORTMAN

The man who graduates today and stops learning tomorrow is uneducated the day after.

—NEWTON D. BAKER

Every successful learning initiative requires key people to allocate hours to new types of activities: reflection, planning, collaborative work, and training.

—PETER SENGE, FROM HIS BOOK THE DANCE OF CHANGE (1999)

If you can't learn to do it well, learn to enjoy doing it badly.

—ASHLEIGH BRILLIANT, ENGLISH AUTHOR AND SYNDICATED CARTOONIST

The classroom, not the trench, is the frontier of freedom now and forevermore.

—LYNDON B. JOHNSON

Restraint and discipline and examples of virtue and justice. These are the things that form the education of the world.

—EDMUND BURKE

To say "well done" to any bit of good work is to take hold of the powers which have made the effort and strengthen them beyond our knowledge.

—PHILLIPS BROOKS

Results are better than intentions.

—DR. PHIL MCGRAW

It was an initiation into the love of learning, of learning how to learn, that was revealed to me by my BLS masters as a matter of interdisciplinary cognition—that is, learning to know something by its relation to something else.

—LEONARD BERNSTEIN, ON THE BOSTON LATIN SCHOOL, AS QUOTED IN THE *NEW YORK TIMES* (1984)

A little learning is a dangerous thing; drink of it deeply, or taste it not, for shallow thoughts intoxicate the brain, and drinking deeply sobers us again.

—ALEXANDER POPE

They know enough who know how to learn.

—HENRY ADAMS

To every answer you can find a new question.

—YIDDISH PROVERB

The very fact of its finding itself in agreement with other minds perturbs it, so that it hunts for points of divergence, feeling the urgent need to make it clear that at least it reached the same conclusions by a different route.

—SIR HERBERT BUTTERFIELD, IN HIS 1961 RETIREMENT ADDRESS

He who is ashamed of asking is ashamed of learning.

—DANISH PROVERB

The artificial method of learning is to hear what other people say, to learn and to read, and so to get your head crammed full of general ideas before you have any sort of extended acquaintance with the world as it is, and as you may see it for yourself.

—ARTHUR SCHOPENHAUER, FROM "ON EDUCATION," *STUDIES IN PESSIMISM* (1851)

We cannot seek or attain health, wealth, learning, justice, or kindness in general. Action is always specific, concrete, individualized, unique.

—BENJAMIN JOWETT

Much learning does not teach understanding.

—HERACLITUS

If you employed study, thinking, and planning time daily, you could develop and use the power that can change the course of your destiny.

—W. CLEMENT STONE

Whether one has natural talent or not, any learning period requires the willingness to suffer uncertainty and embarrassment.

—GAIL SHEEHY

Let us rise up and be thankful, for if we didn't learn a lot today, at least we learned a little, and if we didn't learn a little, at least we didn't get sick, and if we got sick, at least we didn't die; so let us all be thankful.

—BUDDHA

The brighter you are, the more you have to learn.

—DON HEROLD

Creativity is a type of learning process where the teacher and pupil are located in the same individual.

—ARTHUR KOESTLER

Apply yourself. Get all the education you can, but then, by God, do something. Don't just stand there; make it happen.

—LEE IACOCCA

There is divine beauty in learning, just as there is human beauty in tolerance. To learn means to accept the postulate that life did not begin at my birth. Others have been here before me, and I walk in their footsteps.

—ELIE WIESEL

Nature without learning is blind, learning apart from nature is fractional, and practice in the absence of both is aimless.

—PLUTARCH

He not only overflowed with learning, but stood in the slop.

—SYDNEY MITH OF MACAULAY

I learned to make my mind large, as the universe is large, so that there is room for paradoxes.

—MAXINE HONG KINGSTON

I will study and get ready and someday my chance will come.

—ABRAHAM LINCOLN

If you stuff yourself full of poems, essays, plays, stories, novels, films, comic strips, magazines, music, you automatically explode every morning like Old Faithful. I have never had a dry spell in my life, mainly because I feed myself well, to the point of bursting. I wake early and hear my morning voices leaping around in my head like jumping beans. I get out of bed to trap them before they escape.

—RAY BRADBURY

That which we obtain too easily, we esteem too lightly.

—THOMAS PAINE

I do not pray for a lighter load, but for a stronger back.

—PHILLIPS BROOKS

In times of change, learners inherit the earth; while the learned find themselves beautifully equipped to deal with a world that no longer exists.

—ERIC HOFFER

The only person who is educated is the one who has learned how to learn and change.

—CARL ROGERS

Whoever neglects learning in his youth, loses the past and is dead to the future.

—EURIPIDES

We do not learn by inference and deduction and the application of mathematics to philosophy, but by direct intercourse and sympathy.

—HENRY DAVID THOREAU, FROM HIS BOOK *NATURAL HISTORY OF MASSACHUSETTS* (1842)

At present there are differences of opinion . . . for all people do not agree as to the things that the young ought to learn, either with a view to virtue or with a view to the best life, nor is it clear whether their studies should be regulated more with regard to intellect or with regard to character.

—ARISTOTLE

In all the things we learn only from those whom we love.

—Johann Wolfgang von Goethe

It is my firm conviction that a man can learn more about poetry by really knowing and examining a few of the best poems than by meandering about among a great many.

—Ezra Pound, from his book *ABC of Reading* (1934)

Develop a passion for learning. If you do, you will never cease to grow.

—Anthony J. D'Angelo, from his book *The College Blue Book* (1995)

Study to be quiet.

—Izaak Walton, from his book *The Compleat Angler* (1653)

If you rest, you rust.

—HELEN HAYES, FROM HER BOOK *MY LIFE IN THREE ACTS* (1990)

I know of no more encouraging fact than the unquestionable ability of man to elevate his life by conscious endeavor.

—HENRY DAVID THOREAU

The proper study of mankind is man.

—ALEXANDER POPE

In old days men studied for the sake of self-improvement; nowadays men study in order to impress other people.

—CONFUCIUS

We are commanded to love God with all our minds, as well as with all our hearts, and we commit a great sin if we forbid or prevent that cultivation of the mind in others which would enable them to perform this duty.

> —ANGELINA GRIMKE

All men who have turned out worth anything have had the chief hand in their own education.

> —SIR WALTER SCOTT

No one can become really educated without having pursued some study in which he took no interest.

> —T. S. ELIOT

The beginning is the most important part of the work.

> —PLATO

Gie me ae spark o' Nature's fire.
That's a' the learning I desire.

—ROBERT BURNS, FROM "EPISTLE TO J. LAPRAIK," *POEMS, MAINLY IN THE SCOTTISH DIALECT* (1786)

The best learners . . . often make the worst teachers. They are, in a very real sense, perceptually challenged. They cannot imagine what it must be like to struggle to learn something that comes so naturally to them.

—STEPHEN BROOKFIELD

To make headway, improve your head.

—B. C. FORBES

The same man cannot be skilled in everything, each has his own special excellence.

—EURIPIDES

Everyone is ignorant, only on different subjects.

—WILL ROGERS

—————◆—————

An excellent plumber is infinitely more admirable than an incompetent philosopher.

—JOHN W. GARDNER

—————◆—————

It iz better tew know nothing than two know what ain't so.

—JOHN BILLINGS, FROM "SOLLUM THOUGHTS," *EVERYBODY'S FRIEND* (1874)

—————◆—————

Opposites are not contradictory but complementary.

—NIELS BOHR

—————◆—————

I had started also studying because I wanted to learn more about power and fighting.

—Lou Reed

We must learn our limits. We are all something, but none of us are everything.

—Blaise Pascal

Get over the idea that only children should spend their time in study. Be a student so long as you still have something to learn, and this will mean all your life.

—Henry L. Doherty

Simply making consistent investments in our self-education and knowledge banks pays major dividends throughout our lives.

—Jim Rohn, motivational coach

What a relief it was to discover that I wasn't really an idiot! I simply had a learning disability.

—JOHN H. JOHNSON, FOUNDER OF THE LARGEST AFRICAN AMERICAN PUBLISHING COMPANY IN AMERICA, JOHNSON PUBLISHING COMPANY

His studies were pursued but never effectually overtaken.

—H. G. WELLS

Poor is the pupil who does not surpass his master.

—LEONARDO DA VINCI

There is no subject so old that something new cannot be said about it.

—FYODOR DOSTOEVSKY

There studious let me sit,
And hold high converse with the mighty dead.

—JAMES THOMSON

Cultivate the habit of attention and try to gain opportunities to hear wise men and women talk. Indifference and inattention are the two most dangerous monsters that you ever meet. Interest and attention will insure to you an education.

—ROBERT A. MILLIKAN

It is important that students bring a certain ragamuffin, barefoot irreverence to their studies; they are not here to worship what is known, but to question it.

—JACOB BRONOWSKI

Learned men are the cisterns of knowledge, not the fountainheads.

—JAMES NORTHCOTE

A wretched soul, bruis'd with adversity,
We bid be quiet, when we hear it cry;
But were we burthen'd with like weight of pain,
As much, or more, we should ourselves complain.

—WILLIAM SHAKESPEARE

Sufficient unto the day is the rigor thereof.

—ELIAKIM H. MOORE

God not only plays dice. He also sometimes throws the dice where they cannot be seen.

—STEPHEN HAWKING

One should always generalize.

—CARL JACOBI

Better is the enemy of good.

—VOLTAIRE

Love not what you are but only what you may become.

—MIGUEL DE CERVANTES

There is always room at the top.

—DANIEL WEBSTER

Lack of something to feel important about is almost the greatest tragedy a man may have.

—ARTHUR E. MORGAN

The barriers are not erected which can say to aspiring talents and industry, "Thus far and no farther."

—LUDWIG VAN BEETHOVEN

Nothing would be done, at all, if we waited until we could do it so well that no one could find fault with it.

—JOHN HENRY CARDINAL NEWMAN

CHAPTER SIX

Classroom Perspectives

Education: n., the process of nourishing or rearing.

—*THE SHORTER OXFORD ENGLISH DICTIONARY*

———⬗◆⬖———

One's work may be finished some day, but one's education never.

—ALEXANDRE DUMAS

———⬗◆⬖———

Education is man's going forward from cocksure ignorance to thoughtful uncertainty.

—KENNETH G. JOHNSON

———⬗◆⬖———

The task of education is to make the individual so firm and sure that, as a whole being, he can no longer be diverted from his path.

—FRIEDRICH NIETZSCHE, FROM HIS BOOK *HUMAN, ALL TOO HUMAN* (1878)

———⬗◆⬖———

Education is bitter but the fruit is sweet.

—AGUSTIN MARISSA

Education is light, lack of it darkness.

—RUSSIAN PROVERB

There is much to be said for apathy in education.

—E. M. FORSTER

Your Education is worth what You are worth.

—ANONYMOUS

The educated differ from the uneducated as much as the living from the dead.

—ARISTOTLE

Real education must ultimately be limited to men who insist on knowing—the rest is mere sheep-herding.

—EZRA POUND

Education is a specifically human activity. Unlike other animals, man inherits something over and above what is transmitted to him automatically by physical and psychic heredity.

—ARNOLD J. TOYNBEE, AS QUOTED IN *THE TEACHER AND THE TAUGHT* (1963)

Education: Being able to differentiate between what you do know and what you don't. It's knowing where to go to find out what you need to know; and it's knowing how to use the information once you get it.

—WILLIAM FEATHER

Education is the point at which we decide whether we love the world enough to assume responsibility for it.

—Hannah Arendt

Real education should educate us out of self into something far finer; into a selflessness which links us with all humanity.

—Nancy Astor, the first woman to serve as a member of the British House of Commons

Education is the power to think clearly, the power to act well in the world's work, and the power to appreciate life.

—Brigham Young

Education is an ornament in prosperity and a refuge in adversity.

—Aristotle

We need education in the obvious more than investigation of the obscure.

—OLIVER WENDELL HOLMES, JR., IN A SPEECH AT A DINNER OF THE
HARVARD LAW SCHOOL ASSOCIATION OF NEW YORK, 1913

An education isn't how much you have committed to memory, or even how much you know. It's being able to differentiate between what you know and what you don't.

—MALCOLM S. FORBES

To repeat what others have said, requires education; to challenge it, requires brains.

—MARY PETTIBONE POOLE

An educated man is one who can entertain a new idea, entertain another person, and entertain himself.

—SYDNEY WOOD

The very spring and root of honesty and virtue lie in good education.

—PLUTARCH

Education is the art of making man ethical.

—GEORG HEGEL, IN HIS BOOK *THE PHILOSOPHY OF RIGHT* (1821)

Education should be constructed on two bases: morality and prudence.
Morality in order to assist virtue, and prudence in order to defend
you against the vices of others. In tipping the scales toward morality,
you merely produce dupes and martyrs. In tipping the other way, you
produce egotistical schemers.

—NICOLAS CHAMFORT

Intelligence plus character—that is the goal of true education.

—MARTIN LUTHER KING, JR.

Knowledge has outstripped character development, and the young today are given an education rather than an upbringing.

—ILYA EHRENBURG

All genuine education is liberating, and certainly needs freedom and discipline.

—REGINALD D. ARCHAMBAULT, FROM HIS BOOK *JOHN DEWEY ON EDUCATION* (1964)

Education has for its object the formation of character.

—HERBERT SPENCER

An educated man . . . is thoroughly inoculated against humbug, thinks for himself, and tries to give his thoughts, in speech or on paper, some style.

—ALAN SIMPSON, ON BECOMING PRESIDENT OF VASSAR COLLEGE

The true purpose of education is to cherish and unfold the seed of immortality already sown within us; to develop, to their fullest extent, the capacities of every kind with which the God who made us has endowed us.

—ANNA JAMES

Intelligence appears to be the thing that enables a man to get along without education. Education appears to be the thing that enables a man to get along without the use of his intelligence.

—A. E. WIGGAN

The quality of strength lined with tenderness is an unbeatable combination, as are intelligence and necessity when unblunted by formal education.

—MAYA ANGELOU

True education makes for inequality; the inequality of individuality, the inequality of success, the glorious inequality of talent, of genius.

—FELIX E. SCHELLING, AMERICAN EDUCATOR

The only real education comes from what goes counter to you.

—ANDRÉ GIDE

The principal goal of education is to create men who are capable of doing new things, not simply of repeating what other generations have done—men who are creative, inventive, and discoverers.

—JEAN PIAGET

The office of the scholar is to cheer, to raise, and to guide men by showing them facts amid appearances.

—RALPH WALDO EMERSON, FROM HIS BOOK THE AMERICAN SCHOLAR; SELF-RELIANCE; COMPENSATION (1837)

The secret of all success is to know how to deny yourself. Prove that you can control yourself, and you are an educated man; and without this all other education is good for nothing.

—R. D. HITCHCOCK

Education is the process of casting false pearls before real swine.

—IRWIN EDMAN

There is nothing so stupid as an educated man, if you get off the thing that he was educated in.

—WILL ROGERS

He is to be educated because he is a man, and not because he is to make shoes, nails, and pins.

—WILLIAM ELLERY CHANNING

Education is freedom.

—ANDRÉ GIDE

Education makes people easy to lead, but difficult to drive; easy to govern, but impossible to enslave.

—HENRY PETER BROUGHAN

The highest result of education is tolerance.

—HELEN KELLER

It is very nearly impossible . . . to become an educated person in a country so distrustful of the independent mind.

—JAMES BALDWIN

If you say you understand something, then you can explain what you understand to others. Anything short of that is deception, not understanding. Education, above all, should not be about fostering deception.

—R. J. KIZLIK

Education is a method whereby one acquires a higher grade of prejudices.

—LAURENCE J. PETER

Education is the process of driving a set of prejudices down your throat.

—MARTIN H. FISCHER

Next in importance to freedom and justice is popular education, without which neither freedom nor justice can be permanently maintained.

—JAMES A. GARFIELD

Only the educated are free.

—Epictetus

The whole purpose of education is to turn mirrors into windows.

—Sydney J. Harris

Education is simply the soul of a society as it passes from one generation to another.

—G. K. Chesterton

I read Shakespeare and the Bible and I can shoot dice. That's what I call a liberal education.

—Tallulah Bankhead

The primary purpose of a liberal education is to make one's mind a pleasant place in which to spend one's time.

—SYDNEY J. HARRIS

The liberally educated person is one who is able to resist the easy and preferred answers not because he is obstinate but because he knows others worthy of consideration.

—ALLAN BLOOM

The gains in education are never really lost. Books may be burned and cities sacked, but truth, like the yearning for freedom, lives in the hearts of humble men.

—FRANKLIN DELANO ROOSEVELT

Formal education is but an incident in the lifetime of an individual. Most of us who have given the subject any study have come to realize that education is a continuous process ending only when ambition comes to a halt.

—R. I. REES

Vitally important for a young man or woman is, first, to realize the value of education and then to cultivate earnestly, aggressively, ceaselessly, the habit of self-education.

—B. C. FORBES

An educational system isn't worth a great deal if it teaches young people how to make a living but doesn't teach them how to make a life.

—ANONYMOUS

Education in our times must try to find whatever there is in students that might yearn for completion, and to reconstruct the learning that would enable them autonomously to seek that completion.

—ALLAN BLOOM

The main failure of education is that it has not prepared people to comprehend matters concerning human destiny.

—Norman Cousins

⬥

To succeed, you will soon learn, as I did, the importance of a solid foundation in the basics of education—literacy, both verbal and numerical, and communication skills.

—Alan Greenspan

⬥

Education is the drawing out of the soul.

—Ralph Waldo Emerson

⬥

The ultimate end of education is happiness or a good human life, a life enriched by the possession of every kind of good, by the enjoyment of every type of satisfaction.

—Mortimer J. Adler

⬥

Education is the manifestation of the perfection already in man.

—SWAMI VIVEKANANDA

The great secret of education is to make the exercises of the body and the mind serve as relaxation to each other.

—JEAN-JACQUES ROUSSEAU

The most important outcome of education is to help students become independent of formal education.

—PAUL E. GRAY, PRESIDENT OF THE MASSACHUSETTS INSTITUTE OF TECHNOLOGY

A wise system of education will at last teach us how little man yet knows, how much he has still to learn.

—SIR JOHN LUBBOCK

Without education, you're not going anywhere in this world.

    —MALCOLM X

Education is not preparation for life; education is life itself.

    —JOHN DEWEY

Invest in yourself, in your education. There's nothing better.

    —SYLVIA PORTER

Education is one of the few things a person is willing to pay for and not get.

    —WILLIAM LOWE BRYAN

A good education is like a savings account; the more you put into it, the richer you are.

—Anonymous

Education costs money, but then so does ignorance.

—Sir Claude Moser

Genius without education is like silver in the mine.

—Benjamin Franklin

Formal education will make you a living; self-education will make you a fortune.

—Jim Rohn, motivational coach

If you think education is expensive, try ignorance.

>—DEREK BOK, FROM HIS BOOK *UNIVERSITIES AND THE FUTURE OF AMERICA* (1990)

The day someone quits school he is condemning himself to a future of poverty.

>—JAIME ESCALANTE, MATH TEACHER AND BASIS FOR THE FILM *STAND AND DELIVER* (1988)

The great aim of education is not knowledge but action.

>—HERBERT SPENCER

Information cannot replace education.

>—EARL KIOLE

An educated person is one who has learned that information almost always turns out to be at best incomplete and very often false, misleading, fictitious, mendacious—just dead wrong.

—RUSSELL BAKER

Education is not the answer to the question. Education is the means to the answer to all questions.

—WILLIAM ALLIN

Schooling, instead of encouraging the asking of questions, too often discourages it.

—MADELEINE L'ENGLE

The one real goal of education is to leave a person asking questions.

—MAX BEERBOHM

The one real object of education is to have a man in the condition of continually asking questions.

—BISHOP MANDELL CREIGHTON

It is the mark of an educated mind to be able to entertain a thought without accepting it.

—ARISTOTLE

One of the greatest problems of our time is that many are schooled but few are educated.

—THOMAS MOORE

Nothing in education is so astonishing as the amount of ignorance it accumulates in the form of facts.

—HENRY ADAMS

Education is that which discloses to the wise and disguises from the foolish their lack of understanding.

—AMBROSE BIERCE

Education consists mainly of what we have unlearned.

—MARK TWAIN

Much that passes for education is not education at all but ritual. The fact is that we are being educated when we know it least.

—DAVID P. GARDNER

Anyone who has passed through the regular gradations of a classical education, and is not made a fool by it, may consider himself as having had a very narrow escape.

—WILLIAM HAZLITT, FROM "ON THE IGNORANCE OF THE LEARNED," *TABLE TALK* (1822)

There is a great danger in the present day lest science-teaching should degenerate into the accumulation of disconnected facts and unexplained formulae, which burden the memory without cultivating the understanding.

—J. D. EVERETT

Many instructional arrangements seem "contrived" but there is nothing wrong with that. It is the teacher's function to contrive conditions under which students learn. It has always been the task of formal education to set up behavior which would prove useful or enjoyable later in a student's life.

—B. F. SKINNER, FROM HIS BOOK *SCIENCE AND HUMAN BEHAVIOR* (1953)

We no longer send our young to them primarily to be taught and given the tools of thought, no longer primarily to be informed and acquire knowledge; but to be "socialized."

—ROBERT LINDNER

Scholarship is polite argument.

—PHILIP RIEFF

Education is the ability to listen to almost anything without losing your temper.

—ROBERT FROST

One of the benefits of a college education is to show the boy its little avail.

— RALPH WALDO EMERSON

The very spring and root of honesty and virtue lie in good education.

—TITUS VESPASIANUS

Education, properly understood, is that which teaches discernment.

—JOSEPH ROUX

There is only one curriculum, no matter what the method of education: what is basic and universal in human experience and practice, the underlying structure of culture.

—PAUL GOODMAN

Upon the subject of education, not presuming to dictate any plan or system respecting it, I can only say that I view it as the most important subject which we as a people may be engaged in.

— ABRAHAM LINCOLN

The best education consists in immunizing people against systematic attempts at education.

—PAUL KARL FEYERABEND

They teach in academies far too many things, and far too much that is useless.

—JOHANN WOLFGANG VON GOETHE

Education is like a double-edged sword. It may be turned to dangerous uses if it is not properly handled.

—WU TING-FANG

Education can be dangerous. It is very difficult to make it not dangerous. In fact, it is almost impossible.

—ROBERT M. HUTCHINS

Education would be so much more effective if its purpose were to ensure that by the time they leave school every boy and girl should know how much they don't know, and be imbued with a lifelong desire to know it.

—SIR WILLIAM HALEY

Education is the period during which you are being instructed by somebody you do not know, about something you do not want to know.

—G. K. CHESTERTON

The well-meaning people who talk about education as if it were a substance distributable by coupon in large or small quantities never exhibit any understanding of the truth that you cannot teach anybody anything that he does not want to learn.

—GEORGE SAMPSON

Education is our passport to the future, for tomorrow belongs to the people who prepare for it today.

—MALCOLM X

I am convinced that it is of primordial importance to learn more every year than the year before. After all, what is education but a process by which a person begins to learn how to learn?

—PETER USTINOV

Education is the ability to meet life's situations.

—Dr. John G. Hibben, former president of Princeton University

The best educated human being is the one who understands most about the life in which he is placed.

—Helen Keller

Let us think of education as the means of developing our greatest abilities, because in each of us there is a private hope and dream which, fulfilled, can be translated into benefit for everyone and greater strength for our nation.

—John F. Kennedy

Education is what survives when what has been learned has been forgotten.

—B. F. Skinner

The education of a man is never completed until he dies.

—ROBERT E. LEE

A final reason for making education a process of self-instruction, and by consequence a process of pleasurable instruction, we may advert to the fact that, in proportion as it is made so, is here a probability that it will not cease when school days end.

—HERBERT SPENCER

Education is the best provision for old age.

—ARISTOTLE

There is no end to education. We are all in the Kindergarten of God.

—ELBERT HUBBARD, FROM *THE NOTE BOOK OF ELBERT HUBBARD* (1927)

No man who worships education has got the best out of education.
. . . Without a gentle contempt for education, no man's education is
complete.

—G. K. Chesterton

Education, like neurosis, begins at home.

—Milton Sapirstein

You speak of beginning the education of your son. The moment he was
able to form an idea his education was already begun.

—Anna Laetitia Barbauld

What the child says, he has heard at home.

—African proverb

Who takes the child by the hand takes the mother by the heart.

 —GERMAN PROVERB

One mother can achieve more than a hundred teachers.

 —JEWISH PROVERB

The family fireside is the best of schools.

 —ARNOLD H. GLASOW

I doubt that we can ever successfully impose values or attitudes or behaviors on our children—certainly not by threat, guilt, or punishment. But I do believe they can be induced through relationships where parents and children are growing together. Such relationships are, I believe, build on trust, example, talk, and caring.

 —FRED ROGERS

The best kind of sex education is life in a loving family.

—ROSEMARY HAUGHTON

Education is the mother and the father.

—MOTTO OF THE "LOST BOYS OF THE SOUTHERN SUDAN"

My grandmother wanted me to have an education, so she kept me out of school.

—MARGARET MEAD

The group consisting of mother, father, and child is the main educational agency of mankind.

—MARTIN LUTHER KING, JR.

School is an invaluable adjunct to the home, but it is a wretched substitute for it.

—THEODORE ROOSEVELT

Parents must acknowledge that the schooling which will be best for their children in the twenty-first century, must be very different from the schooling they experienced themselves.

—ANDY HARGREAVES AND MICHAEL FULLAN, FROM THEIR BOOK *WHAT'S WORTH FIGHTING FOR OUT THERE?* (1998)

Showing up at school already able to read is like showing up at the undertaker's already embalmed: people start worrying about being put out of their jobs.

—FLORENCE KING

They say that we are better educated than our parents' generation. What they mean is that we go to school longer. It is not the same thing.

—RICHARD YATES

There are three important qualities of a good family. These are love, cooperation, and positive expectations. So it should be in a good school.

—WILLIAM COOPER SMITH

Education begins at home. You can't blame the school for not putting into your child what you don't put into him.

—GEOFFREY HOLDER

My schooling not only failed to teach me what it professed to be teaching, but prevented me from being educated to an extent which infuriates me when I think of all I might have learned at home by myself.

—GEORGE BERNARD SHAW

Examinations are formidable even to the best prepared, for the greatest fool may ask more than the wisest man can answer.

—CHARLES CALEB COLTON

Trying to teach children without involving parents is like raking leaves in high wind.

—DR. KIMBERLY MUHAMMAD-EARL

I suppose it is because nearly all children go to school nowadays, and have things arranged for them, that they seem so forlornly unable to produce their own ideas.

—AGATHA CHRISTIE

This is the great vice of academicism, that it is concerned with ideas rather than with thinking.

—LIONEL TRILLING

It has been said that the primary function of schools is to impart enough facts to make children stop asking questions. Some, with whom the schools do not succeed, become scientists.

—Knut Schmidt-Nielsen

The chief wonder of education is that it does not ruin everybody concerned in it, teachers and taught.

—Henry Brooks Adams

Education is what happens to the other person, not what comes out of the mouth of the educator.

—Miles Horton

Much education today is monumentally ineffective. All too often we are giving young people cut flowers when we should be teaching them to grow their own plants.

—John W. Gardner

Teachers should be able to teach subjects, not manuals merely.

—HORACE MANN, AS QUOTED BY LAWRENCE A. CREMIN IN *THE REPUBLIC AND THE SCHOOL* (1957)

Education is not the piling of learning, information, data, facts, skills, or abilities—that's training or instruction—but is rather a making visible what is hidden as a seed.

—THOMAS MOORE

Ideas, facts, relationships, stories, histories, possibilities, artistry in words, in sounds, in form, and in color, crowd into the child's life, stir his feelings, excite his appreciation, and incite his impulses to kindred activities. It is a saddening thought that on this golden age there falls so often the shadow of the crammer.

—ALFRED NORTH WHITEHEAD, AS QUOTED IN *THE TEACHER AND THE TAUGHT* (1963)

Education is not something which the teacher does . . . it is a natural process which develops spontaneously in the human being.

—MARIA MONTESSORI

All genuine learning is active, not passive. It involves the use of the mind, not just the memory. It is a process of discovery, in which the student is the main agent, not the teacher.

—MORTIMER J. ADLER

The modern child, when asked what he learned today, replies, "Nothing, but I gained some meaningful insights.

—BILL VAUGHAN, IN *THE PAIDEIA PROPOSAL: AN EDUCATIONAL MANIFESTO* (1982)

The most effective kind of education is that a child should play amongst lovely things.

—PLATO

One of the first things schoolchildren in Texas learn is how to compose a simple declarative sentence without the word "shit" in it.

—ANONYMOUS

Phonetics, word associations, sentence structure, and all the techniques of good reading must be taught and drilled, but do not let us confuse these with reading. As teachers, let us learn how to prepare our reading lessons so that they serve to stir and strengthen the wings of imagination which may help our children to read the reality of life when they enter it as adult human beings.

—HENRY BARNES

All of us learn to write in the second grade. Most of us go on to greater things.

—BOBBY KNIGHT

Schools must stop being holding pens to keep energetic young people off the job market and off the streets. We stretch puberty out a long, long time.

—Toni Morrison

Parochial schools gave me a good early education. They made it possible for me to begin writing stories and even one novel at the age of eleven.

—Jack Kerouac

Some are bewildered in the maze of schools,
And some made coxcombs nature meant but fools.

—Alexander Pope

Garp knew what to take for courses and whom to have for teachers. That is often the difference between doing well or poorly in a school. He was not really a gifted student but he had direction.

—John Irving, from his book *The World According to Garp* (1978)

School buildings mirror our educational concepts. American has a predilection for straight lines, rectangles, squared-off blocks, and nowhere is this more true than in the usual schoolhouse.

> —J. LLOYD TRUMP, AS QUOTED IN *THE TEACHER AND THE TAUGHT* (1963)

The chief reason for going to school is to get the impression fixed for life that there is a book side for everything.

> —ROBERT FROST

The objective of education is to prepare the young to educate themselves throughout their lives.

> —ROBERT MAYNARD HUTCHINS

Education: What remains after you have forgotten all that you have been taught.

—Lord Halifax, aristocrat, politician, and war secretary of Britain during World War II

The function of education is to help you from childhood not to imitate anybody, but be yourself all the time.

—Jiddu Krishnamurti

The aim of education should be to teach us rather how to think, than what to think—rather to improve our minds, so as to enable us to think for ourselves, than to load the memory with thoughts of other men.

—Bill Beattie

Education must not simply teach work—it must teach life.

—W. E. B. Du Bois

I'm sure the reason such young nitwits are produced in our schools is because they have no contact with anything of any use in everyday life.

—PETRONIUS

Education does not mean teaching people to know what they do not know; it means teaching them to behave as they do not behave.

—JOHN RUSKIN

Education must have an end in view, for it is not an end in itself.

—SYBIL MARSHALL

At best, most college presidents are running something that is somewhere between a faltering corporation and a hotel.

—LEON BOTSTEIN

I find the three major administrative problems on a campus are sex for the students, athletics for the alumni, and parking for the faculty.

—CLARK KERR

University politics are vicious precisely because the stakes are so small.

—WALLACE SAYRE

Education is a state-controlled manufactory of echoes.

—NORMAN DOUGLAS

They wanted a great university without building a great university. They knew a lot about football, but not a lot about academia.

—BRAD CARTER, ON THE NCAA'S SUSPENSION OF SOUTHERN METHODIST UNIVERSITY'S FOOTBALL PROGRAM, AS QUOTED IN THE NEW YORK TIMES (1987)

It will be a great day when our schools get all the money they need and the Air Force has to hold a bake sale to buy a bomber.

—ANONYMOUS

It is not in the power of one generation to form a complete plan of education.

—IMMANUEL KANT, AS QUOTED IN *THE TEACHER AND THE TAUGHT* (1963)

Uniting a school behind an academic endeavor is no easy task.

—FRANK PAJARES

Academy: A modern school where football is taught.

—AMBROSE BIERCE

Some men are graduated from college *cum laude*, some are graduated *summa cum laude*, and some are graduated *mirabile dictu*.

—WILLIAM HOWARD TAFT

A whaleship was my Yale College and my Harvard.

—HERMAN MELVILLE, FROM *MOBY-DICK* (1851)

I am not impressed by the Ivy League establishments. Of course they graduate the best—it's all they'll take, leaving to others the problem of educating the country. They will give you an education the way the banks will give you money—provided you can prove to their satisfaction that you don't need it.

—PETER DE VRIES

Four years was enough of Harvard. I still had a lot to learn, but had been given the liberating notion that now I could teach myself.

—JOHN UPDIKE

I had a good education but it never went to my head, somehow. It should be a journey ending up with you at a different place. It didn't take with me. My degree was a kind of inoculation. I got just enough education to make me immune from it for the rest of my life.

—ALAN BENNETT

Undergraduates owe their happiness chiefly to the consciousness that they are no longer at school. The nonsense which was knocked out of them at school is all put gently back at Oxford or Cambridge.

—MAX BEERBOHM

Colleges . . . have their indispensable office—to teach elements. But they can only highly serve us when they aim not to drill, but to create; when they gather from afar every ray of various genius to their hospitable halls, and by the concentrated fires set the hearts of their youth on flame.

—RALPH WALDO EMERSON, FROM HIS BOOK *THE AMERICAN SCHOLAR; SELF-RELIANCE; COMPENSATION* (1837)

You can lead a boy to college, but you cannot make him think.

—ELBERT HUBBARD

—◆—

I'm still waiting for some college to come up with a march protesting student ignorance.

—PAUL LARMER, IN THE *CHICAGO TRIBUNE*

—◆—

A Harvard education consists of what you learn at Harvard while you are not studying.

—JAMES B. CONANT

—◆—

I think everyone should go to college and get a degree and then spend six months as a bartender and six months as a cabdriver. Then they would really be educated.

—AL MCGUIRE

—◆—

I prefer the company of peasants because they have not been educated sufficiently to reason incorrectly.

—MICHEL DE MONTAIGNE

It is only the ignorant who despise education.

—PUBLILIUS SYRUS

A pine bench, with Mark Hopkins at one end of it and me at the other, is a good enough college for me!

—JAMES A. GARFIELD, IN A SPEECH DURING A WILLIAMS COLLEGE
ALUMNI DINNER, NEW YORK CITY, 1871

The real University is a state of mind. It is that great heritage of rational thought that has been brought down to us through the centuries and which does not exist at any specific location. . . . The real University is nothing less than the continuing body of reason itself.

—ROBERT M. PIRSIG, FROM HIS BOOK *ZEN AND THE ART OF MOTORCYCLE MAINTENANCE* (1974)

A university is what a college becomes when the faculty loses interest in students.

—JOHN CIARDI

A college education shows a man how little other people know.

—THOMAS CHANDLER HALIBURTON

It is time that we had uncommon schools, that we did not leave off our education when we begin to be men and women. It is time that villages were universities, and their elder inhabitants the fellows of universities.

—HENRY DAVID THOREAU, FROM HIS BOOK *WALDEN; OR LIFE IN THE WOODS* (1854)

College isn't the place to go for ideas.

—HELEN KELLER

———✦———

A university education should equip one to entertain three things: a friend, an idea, and one's self.

—THOMAS EHRLICH AND JULIET FRY, FROM "MR. CARNEGIE'S GIFT,"
MR. DOOLEY'S OPINIONS (1901)

———✦———

Courses in education given at . . . teachers' colleges have traditionally been used as a substitute for genuine scholarship. In my opinion, much of the so-called science of "education" was invented as a necessary mechanism for enabling semieducated people to act as tolerable teachers.

—SLOAN WILSON

———✦———

Everywhere I go I'm asked if I think the university stifles writers. My opinion is that they don't stifle enough of them. There's many a bestseller that could have been prevented by a good teacher.

—FLANNERY O'CONNOR

Our American professors like their literature clear and cold and pure and very dead.

—SINCLAIR LEWIS, IN HIS NOBEL PRIZE ADDRESS, 1930

Nor can I do better, in conclusion, than impress upon you the study of Greek literature, which not only elevates above the vulgar herd, but leads not infrequently to positions of emolument.

—THOMAS GAISFORD, IN A CHRISTMAS DAY SERMON IN THE CATHEDRAL, OXFORD

Our principal writers have nearly all been fortunate in escaping regular education.

—Hugh MacDiarmid

———✦———

The discipline of colleges and universities is in general contrived, not for the benefit of the students, but for the interest or more properly speaking, for the ease of the masters.

—Adam Smith from *Wealth of Nations* (1776)

———✦———

School has not given me anything. I have always been suspicious of teachers. I do not know why.

—Werner Herzog

———✦———

I am inclined to think that one's education has been in vain if one fails to learn that most schoolmasters are idiots.

—Hesketh Pearson

———✦———

Our problem as educators is that far too often we begin the academic year worrying more about our courses and about our academic responsibilities than about our students, those fragile human beings who sit across from us and stare, waiting to learn and eager to know.

—FRANK PAJARES

Class discussion: letting twenty young blockheads and two cocky neurotics discuss something that neither their teacher nor they know.

—VLADIMIR NABOKOV

Education is too important to be left solely to the educators.

—FRANCIS KEPPEL

I spent fourteen months at Magdalen College: they proved the fourteen months the most idle and unprofitable of my whole life.

—EDWARD GIBBON, FROM HIS BOOK *MEMOIRS OF MY LIFE* (1796)

To my astonishment I was informed on leaving college that I had studied navigation!—why if I had taken one turn down the harbour—I should have known more about it.

> —HENRY DAVID THOREAU, FROM HIS BOOK *WALDEN; OR LIFE IN THE WOODS* (1854)

A man who has never gone to school may steal from a freight car; but if he has a university education, he may steal the whole railroad.

> —THEODORE ROOSEVELT

Happy the natural college thus self-instituted around every natural teacher; the young men of Athens around Socrates.

> —RALPH WALDO EMERSON

One of the marks of the new school and the new university will be the provision of hours of withdrawal, not spent in classroom study or in sport, in the midst of its regular work day: a period of concentration and reflection, in which the work of active selection and spiritual assimilation can go on.

—LEWIS MUMFORD

For the most part, colleges are places where pebbles are polished and diamonds are dimmed.

—ROBERT GREEN INGERSOLL

Since the literature demonstrates the value of grouping students by ability, while few if any studies support restricting grouping to common ages, it is ironic that so many schools are moving from the former to the latter.

—MIKE ROBISON

All schools, all colleges, have two great functions: to confer, and to conceal, valuable knowledge. The theological knowledge which they conceal cannot justly be regarded as less valuable than that which they reveal. That is, when a man is buying a basket of strawberries it can profit him to know that the bottom half of it is rotten.

—MARK TWAIN

Universities should be safe havens where ruthless examination of realities will not be distorted by the aim to please or inhibited by the risk of displeasure.

—KINGMAN BREWSTER, IN HIS INAUGURAL ADDRESS AT YALE UNIVERSITY, 1964

Universities are, of course, hostile to geniuses, who seeing and using ways of their own, discredit the routine.

—RALPH WALDO EMERSON

Any attempt to reform the university without attending to the system of which it is an integral part is like trying to do urban renewal in New York City from the twelfth story up.

—Ivan Illich

A university's essential character is that of being a center of free inquiry and criticism—a thing not to be sacrificed for anything else.

—Richard Hofstadter, in his commencement address at Columbia University (1968)

The most conservative persons I ever met are college undergraduates.

—Woodrow Wilson

The university is the last remaining platform for national dissent.

—Leon Eisenberg

The real struggle is not between East and West, or capitalism and communism, but between education and propaganda.

—MARTIN BUBER

The function of a University is to enable you to shed details in favor of principles.

—ANONYMOUS

At college age, you can tell who is best at taking tests and going to school, but you can't tell who the best people are. That worries the hell out of me.

—BARNABY C. KEENEY

You think, 'cause you been to college, you know better than anybody.

—RICHARD HENRY DANA, JR., FROM HIS BOOK *TWO YEARS BEFORE THE MAST* (1840)

If a man is a fool, you don't train him out of being a fool by sending him to university. You merely turn him into a trained fool, ten times more dangerous.

—DESMOND BAGLEY

The once universal practice of learning by rote is daily falling into discredit.

—HERBERT SPENCER

Colleges are like old-age homes, except for the fact that more people die in colleges.

—BOB DYLAN, AS QUOTED IN *PLAYBOY* (1966)

The bachelor's degree is not the end of the educational journey, but just another milestone.

—KENNETH C. GREEN, DIRECTOR OF THE CAMPUS COMPUTING PROJECT

You are educated. Your certification is in your degree. You may think of it as the ticket to the good life. Let me ask you to think of an alternative. Think of it as your ticket to change the world.

—TOM BROKAW

Nine-tenths of education is encouragement.

—ANATOLE FRANCE

Ask not what your school can do for you, but what you can do for your school.

—GEORGE ST. JOHN, AS QUOTED BY G. WILLIAMS DOMHOFF IN *WHO RULES AMERICA NOW?: A VIEW FOR THE '80s* (1983)

Training is everything. The peach was once a bitter almond; cauliflower is nothing but cabbage with a college education.

—MARK TWAIN

We are shut up in schools and college recitation rooms for ten or fifteen years, and come out at last with a bellyful of words and do not know a thing.

  —RALPH WALDO EMERSON

The business schools reward difficult complex behavior more than simple behavior, but simple behavior is more effective.

  —WARREN BUFFETT

I was able to find nontraditional methods in the traditional setting of business school. All of use were subject to three "cold calls" and our performance would determine one-third of our grade. Bill could nail us at any time, in class or in the hallway, at a bar or at the apartment, and you had to answer. Incidentally, as tough as his course was, it was the most oversubscribed in the school.

  —JOHN KELLY, ON BILL COCKRUM, FINANCE PROFESSOR AT ANDERSON BUSINESS SCHOOL AND INNOVATOR OF THE COLD CALL METHOD OF ASSESSMENT (2002)

No one can look back on his schooldays and say with truth that they were altogether unhappy.

—GEORGE ORWELL

I won't say ours was a tough school, but we had our own coroner. We used to write essays like: What I'm going to be if I grow up.

—LENNY BRUCE

Thank goodness I was never sent to school; it would have rubbed off some of the originality.

—BEATRIX POTTER

I believe that in that first year at Dayton High School I learned more about how to work with people and about myself—than any of the thirty-nine years of coaching that followed.

—JOHN WOODEN, FROM HIS BOOK *MY PERSONAL BEST* (2004)

Show me a man who has enjoyed his schooldays, and I'll show you a bully and a bore.

—ROBERT MORLEY

It is indeed ironic that we spend our school days yearning to graduate and our remaining days waxing nostalgic about our school days.

—ISABEL WAXMAN, AMERICAN EDUCATOR

We have but one rule here and it is that every student must be a gentleman.

—ROBERT E. LEE, TO A STUDENT WHO ASKED FOR A COPY OF THE RULES AT WASHINGTON COLLEGE (NOW WASHINGTON AND LEE UNIVERSITY)

If I ran a school, I'd give the average grade to the ones who gave me all the right answers, for being good parrots. I'd give the top grades to those who made a lot of mistakes and told me about them, and then told me what they learned from them.

—R. BUCKMINSTER FULLER

The shrewd guess, the fertile hypothesis, the courageous leap to a tentative conclusion—these are the most valuable coin of the thinker at work. But in most schools guessing is heavily penalized and is associated somehow with laziness.

—JEROME S. BRUNER

I have never let my schooling interfere with my education.

—MARK TWAIN

If I had learned education I would not have had time to learn anything else.

—CORNELIUS VANDERBILT

But this bridge will only take you halfway there—The last few steps you'll have to take alone.

> —SHEL SILVERSTEIN, FROM "THIS BRIDGE," *A LIGHT IN THE ATTIC* (1981)

CHAPTER SEVEN

Life Lessons

Gentlemen: I have not had your advantages. What poor education I have received has been gained at the University of Life.

—HORATIO BOTTOMLEY, IN A SPEECH AT THE OXFORD UNION, 1920

Not art, not books, but life itself is the true basis of . . . education.

—JOHANN HEINRICH PESTALOZZI

We need to be the authors of our own life.

—PETER SENGE, AUTHOR OF *THE DANCE OF CHANGE* (1999)

Experience is the teacher of all things.

—JULIUS CAESAR

I may have said the same thing before. . . . But my explanation, I am sure, will always be different.

—OSCAR WILDE

The best of all teachers, experience.

—PLINY THE YOUNGER

Results! Why, man, I have gotten a lot of results. I know several thousand things that won't work.

—THOMAS EDISON

"Experience iz a good schoolmaster," but reason iz a better one.

—JOSH BILLINGS, FROM "INK BRATS," *EVERYBODY'S FRIEND: JOSH BILLINGS' ENCYCLOPEDIA AND PROVERBIAL PHILOSOPHY OF WIT AND HUMOR* (1874)

The only thing experience teaches us is that experience teaches us nothing.

—André Maurois

Experience is a good teacher, but she sends in terrific bills.

—Minna Antrim

Experience is a good school, but the fees are high.

—Heinrich Heine

I believe that education is a process of living and not a preparation for future living.

—John Dewey

Experience keeps a dear school, yet Fools will learn in no other.

—BENJAMIN FRANKLIN

A moment's insight is sometimes worth a life's experience.

—OLIVER WENDELL HOLMES, SR., FROM HIS BOOK *THE PROFESSOR AT THE BREAKFAST-TABLE* (1860)

Mr. B's F.A.C.T.S. of Life:
Flexibility
Accountability
Cooperation
Trust
Sincerity

—T. BOGUSZ

Our life is an apprenticeship to the truth that around every circle another can be drawn.

—RALPH WALDO EMERSON

Life is ten percent what happens to me and ninety percent how I react to it.

—CHARLES SWINDOLL

It's not the load that breaks you down, it's the way you carry it.

—LOU HOLTZ

It's kind of fun to do the impossible.

—WALT DISNEY

Expecting something for nothing is the most popular form of hope.

—Arnold Glasow

Prepare for the unknown by studying how others in the past have coped with the unforeseeable and the unpredictable.

—George Patton

Look not mournfully into the past, it comes not back again. Wisely improve the present, it is thine. Go forth to meet the shadowy future without fear and with a manly heart.

—Henry Wadsworth Longfellow

First say to yourself what you would be;
and then do what you have to do.

—Epictetus

Only so much do I know, as I have lived. Instantly we know whose words are baded with life, and whose are not.

—RALPH WALDO EMERSON, FROM HIS BOOK *THE AMERICAN SCHOLAR; SELF-RELIANCE; COMPENSATION* (1837)

Discoveries are often made by not following instructions; by going off the main road; by trying the untried.

—FRANK TYGER

The more original a discovery, the more obvious it seems afterward.

—ARTHUR KOESTLER

The moment a person forms a theory, his imagination sees, in every object, only the traits that favor that theory.

—THOMAS JEFFERSON

The most damaging phrase in the language is "It's always been done that way."

—GRACE MURRAY HOPPER

It is not in the stars to hold our destiny, but in ourselves.

—WILLIAM SHAKESPEARE

Winning isn't everything, but wanting to win is.

—VINCE LOMBARDI

Humans are allergic to change. They love to say, "We've always done it this way." I try to fight that. That's why I have a clock on my wall that runs counter-clockwise.

—GRACE MURRAY HOPPER

There are young people out there cutting raw cocaine with chemicals from the local hardware store . . . and each of these new drugs is more addictive, more deadly, and less costly than the last. . . . How is it that we have failed to tap that ingenuity, that sense of experimentation?

—SENATOR KOHL, FROM THE U.S. SENATE HEARING "CRISIS IN MATH AND SCIENCE EDUCATION"

Reinventing the wheel is a process.

—RASHID ELISHA

A talent is formed in stillness, a character in the world's torrent.

—JOHANN WOLFGANG VON GOETHE

The future is yet full of trial and success. There is happiness to be enjoyed! There is good to be done! Exchange this false life of thine for a true one.

—NATHANIEL HAWTHORNE

The circumstances that surround a man's life are not important. How that man responds to those circumstances is important. His response is the ultimate determining factor between success and failure.

—BOOKER T. WASHINGTON

In leadership, there are no words more important that trust. In any organization, trust must be developed among every member of the team if success is going to be achieved.

—MIKE KRZYZEWSKI, COLLEGE BASKETBALL COACH

You must understand the whole of life, not just one little part of it. That is why you must read, that is why you must look at the skies, that is why you must sing and dance, and write poems, and suffer, and understand, for all that is life.

—JIDDU KRISHNAMURTI

I really consider life to be like studying. The first thing I look up when I'm out of town is the local museum. You can always continue to learn.

—SARAH MICHELLE GELLAR

⎯⎯◆⎯⎯

You live your life between your ears.

—BEBE MOORE CAMPBELL

⎯⎯◆⎯⎯

All of the top achievers I know are lifelong learners . . . looking for new skills, insights, and ideas. If they're not learning, they're not growing . . . not moving toward excellence.

—DENIS WAITLEY

⎯⎯◆⎯⎯

We now accept the fact that learning is a lifelong process of keeping abreast of change. And the most pressing task is to teach people how to learn.

—PETER F. DRUCKER

There is more to life than increasing its speed.

—GANDHI

Perhaps the angels who fear to tread where fools rush in used to be fools who rushed in.

—FRANKLIN P. JONES

The very least you can do in your life is to figure out what you hope for. And the most you can do is live inside that hope. Not admire it from a distance but live right in it, under its roof.

—BARBARA KINGSOLVER, FROM HER BOOK *ANIMAL DREAMS* (1997)

No matter how deep a study you make, what you really have to rely on is your own intuition and when it comes down to it, you really don't know what's going to happen until you do it.

—KONOSUKE MATSUSHITA, AS QUOTED IN *MATSUSHITA LEADERSHIP* (1997)

The happiest life is that which constantly exercises and educates what is best in us.

—PHILIP G. HAMERTON, AUTHOR OF *INTELLECTUAL LIFE* (1981)

Life is a wonderful thing to talk about, or to read about in history books—but it is terrible when one has to live it.

—JEAN ANOUILH

Some people study all their life, and at their death have learned everything but to think.

—DEMERGUE

One of life's most painful moments comes when we must admit that we didn't do our homework, that we are not prepared.

—MERLIN OLSEN

One must learn by doing the thing; for though you think you know it, you have no certainty, until you try.

—SOPHOCLES

Any place that anyone young can learn something useful from someone with experience is an educational institution.

—AL CAPP

Knowledge can only be got in one way, the way of experience; there is no other way to know.

—SWAMI VIVEKANANDA, AS QUOTED IN *LIVING AT THE SOURCE YOGA: TEACHINGS OF VIVEKANANDA* (1993)

Most of the most important experiences that truly educate cannot be arranged ahead of time with any precision.

—HAROLD TAYLOR

Time is a great teacher, but unfortunately it kills all its pupils.

—LOUIS HECTOR BERLIOZ

It's never too late to start over, never too late to be happy.

—JANE FONDA

If the past cannot teach the present and the father cannot teach the son, then history need not have bothered to go on, and the world has wasted a great deal of time.

—RUSSELL HOBAN

We are inheritors of a past that gives us every reason to believe that we will succeed.

—ANONYMOUS

Yesterday is a dream, tomorrow but a vision. But today well lived makes every yesterday a dream of happiness, and every tomorrow a vision of hope. Look well, therefore, to this day.

—SANSKRIT PROVERB

Time is the currency of teaching. We barter with time. Every day we make small concessions, small tradeoffs, but, in the end, we know it's going to defeat us.

—ERNEST L. BOYER

The problem with doing something right the first time is that nobody appreciates how difficult it was.

—WALT WEST

Wait for the wisest of all counselors: time.

—PERICLES

The adult with a capacity for true maturity is one who has grown out of childhood without losing childhood's best traits.

—JOSEPH STONE

He who has no hair on his lip cannot be trusted to do anything well.

—CHINESE PROVERB

Maturity is not a goal, but rather a process.

—DR. LEO BUSCAGLIA

No one will live all his life in the world into which he was born, and no one will die in the world in which he worked in his maturity.

—MARGARET MEAD, AS QUOTED IN *THE TEACHER AND THE TAUGHT* (1963)

All that I know I learned after I was thirty.

—GEORGES CLEMENCEAU

They always say that time changes things, but you actually have to change them yourself.

—ANDY WARHOL

Lives of great men all remind us
We can make our lives sublime,
And, departing, leave behind us
Footprints on the sands of time.

—HENRY WADSWORTH LONGFELLOW

Time, as it grows old, teaches all things.

—AESCHYLUS

Vague and nebulous is the beginning of all things, but not their end.

—KAHLIL GIBRAN

He would not be ashamed of dying. . . . He could be research. A human textbook. *Study me in my slow and patient demise. Watch what happens to me. Learn with me.*

—MITCH ALBOM, FROM HIS BOOK *TUESDAYS WITH MORRIE* (1997)

Times of great calamity and confusion have ever been productive of the greatest minds. The purest ore is produced from the hottest furnace, and the brightest thunderbolt is elicited from the darkest storm.

—CHARLES CALEB COLTON

Everything comes gradually and at its appointed hour.

—OVID

Experience . . . has ways of *boiling over*, and making us correct our present formulas.

—WILLIAM JAMES, FROM HIS BOOK *PRAGMATISM* (1907)

Experience is a great advantage. The problem is that when you get the experience, you're too damned old to do anything about it.

—JIMMY CONNORS, FORMER AMERICAN TENNIS CHAMPION

We ought not to look back unless it is to derive useful lessons from past errors, and for the purpose of profiting by dear-bought experience.

—GEORGE WASHINGTON

The past must be a springboard, not a sofa.

—HAROLD MACMILLAN

Events seen and participated in leave disproportionate impressions. Furthermore . . . the lessons drawn from firsthand experience are overgeneralized. So if people do not learn enough from what happens to others, they learn too much from what happens to them.

—ROBERT JERVIS

Experience enables you to recognize a mistake when you make it again.

—FRANKLIN P. JONES

As we experience the world, so we act.

—R. D. LAING, FROM HIS BOOK *THE POLITICS OF EXPERIENCE* (1967)

The world doesn't fear a new idea. It can pigeonhole any idea. But it can't pigeonhole a real new experience.

—D. H. LAWRENCE, FROM HIS BOOK *STUDIES IN CLASSIC AMERICAN LITERATURE* (1923)

a man who is so dull
that he can only learn by personal experience
is too dull to learn
anything important by experience.

—Don Marquis, from "Archy on this and that," *Archy Does His Part* (1935)

We can learn from experience if we are ready to adapt that experience to changed conditions.

—J. C. Masterman, from his book *The Double-Cross System in the War of 1939 to 1945* (1972)

Learn why the world wags and what wags it. That is the only thing which the mind can never exhaust, never alienate, never be tortured by, never fear or distrust, and never dream of regretting. Learning is the only thing for you. Look what a lot of things there are to learn.

—T. H. White, from his book *The Once and Future King*

We shall never learn to feel and respect our real calling and destiny, unless we have taught ourselves to consider every thing as moonshine, compared with the education of the heart.

—Sir Walter Scott

Learn not only to find what you like, learn to like what you find.

—Anthony J. D'Angelo, from his book *The College Blue Book* (1995)

If you do not expect it, you will not find the unexpected, for it is hard to find and difficult.

—Heraclitus

To do just the opposite is a form of imitation.

—Georg Christoph Lichtenberg

I am always doing that which I cannot do, in order that I may learn how to do it.

—PABLO PICASSO

⟫⟨

The things we know best are the things we haven't been taught.

—MARQUIS DE VAUVENARGUES

⟫⟨

If it be knowledge or wisdom one is seeking, then one had better go direct to the source. And the source is not the scholar or philosopher, not the master, saint, or teacher, but life itself—direct experience of life.

—HENRY MILLER, FROM THE PREFACE TO *THE BOOKS IN MY LIFE* (1952)

⟫⟨

This instrument (radio) can teach. It can illuminate, yes, and it can even inspire. But it can do so only to the extent that humans are determined to use it to those ends. Otherwise it's nothing but wires and lights in a box.

—EDWARD R. MURROW

We must not study ourselves while having an experience.

—FRIEDRICH NIETZSCHE

I like to think of my behavior in the sixties as a "learning experience." Then again, I like to think of anything stupid I've done as a "learning experience." It makes me feel less stupid.

—P. J. O'ROURKE, FROM "SECOND THOUGHTS ABOUT THE SIXTIES," GIVE WAR A CHANCE (1992)

The Law of Primacy . . . states that the earlier an experience the more potent its effect since it influences how later experiences will be interpreted.

—J. A. C. BROWN, FROM HIS BOOK *TECHNIQUES OF PERSUASION: FROM PROPAGANDA TO BRAINWASHING* (1963)

We are human because, at a very early stage in the history of the species, our ancestors discovered a way of preserving and disseminating the results of experience.

—ALDOUS HUXLEY, FROM "KNOWLEDGE AND UNDERSTANDING," *TOMORROW AND TOMORROW AND TOMORROW AND OTHER ESSAYS* (1956)

If men could learn from history, what lessons it might teach us! But passion and party blind our eyes, and the light which experience gives is a lantern on the stern, which shines only the waves behind us!

—SAMUEL TAYLOR COLERIDGE, FROM *SPECIMENS OF THE TABLE TALK OF SAMUEL TAYLOR COLERIDGE* (1836)

Education is a progressive discovery of our own ignorance.

—WILL DURANT

Life at university, with its intellectual and inconclusive discussions at a postgraduate level is on the whole a bad training for the real world. Only men of very strong character surmount this handicap.

—PAUL CHAMBERS, JAZZ BASSIST

The first rule of discovery is to have brains and good luck. The second rule of discovery is to sit tight and wait till you get a bright idea.

—GEORGE POLYA

Experience is not what happens to you. It is what you do with what happens to you.

—ALDOUS HUXLEY

She had some experience of the world, and the capacity for reflection that makes such experience profitable.

—JEAN-JACQUES ROUSSEAU, FROM HIS BOOK *CONFESSIONS* (1781)

Our experience is composed rather of illusions lost than of wisdom acquired.

—JOSEPH ROUX, FROM HIS BOOK *MEDITATIONS OF A PARISH PRIEST* (1886)

When a man with money meets a man with experience, the man with the experience ends up with the money and the man with the money ends up with the experience.

—ANONYMOUS

There's no educational value in the second kick of a mule.

—AMERICAN PROVERB

If you would know the road ahead, ask someone who has traveled it.

—CHINESE PROVERB

Once burned, twice shy.

—ENGLISH PROVERB

Don't be discouraged by failure. It can be a positive experience. Failure is, in a sense, the highway to success, inasmuch as every discovery of what is false leads us to seek earnestly after what is true, and every fresh experience points out some form of error, which we shall afterwards carefully avoid.

—JOHN KEATS

And you know, life is a constant learning experience. I learn so much with my kids. I read tons of books and study what they're studying.

—REESE WITHERSPOON

Wisdom is the daughter of experience.

—LEONARDO DA VINCI

You cannot acquire experience by making experiments. You cannot create experience. You must undergo it.

—ALBERT CAMUS

I want to stone these people who have life-changing experiences, and it all happens right away. For me, it has been a process, a long process of learning and study.

—WILLIE AAMES

A failure is a man who has blundered, but is not able to cash in on the experience.

—ELBERT HUBBARD

The important thing in life is not the triumph but the struggle.

—PIERRE DE COUBERTIN, HISTORIAN AND FOUNDER OF THE MODERN
OLYMPIC GAMES

There is no education like adversity.

—BENJAMIN DISRAELI

These then are my last words to you: be not afraid of life. Believe that life
is worth living and your belief will help create the fact.

—WILLIAM JAMES

If you truly want to bless others in your life, you must seek out those
experiences that keep you motivated and inspired, and then share them.

—THOMAS KINKADE

Only by being permitted to experience the consequences of his actions will the child acquire a sense of responsibility; and within the limits marked by the demands of his safety this must be done.

—ROBERT LINDNER, FROM HIS BOOK *PRESCRIPTION FOR REBELLION* (1952)

Get the child interested in avoiding insufficient or superfluous efforts. If in this way you train him to calculate the effects of all his movements, and to correct his mistakes by experience, is it not clear that the more he does the wiser he will become?

—JEAN-JACQUES ROUSSEAU, FROM HIS BOOK *TREATISE ON EDUCATION* (1762)

Our errors are surely not such awfully solemn things. In a world where we are so certain to incur them in spite of all our caution, a certain lightness of heart seems healthier than this excessive nervousness on their behalf.

—WILLIAM JAMES, FROM HIS BOOK *THE WILL TO BELIEVE* (1897)

Students who experience repeated success in school are likely to develop positive feelings about their abilities, while those who encounter failure tend to develop negative views of themselves.

—WILLIAM PURKEY

With just a little education and practice on how to manage your emotions, you can move into a new experience of life so rewarding that you will be motivated to keep on managing your emotional nature in order to sustain it. The payoff is delicious in terms of improved quality of life.

—DOC CHILDRE

You can get all A's and still flunk life.

—WALKER PERCY

The best education in the world is that got by struggling to get a living.

—WENDELL PHILLIPS, ABOLITIONIST AND ORATOR

The knowledge of the world is only to be acquired in the world, and not in a closet.

—LORD CHESTERFIELD

Experience is a hard teacher, because she gives the test first, the lesson afterward.

—VERNON LAW, RETIRED PROFESSIONAL BASEBALL PLAYER

It's okay to make mistakes. Mistakes are our teachers—they help us to learn.

— JOHN BRADSHAW

Tell me and I forget. Show me and I remember. Involve me and
I understand.

—CHINESE PROVERB

I got a fortune cookie that said, "To remember is to understand."
I have never forgotten it. A good judge remembers what it was like to
be a lawyer. A good editor remembers being a writer. A good parent
remembers what it was like to be a child.

—ANNA QUINDLEN

You can observe a lot by just looking around.

—YOGI BERRA

People learn more quickly by doing something or seeing something done.

—GILBERT HIGHET

The essence of intelligence is skill in extracting meaning from everyday experience.

—ANONYMOUS

We learn geology the morning after the earthquake.

—RALPH WALDO EMERSON, FROM "CONSIDERATIONS BY THE WAY," *THE CONDUCT OF LIFE* (1860)

I have learned silence from the talkative, toleration from the intolerant, and kindness from the unkind; yet, strange, I am ungrateful to these teachers.

—KAHLIL GIBRAN

I learned that is the weak who are cruel, and that gentleness is to be expected only from the strong.

—LEO ROSTEN

The main part of intellectual education is not the acquisition of facts but learning how to make facts live.

—OLIVER WENDELL HOLMES

Men must be taught as if you taught them not, And things unknown proposed as things forgot.

—ALEXANDER POPE

I have learned throughout my life as a composer chiefly through my mistakes and pursuits of false assumptions, not my exposure to founts of wisdom and knowledge.

—IGOR STRAVINSKY

There are two types of education. One should teach us how to make a living, and the other how to live.

—JOHN ADAMS

I would rather live in a world where my life is surrounded by mystery than live in a world so small that my mind could comprehend it.

—HENRY EMERSON FOSDICK

You will never stub your toe standing still. The faster you go, the more chance there is of stubbing your toe, but the more chance you have of getting somewhere.

—CHARLES F. KETTERING

If you can spend a perfectly useless afternoon in a perfectly useless manner, you have learned how to live.

—LIN YUTANG

You can get help from teachers, but you are going to have to learn a lot by yourself, sitting alone in a room.

—THEODOR "DR. SEUSS" GEISEL

A sufficient experimental training was believed to have been provided as long as the student had been introduced to the results of past experiments or had been allowed to watch demonstration experiments conducted by his teacher, as though it were possible to sit in rows on a wharf and learn to swim merely by watching grown-up swimmers in the water.

—JEAN PIAGET

A fall from the third floor hurts as much as a fall from the hundredth. If I have to fall, may it be from a high place.

—PAULO COELHO

Worrying is the most natural and spontaneous of all human functions. It is time to acknowledge this, perhaps even to learn to do it better.

—LEWIS THOMAS

A good scare is worth more than good advice.

—EDGAR WATSON HOWE

Education is what you get from reading the fine print. Experience is what you get if you don't.

—PETE SEEGER

———◦———

There are three schoolmasters for everybody that will employ them—the senses, intelligent companions, and books.

—HENRY WARD BEECHER

———◦———

It is by teaching that we teach ourselves, by relating that we observe, by affirming that we examine, by showing that we look, by writing that we think, by pumping that we draw water into the well.

—HENRI-FRÉDÉRIC AMIEL

———◦———

Give a man a fish and you feed him for a day. Teach him how to fish and you feed him for a lifetime.

—LAO-TZU

———◦———

Excellence is a better teacher than mediocrity. The lessons of the ordinary are everywhere. Truly profound and original insights are to be found only in studying the exemplary.

—WARREN G. BENNIS

All Scripture is inspired by God and profitable for teaching, for reproof, for correction, and for training in righteousness, that the man of God may be complete, equipped for every good work.

—PAUL, 2 TIMOTHY 3:16

The educator must above all understand how to wait; to reckon all effects in the light of the future, not of the present.

—ELLEN KEY

Too often we give children answers to remember rather than problems to solve.

—ROGER LEWIN

⟦⟧

Come forth into the light of things, let nature be your teacher.

—WILLIAM WORDSWORTH

⟦⟧

We have to look for routes of power our teachers never imagined, or were encouraged to avoid.

—THOMAS PYNCHON, FROM HIS BOOK *GRAVITY'S RAINBOW* (1973)

⟦⟧

To live for a long time close to great minds is the best kind of education.

—JOHN BUCHAN, FROM HIS BOOK *MEMORY HOLD-THE-DOOR* (1940)

⟦⟧

I studied the lives of great men and famous women; and I found that the men and women who got to the top were those who did the jobs they had in hand, with everything they had of energy and enthusiasm and hard work.

—HARRY S. TRUMAN

If I have seen farther than other men, it is because I have stood on the shoulders of giants.

—ISAAC NEWTON

Small deeds done are better than great deeds planned.

—PETER MARSHALL

It is the surmounting of difficulties that make heroes.

—LOUIS KOSSUTH, HUNGARIAN REVOLUTIONARY HERO

Education is an admirable thing, but it is well to remember from time to time that nothing that is worth knowing can be taught.

—OSCAR WILDE

The greatest education in the world is watching the masters at work.

—MICHAEL JACKSON

There is a time in every man's education when he arrives at the conviction that envy is ignorance; that imitation is suicide; that he must take himself for better, for worse, as his portion; that though the wide universe is full of good, no kernel of nourishing corn can come to him but through his toil bestowed on that plot of ground which is given to him to till. The power which resides in him is new in nature, and none but he knows what that is which he can do, nor does he know until he has tried.

—RALPH WALDO EMERSON, FROM HIS BOOK *SELF-RELIANCE* (1839)

No one could make a greater mistake than those who did nothing because they could do only a little.

—EDMUND BURKE

I do not cast my eyes away from my troubles. I pack them in as little compass as I can for myself, and never let them annoy others.

—ROBERT SOUTHEY

Sweet are the uses of adversity,
Which like the toad, ugly and venomous,
Wears yet a precious jewel in his head.

—WILLIAM SHAKESPEARE

Inside every problem are the seeds of innovative solutions.

—REED MARKHAM

Wherever we look upon this earth, the opportunities take shape within the problems.

—NELSON A. ROCKEFELLER

The mark of a well-educated person is not necessarily in knowing all the answers, but in knowing where to find them.

—DOUGLAS EVERETT

Recognizing the correct answer out of a predetermined list of responses is fundamentally different from the act of reading, or writing, or speaking, or reasoning, or dancing, or anything else that human beings do in the real world.

—LINDA DARLING-HAMMOND, FROM "MAD-HATTER TESTS OF GOOD TEACHING," THE *NEW YORK TIMES* (1984)

The shortest answer is doing.

—George Herbert

—◆—

It is not enough for me to answer questions; I want to know how to answer the one question that seems to encompass everything I face: What am I here for?

—Abraham Joshua Heschel, from his book *Who Is Man?* (1965)

—◆—

The day after never we will have an explanation.

—Henry David Thoreau, from his journal dated November 8, 1857

—◆—

You are also asking me questions and I hear you,
I answer that I cannot answer, you must find out for yourself.

—Walt Whitman, from his poem "Song of Myself" (1855)

—◆—

It is not a question of how much a man knows, but what use he can make of what he knows.

—Josiah Gilbert Holland, from "Self-Help," *Plain Talks on Familiar Subjects* (1866)

Ask me no questions, and I'll tell you no fibs.

—Oliver Goldsmith, from his book *She Stoops to Conquer: Or, the Mistakes of Night* (1773)

He knows who says: we do not know.

—Upanishads

We know what we are, but know not what we may be.

—William Shakespeare

My name is Sherlock Holmes. It is my business to know what other people don't know.

—Sir Arthur Conan Doyle, from "The Adventure of a Carbuncle," *The Adventures of Sherlock Holmes* (1892)

If you don't know where you are going, you'll end up someplace else.

—Yogi Berra

Now there is one outstandingly important fact regarding Spaceship Earth, and that is that no instruction book came with it.

—Buckminster Fuller

There is a theory which states that if ever anybody discovers exactly what the universe is for and why it is here, it will instantly disappear and be replaced by something even more bizarre and inexplicable. There is another theory which states that this has already happened.

—DOUGLAS ADAMS, FROM HIS BOOK *THE HITCHHIKER'S GUIDE TO THE GALAXY* (1995)

The universe is full of magical things patiently waiting for our wits to grow sharper.

—EDEN PHILLPOTTS

When you want something, all the universe conspires in helping you to achieve it.

—PAULO COELHO

The thing always happens that you really believe in; and the belief in a thing makes it happen.

—FRANK LOYD WRIGHT

Only the hand that erases can write the true thing.

—JOHANNES ECKHART O. P.

Throughout the centuries there were men who took first steps down new roads armed with nothing but their own vision.

—AYN RAND

The noblest search is the search for excellence.

—LYNDON B. JOHNSON

What is now proved was once only imagined.

—WILLIAM BLAKE

Rebellion against your handicaps gets you nowhere. Self-pity gets you nowhere. One must have the adventurous daring to accept oneself as a bundle of possibilities and undertake the most interesting game in the world—making the most of one's best.

—HARRY EMERSON FOSDICK

When we feel stuck, going nowhere—even starting to slip backward— we may actually be backing up to get a running start.

—DAN MILLMAN, AUTHOR OF *WAY OF THE PEACEFUL WARRIOR* (1980)

Even if I knew that tomorrow the world would go to pieces, I would still plant my apple tree.

—MARTIN LUTHER

Not all who wander are lost.

—J. R. R. TOLKIEN

———————

Meeting people unlike oneself does not enlarge one's outlook; it only confirms one's idea that one is unique.

—ELIZABETH BOWEN

———————

I will not permit people to narrow and degrade my soul by making me hate them.

—BOOKER T. WASHINGTON

———————

I love the man that can smile in trouble, that can gather strength from distress, and grow brave by reflection. 'Tis the business of little minds to shrink, but he whose heart is firm, and whose conscience approves his conduct, will pursue his principles unto death.

—THOMAS PAINE

———————

Keep away from people who try to belittle your ambitions. Small people always do that, but the really great make you feel that you, too, can become great.

—MARK TWAIN

When getting ready to reason with a man, I spend one-third of my time thinking about myself and what I am going to say and two-thirds thinking about him and what he is going to say.

—ABRAHAM LINCOLN

There are two sides to every story and TRUTH lies somewhere in the middle.

—JEAN GATI

The smarter the guy, the bigger the rascal.

—WILL ROGERS

The smarter you are, the smaller your strike zone.

—ANONYMOUS

There is no reason why we can't accept who we are. We are who we are for a reason. But we all want to be different in one way or another. We judge and we get judged. . . . There is no normal, but we all cry and we all dream the same.

—BRIAN CALLABRO

The easiest thing in the world is to be you. The most difficult thing to be is what other people want you to be. Don't let them put you in that position.

—DR. LEO BUSCAGLIA

Sometimes one man with courage is a majority.

—ANDREW JACKSON

Reflect upon your present blessings, of which every man has plenty; not on your past misfortunes, of which all men have some.

—CHARLES DICKENS

Be not angry that you cannot make others as you wish them to be, since you cannot make yourself as you wish to be.

—THOMAS À KEMPIS

You must either modify your dreams or magnify your skills.

—JIM ROHN, MOTIVATIONAL COACH

Labor to keep alive in your breast that little spark of celestial fire called conscience.

—GEORGE WASHINGTON

In the midst of winter, I found there was within me an invincible summer.

—ALBERT CAREB

—⟐—

They merit more praise who know how to suffer misery than those who temper themselves in contentment.

—PIETRO ARETINO

—⟐—

A man should have any number of little aims about which he should be conscious and for which he should have names, but he should have neither name for, nor consciousness concerning, the main aim of his life.

—SAMUEL BUTLER

—⟐—

The best and most beautiful things in the world cannot be seen or even touched. They must be felt with the heart.

—HELEN KELLER

—⟐—

It is such a secret place, the land of tears.

—Antoine de Saint-Exupéry

Disillusion comes only to the illusioned. One cannot be disillusioned of what one never put faith in.

—Dorothy Thompson

Friendship is the hardest thing in the world to explain. It's not something you learn in school. But if you haven't learned the meaning of friendship, you really haven't learned anything.

—Muhammad Ali

The best way to know life is to love many things.

—Vincent Van Gogh

The best index to a person's character is a) how he treats people who can't do him any good and b) how he treats people who can't fight back.

—ABIGAIL VAN BUREN ("DEAR ABBY")

Character may be manifested in the great moments, but it is made in the small ones.

—PHILLIPS BROOKS

Habits change into character.

—OVID

Discipline is the soul of an army. It makes small numbers formidable; procures success to the weak, and esteem to all.

—GEORGE WASHINGTON

A prudent mind can see room for misgiving, lest he who prospers would one day suffer reverse.

—SOPHOCLES

Seek education rather than grades. Seek your best rather than someone else's. Seek friendship rather than acceptance. Seek worth rather than rank. Seek to build rather than to tear down. Seek laughter and love in spite of pain and you will have learned to live.

—JAQUI SHEEHAN

Learning to love and accept ourselves is basic to human education. So is learning to language emotion in a positive way. Ultimately when we learn to truly love and accept ourselves, we'll be able to live well and love each other and every thing we encounter.

—BARBARA HOBERMAN LEVINE, FROM HER BOOK *YOUR BODY BELIEVES EVERY WORD YOU SAY* (1991)

All paths are the same. They lead nowhere. They are paths going through the brush or into the brush or under the brush. "Does this path have a heart?" is the only question. If it does, then the path is good. If it doesn't, then it is of no use.

—CARLOS CASTANEDA

He who cherishes a beautiful vision, a lofty ideal in his heart, will one day realize it.

—JAMES ALLEN

I think everyone should experience defeat at least once during their career. You learn a lot from it.

—LOU HOLTZ

Problems are only opportunities in work clothes.

—HENRY J. KAISER

The race is not to the swift, nor the battle to the strong.

—Proverb

No one has ever drowned in sweat.

—Lou Holtz

Hard work, dedication, and desire don't guarantee you a thing, but without them you don't stand a chance.

—Pat Riley

Go ahead and do the impossible. It's worth the look on the faces of those who said you couldn't.

—Walter Bagehot

We cannot do everything at once, but we can do something at once.

—CALVIN COOLIDGE

People look at you and me to see what they are supposed to be. And, if we don't disappoint them, maybe, just maybe, they won't disappoint us.

—WALT DISNEY

Do not let anyone look down on you because you are young, but set an example for all believers in speech, in life, in love, in faith, and in purity.

—ST. PAUL

It is our choices, Harry, that show what we truly are, far more than our abilities.

—J. K. ROWLING

It wasn't raining when Noah built the ark.

—Howard Ruff

If I opened a film school, I would make everyone earn their tuition themselves by working . . . out where there is real life. Earn it as a bouncer in a sex club or as a warden in a lunatic asylum. . . . That makes you more of a filmmaker than three years of film school.

—Werner Herzog

Today, many companies are reporting that their number one constraint on growth is the inability to hire workers with the necessary skills.

—Bill Clinton

Whenever you are asked if you can do a job, tell 'em "Certainly, I can!" Then get busy and find out how to do it.

—Theodore Roosevelt

Hide not your talents, they for use were made. What's a sun-dial in the shade?

—BENJAMIN FRANKLIN

One is always a long way from solving a problem until one actually has the answer.

—STEPHEN HAWKING

Go to the edge of the cliff and jump off. Build your wings on the way down.

—RAY BRADBURY

Nothing is particularly hard if you divide it into small jobs.

—HENRY FORD

To become an able and successful man in any profession, three things are necessary: nature, study, and practice.

—HENRY WARD BEECHER

Luctor et Emergo ("I struggle and I come through").

—MOTTO OF NOTRE DAME COLLEGE OF SASKATCHEWAN

A common mistake among those who work in sport is spending a disproportionate amount of time on "x's and o's" as compared to time spent learning about people.

—MIKE KRZYZEWSKI, COLLEGE BASKETBALL COACH

In knowledge-intensive business settings, where every manager has to oversee massive amounts of information as well as people, facilitating the use of psychic energy becomes a primary concern.

—MIHALY CSIKSZENTMIHALYI

Even in such technical lines as engineering, about 15% of one's financial success is due one's technical knowledge and about 85% is due to skill in human engineering, to personality and the ability to lead people.

—DALE CARNEGIE

Our deepest fear is not that we are inadequate. Our deepest fear is that we are powerful beyond measure. It is our light, not our darkness that most frightens us. . . . Your playing small doesn't serve the world.

—NELSON MANDELA

Failure should be our teacher, not our undertaker. Failure is delay, not defeat. It is a temporary detour, not a dead end. Failure is something we can avoid only by saying nothing, doing nothing, and being nothing.

—DENIS WAITLEY

Many people dream of success. To me, success can only be achieved through repeated failure and introspection.

—SOICHIRO HONDA

The great and glorious masterpiece of man is to know how to live to purpose.

—MICHEL DE MONTAIGNE

Ah, but a man's reach should exceed his grasp, or what's a heaven for?

—ROBERT BROWNING

Don't bunt. Aim out of the ballpark.

—DAVID OGILVY

The difference between perseverance and obstinacy is that one often comes from a strong will, and the other from a strong won't.

—HENRY WARD BEECHER

———◆———

We all have ability. The difference is how we use it.

—STEVIE WONDER

———◆———

The best place to succeed is where you are with what you have.

—CHARLES SCHWAB

———◆———

Effective people are not problem-minded; they're opportunity minded. They feed opportunities and starve problems.

—STEPHEN COVEY

———◆———

All growth depends upon activity. There is no development physically or intellectually without effort, and effort means work.

—CALVIN COOLIDGE

————◆————

Ability will never catch up with the demand for it.

—MALCOLM S. FORBES

————◆————

Think of yourself as on the threshold of unparalleled success. A whole clear, glorious life lies before you. Achieve! Achieve!

—ANDREW CARNEGIE

————◆————

You don't become enormously successful without encountering some really interesting problems.

—MARK VICTOR HANSEN, AMERICAN MOTIVATIONAL SPEAKER AND COCREATOR OF THE "CHICKEN SOUP FOR THE SOUL" BOOK SERIES

————◆————

Obedience is the mother of success, and success the parent of salvation.

—AESCHYLUS

About the only problem with success is that it does not teach you how to deal with failure.

—TOMMY LASORDA

Build up your weaknesses until they become your strong points.

—KNUTE ROCKNE

How you respond to the challenge in the second half will determine what you become after the game, whether you are a winner or a loser.

—LOU HOLTZ

Most people have the will to win, few have the will to prepare to win.

—BOBBY KNIGHT

Start a crusade in your life to be your very best.

—WILLIAM DANFORTH

One can succeed at almost anything for which he has enthusiasm.

—CHARLES SCHWAB

You always pass failure on the way to success.

—MICKEY ROONEY

Success isn't permanent, and failure isn't fatal.

—MIKE DITKA

Failures do what is tension relieving, while winners do what is goal achieving.

—DENIS WAITLEY

I cannot give you the formula for success, but I can give you the formula for failure—which is: Try to please everybody.

—HERBERT BAYARD SWOPE

Success is the sum of small efforts, repeated day in and day out.

—ROBERT COLLIER

I attribute my success to this—I never gave or took any excuse.

—FLORENCE NIGHTINGALE

I therefore admonish my students in Europe and America: Don't aim at success—the more you aim at it and make it a target, the more you are going to miss it. For success, like happiness, cannot be pursued; it must ensue.

—VIKTOR FRANKL

Success does not consist in never making blunders, but in never making the same one a second time.

—JOSH BILLINGS

Aim for success, not perfection. Never give up your right to be wrong, because then you will lose the ability to learn new things and move forward with your life. Remember that fear always lurks behind perfectionism.

—DAVID M. BURNS

I learned this, at least, by my experiment: that if one advances confidently in the direction of his dreams, and endeavors to live the life which he has imagined, he will meet with a success unexpected in common hours.

—HENRY DAVID THOREAU

Success is that old ABC—ability, breaks, and courage.

—CHARLES LUCKMAN

Success is the good fortune that comes from aspiration, desperation, perspiration, and inspiration.

—EVAN ESAR

Nothing recedes like success.

—WALTER WINCHELL

My great concern is not whether you have failed, but whether you are content with your failure.

—ABRAHAM LINCOLN

The secret of success in life is for a man to be ready for his opportunity when it comes.

—BENJAMIN DISRAELI

The talent of success is nothing more than doing what you can do, well.

—HENRY WADSWORTH LONGFELLOW

Others can stop you temporarily. You are the only one who can do it permanently.

—ZIG ZIGLAR

"I can't do it" never yet accomplished anything; "I will try" has performed wonders.

—GEORGE P. BURNHAM

The condition of mankind is to be weary of what we do know and afraid of what we do not.

—MARQUIS OF HALIFAX, FROM "OF THE WORLD," *POLITICAL, MORAL AND MISCELLANEOUS REFLECTIONS* (1750)

Far more crucial than what we know or do not know is what we do not want to know.

—ERIC HOFFER, FROM HIS BOOK *THE PASSIONATE STATE OF MIND: AND OTHER APHORISMS* (1954)

If you find a path with no obstacles, it probably doesn't lead anywhere.

—FRANK A. CLARK

Sometimes it is more important to discover what one cannot do, than what one can do.

—LIN YUTANG

Because a thing seems difficult for you, do not think it impossible for anyone to accomplish.

—MARCUS AURELIUS

When you do a thing, do it with all your might. Put your whole soul into it. Stamp it with your own personality. . . . Nothing great was ever achieved without enthusiasm.

—RALPH WALDO EMERSON

If you want to increase your success rate, double your failure rate.

—THOMAS WATSON, SR., FOUNDER OF IBM

Make a true estimate of your own ability, then raise it ten percent.

—NORMAN VINCENT PEALE

Eighty percent of success is showing up.

—JAMES ALLEN, NINETEENTH-CENTURY ENGLISH WRITER

There is only one thing that makes a dream impossible to achieve: the fear of failure.

—PAULO COELHO

All our dreams can come true, if we have the courage to pursue them.

—WALT DISNEY

Always do more than is required of you.

—GEORGE PATTON

Do a little more each day than you think you can.

—LOWELL THOMAS

Whenever you do a thing, act as if all the world were watching.

—THOMAS JEFFERSON

Nobody is bored when he is trying to make something that is beautiful, or to discover something that is true.

—WILLIAM INGE

The great tragedy of life doesn't lie in failing to reach your goals. The great tragedy lies in having no goals to reach.

—BENJAMIN E. MAYS, AS QUOTED BY MARIAN WRIGHT EDELMAN IN THE *NEW YORK TIMES* (1985)

People's behavior makes sense if you think about it in terms of their goals, needs, and motives.

—THOMAS MANN

Talent is like electricity. We don't understand electricity. We use it.

 —MAYA ANGELOU, AS QUOTED IN *BLACK WOMEN WRITERS AT WORK* (1983)

Goals are the fuel in the furnace of achievement.

 —BRIAN TRACY, MOTIVATIONAL COACH AND AUTHOR, FROM HIS BOOK *EAT THAT FROG*

They will rise highest who strive for the highest place.

 —LATIN PROVERB

You are never a loser until you quit trying.

 —MIKE DITKA

When the One Great Scorer comes to write against your name
He makes not that you won or lost
But how you played the game.

—GRANTLAND RICE

Many great actions are committed in small struggles.

—VICTOR HUGO, FROM *LES MISÉRABLES*

If you can't accept losing, you can't win.

—VINCE LOMBARDI

Victory belongs to the most persevering.

—NAPOLEON BONAPARTE

There are no gains without pains.

—ADLAI STEVENSON

There are no gains without pains.

To win without risk is to triumph without glory.

—PIERRE CORNEILLE

If at first you don't succeed, then quit. There's no use being a damn fool about it.

—W. C. FIELDS

If you aren't going all the way, why go at all?

—JOE NAMATH

Nothing can stop the man with the right mental attitude from achieving his goal; nothing on earth can help the man with the wrong mental attitude.

—THOMAS JEFFERSON

Any great work of art revives and readapts time and space, and the measure of its success is the extent to which it makes you an inhabitant of that world—the extent to which it invites you in and lets you breathe its strange, special air.

—LEONARD BERNSTEIN

Creativity often consists of merely turning up what is already there. Did you know that right and left shoes were thought up only a little more than a century ago?

—BERNICE FITZ-GIBBON

The important thing is that a new idea should develop out of what is already there so that it soon becomes an old acquaintance. Old acquaintances aren't by any means always welcome, but at least one can't be mistaken as to who or what they are.

—PENELOPE FITZGERALD

A hunch is creativity trying to tell you something.

—FRANK CAPRA

An essential aspect of creativity is not being afraid to fail.

—DR. EDWIN LAND

Creativity requires the courage to let go of certainties.

—ERICH FROMM

Creativity is more than just being different. Anybody can play weird—that's easy. What's hard is to be as simple as Bach. Making the simple complicated is commonplace—making the complicated simple, awesomely simple—that's creativity.

—CHARLES MINGUS

Creative activity is not a superimposed, extraneous task against which the body, or brain protests, but an orchestration of . . . joyful doing.

—GYORGY KEPES

The art of creation is older than the art of killing.

—EDWARD KOCH

There is a new science of complexity which says that the link between cause and effect is increasingly difficult to trace; that change (planned or otherwise) unfolds in a non-linear ways; that paradoxes and contradictions abound; and that creative solutions arise out of diversity, uncertainty, and chaos.

—ANDY HARGREAVES AND MICHAEL FULLAN, FROM THEIR BOOK
WHAT'S WORTH FIGHTING FOR OUT THERE? (1998)

When Alexander the Great visited Diogenes and asked whether he could do anything for the famed teacher, Diogenes replied: "Only stand out of my light." Perhaps some day we shall know how to heighten creativity. Until then, one of the best things we can do for creative men and women is to stand out of their light.

—JOHN W. GARDNER

Art is not to be taught in Academies. It is what one looks at, not what one listens to, that makes the artist. The real schools should be the streets.

—OSCAR WILDE

It is art that makes life, makes interest, makes importance . . . and I know of no substitute whatever for the force and beauty of its process.

—HENRY JAMES, JR.

The artist is nothing without the gift, but the gift is nothing without work.

—ÉMILE ZOLA

An artist is always out of step with the time. He has to be.

—ORSON WELLES

Inventing is a combination of brains and materials. The more brains you use, the less material you need.

—CHARLES F. KETTERING

There was so much handwriting on the wall that even the wall fell down.

—CHRISTOPHER MORLEY

Quod Erat Demonstrandum ("Which was to be proven").

—EUCLID

Any informed borrower is simply less vulnerable to fraud and abuse.

—ALAN GREENSPAN

Nobody spends somebody else's money as carefully as he spends his own. Nobody uses somebody else's resources as carefully as he uses his own. So if you want efficiency and effectiveness, if you want knowledge to be properly utilized, you have to do it through the means of private property.

—MILTON FRIEDMAN

Basically, our goal is to organize the world's information and to make it universally accessible and useful.

—LARRY PAGE, COFOUNDER OF GOOGLE

At school Mrs. Dickens liked Paul's picture of the sailboat better than my picture of the invisible castle. At singing time she said I sang too loud. At counting time she said I left out sixteen. Who needs sixteen? I could tell it was going to be a terrible, horrible, no good, very bad day.

—JUDITH VIORST, FROM HER BOOK *ALEXANDER AND THE TERRIBLE, HORRIBLE, NO GOOD, VERY BAD DAY* (1972)

CHAPTER EIGHT

Civilized Thoughts

Those who educate children well are more to be honored than parents, for these only gave life, those the art of living well.

—ARISTOTLE

Housework is a breeze. Cooking is a pleasant diversion. Putting up a retaining wall is a lark. But teaching is like climbing a mountain.

—FAWN M. BRODIE

What office is there which involves more responsibility, which requires more qualifications, and which ought, therefore, to be more honorable, than that of teaching?

—HARRIET MARTINEAU

Teaching is the profession that teaches all the other professions.

—ANONYMOUS

If a doctor, lawyer, or dentist had forty people in his office at one time, all of whom had different needs, and some of whom didn't want to be there and were causing trouble, and the doctor, lawyer, or dentist, without assistance, had to treat them all with professional excellence for nine months, then he might have some conception of the classroom teacher's job.

—Donald D. Quinn

A teacher must believe in the value and interest of his subject as a doctor believes in health.

—Gilbert Highet

Experiences in order to be educative must lead out into an expanding world of subject matter, a subject matter of facts or information and of ideas. This condition is satisfied only as the educator views teaching and learning as a continuous process of reconstruction of experience.

—John Dewey

In these days, it is doubtful that any child may reasonably be expected to succeed in life if he is denied the opportunity of an education. Such an opportunity, where the state has undertaken to provide it, is a right which must be made available to all on equal terms.

—EARL WARREN, AS QUOTED IN THE LANDMARK COURT CASE *BROWN V. BOARD OF EDUCATION OF TOPEKA, KANSAS* (1954)

Modern cynics and skeptics . . . see no harm in paying those to whom they entrust the minds of their children a smaller wage than is paid to those to whom they entrust the care of their plumbing.

—JOHN F. KENNEDY

Most teachers have little control over school policy or curriculum or choice of texts or special placement of students, but most have a great deal of autonomy inside the classroom. To a degree shared by only a few other occupations, such as police work, public education rests precariously on the skill and virtue of the people at the bottom of the institutional pyramid.

—TRACY KIDDER

If the object of education were to make pupils think, rather than to make them accept certain conclusions, education would be conducted quite differently; there would be less . . . instruction and more discussion.

—BERTRAND RUSSELL, FROM HIS BOOK *PRINCIPLES OF SOCIAL RECONSTRUCTION* (1916)

We expect teachers to handle teenage pregnancy, substance abuse, and the failings of the family. Then we expect them to educate our children.

—JOHN SCULLEY

Let us reform our schools, and we shall find little need of reform in our prisons.

—JOHN RUSKIN

Upon the education of the people of this country the fate of this country depends.

—BENJAMIN DISRAELI

The sense of duty is the fountain of human rights. In other words, the same inward principle which teaches the former bears witness to the latter. Duties and rights must stand and fall together.

—WILLIAM ELLERY CHANNING

More money is put into prisons than into schools. That, in itself, is the description of a nation bent on suicide. I mean, what is more precious to us than our own children? We are going to build a lot more prisons if we do not deal with the schools and their inequalities.

—JONATHAN KOZOL

Both class and race survive education, and neither should. What is education then? If it doesn't help a human being to recognize that humanity is humanity, what is it for? So you can make a bigger salary than other people?

—BEAH RICHARDS

Good education is the essential foundation of a strong democracy.

—BARBARA BUSH

———⬥———

There is no way, in my opinion, for blacks to focus too much or too obsessively on education. . . . It represents the flip side of failure.

—BOB HERBERT, AS QUOTED IN THE *NEW YORK TIMES*

———⬥———

In a completely rational society, the best of us would aspire to be teachers and the rest of us would have to settle for something less, because passing civilization along from one generation to the next ought to be the highest honor and the highest responsibility anyone could have.

—LEE IACOCCA, FROM HIS BOOK *IACOCCA* (1986)

———⬥———

To educate a man in mind and not in morals is to educate a menace to society.

—THEODORE ROOSEVELT

———⬥———

We cannot enter a learning society, an education age, without giving teachers the recognition they deserve.

—FEDERICO MAYOR, DIRECTOR-GENERAL OF UNESCO FROM
1987 TO 1999

The Great Society is a place where every child can find knowledge to enrich his mind and to enlarge his talents. . . . It is a place where men are more concerned with the quality of their goals than the quantity of their goods.

—LYNDON B. JOHNSON, IN A SPEECH AT THE UNIVERSITY
OF MICHIGAN (1964)

The paradox of education is precisely there—that as one begins to become conscious one begins to examine the society in which he is being educated.

—JAMES BALDWIN, FROM "THE NEGRO CHILD—HIS SELF IMAGE,"
SATURDAY REVIEW (1963)

A liberal education is at the heart of a civilized society, and at the heart of a liberal education is the act of teaching.

—A. BARTLETT GIAMATTI, FROM "THE AMERICAN TEACHER," *HARPER'S* (1980)

A College Degree is a Social Certificate, not proof of competence.

—ELBERT HUBBARD, FROM HIS BOOK *A THOUSAND AND ONE EPIGRAMS* (1911)

The sheltering of upper income children in private schools not only accelerates the deterioration of public education, it hides its consequences from precisely those people who could do something about it.

—HODDING CARTER, FROM "IN PUBLIC SCHOOLS, CLASS WILL TELL," *THE NEW YORK TIMES* (JUNE 13, 1990)

The school's input is all the children. Its output is youths who know their place. . . . No school that is too successful in teaching children not to be prejudiced can continue to be supported by the power order of the society.

—DAN W. DODSON, FROM "AN URGENT CONCERN," *SATURDAY REVIEW*,
MAY 15, 1965

Boarding school graduates go forth . . . into a world of whose richness and subtlety they have no conception. They go forth into it with well-developed bodies, fairly developed minds, and undeveloped hearts.

—E. M. FORSTER, FROM "NOTES ON THE ENGLISH CHARACTER,"
ABINGER HARVEST: A MISCELLANY (1927)

Everywhere the hidden curriculum of schooling initiates the citizens to the myth that bureaucracies guided by scientific knowledge are efficient and benevolent. Everywhere this same curriculum instills in the public the myth that increased production will provide a better life.

—IVAN ILLICH, FROM HIS BOOK *DESCHOOLING SOCIETY* (1970)

In the field of public education, the doctrine of "separate but equal" has no place. Separate educational facilities are inherently unequal.

—EARL WARREN, AS QUOTED IN THE LANDMARK COURT CASE *BROWN V. BOARD OF EDUCATION OF TOPEKA, KANSAS*, 1954

Our education system basically strives for normal—which is too bad. Sometimes the exceptional is classified as abnormal and pushed aside.

—NEIL YOUNG, IN AN INTERVIEW IN *ESQUIRE* (2006)

Knowledge will forever govern ignorance; and a people who mean to be their own governors must arm themselves with the power which knowledge gives.

—JAMES MADISON

The preservation of the means of knowledge among the lowest ranks is of more importance to the public than all the property of the rich men in the country.

—JOHN ADAMS

Education either functions as an instrument which is used to facilitate integration of the younger generation into the logic of the present system and bring about conformity or it becomes the practice of freedom, the means by which men and women deal critically and creatively with reality and discover how to participate in the transformation of their world.

—PAULO FREIRE, BRAZILIAN EDUCATOR AND THEORIST OF EDUCATION

Society, community, family are all conserving institutions. They try to maintain stability, and to prevent, or at least to slow down, change. But the organization of the post-capitalist society of organizations is a destabilizer. Because its function is to put knowledge to work—on tools, processes, and products; on work; on knowledge itself—it must be organized for constant change.

—PETER F. DRUCKER

I am somehow less interested in the weight and convolutions of Einstein's brain than in the near certainty that people of equal talent have lived and died in cotton fields and sweatshops.

—STEPHEN JAY GOULD

The advancement and diffusion of knowledge is the only guardian of true liberty.

—James Madison

My people are going to learn the principles of democracy, the dictates of truth, and the teachings of science. Superstition must go. Let them worship as they will, every man can follow his own conscience provided it does not interfere with sane reason or bid him act against the liberty of his fellow men.

—Mustafa Kemal Ataturk, founder of the Republic of Turkey

When we make college more affordable, we make the American dream more achievable.

—Bill Clinton

It is not the strongest of the species that survive, nor the most intelligent, but the one most responsive to change.

—Charles Darwin

We are approaching a new age of synthesis. Knowledge cannot be merely a degree or a skill. . . . It demands a broader vision, capabilities in critical thinking, and logical deduction, without which we cannot have constructive progress.

—Li Ka Shing, East Asia's richest man and generous philanthropist

Before we can study the central issues of life today, we must destroy the prejudices and fallacies born of previous centuries.

—Leo Tolstoy

I'm very interested in studying cultures and social issues, but as an academic I don't think I would have been too successful.

—George Lucas

The most violent element in society is ignorance.

—Emma Goldman

Anyway, no drug, not even alcohol, causes the fundamental ills of society. If we're looking for the source of our troubles, we shouldn't test people for drugs, we should test them for stupidity, ignorance, greed, and love of power.

—P. J. O'ROURKE

History shows that there is nothing so easy to enslave and nothing so hard to emancipate as ignorance, hence it becomes the double enemy of civilization. By its servility it is the prey of tyranny, and by its credulity it is the foe of enlightenment.

—LEMUEL K. WASHBURN

A society grows great when people plant trees in whose shade they know they shall never sit!

—GREEK PROVERB

Education is for improving the lives of others and for leaving your community and world better than you found it.

—MARIAN WRIGHT EDELMAN

No man has come to true greatness who has not felt that his life belongs to his race, and that which God gives to him, He gives him for mankind.

—PHILLIPS BROOKS

The World is my country, all mankind are my brethren, and to do good is my religion.

—THOMAS PAINE

Urging all of us to open our minds and hearts so that we can know beyond the boundaries of what is acceptable, so that we can think and rethink, so that we can create new vision. I celebrate teaching that enables transgressions—a movement against and beyond boundaries. It is that movement which makes education the practice of freedom.

—"BELL HOOKS," WRITER

America's future will be determined by the home and the school. The child becomes largely what it is taught, hence we must watch what we teach it, and how we live before it.

—JANE ADDAMS, NOBEL PEACE PRIZE–WINNER AND EDUCATOR

To educate a man, is to educate an individual;
To educate a woman, is to educate and liberate a whole nation.

—MALCOLM X

Change does not necessarily assure progress,
But progress implacably requires change.

Education is essential to change,
For education creates both new wants and the ability to satisfy them.

—HENRY STEELE COMMAGER, AMERICAN HISTORIAN

The philosophy of the schoolroom in one generation will be the philosophy of government in the next.

—ABRAHAM LINCOLN

The most dangerous man, to any government, is the man who is able to think things out for himself, without regard to the prevailing superstitions and taboos. Almost invariably he comes to the conclusion that the government he lives under is dishonest, insane and intolerable . . .

—H. L. MENCKEN

The proletarian state must bring up thousands of excellent "mechanics of culture," "engineers of the soul."

—JOSEPH STALIN

Those who corrupt the public mind are just as evil as those who steal from the public purse.

—ADLAI E. STEVENSON

There are many who lust for the simple answers of doctrine or decree. They are on the left and right. They are not confined to a single part of the society. They are terrorists of the mind.

—A. BARTLETT GIAMATTI

The great crisis of education is the crisis of society that in the race for renewed hegemony in the world trading order . . . is concerned most with technical proficiency among its graduates—ensuring workers who will know more and more about less and less in regard to the world they inhabit and the work they do.

—SVI SHAPIRO

Cherishing children is the mark of a civilized society.

—JOAN GANZ COONEY, AMERICAN BUSINESSWOMAN AND TELEVISION
PRODUCER

Develop teachers of fisherman, and you lift all of society.

—FRANKLIN COVEY, BUSINESS CONSULTATION COMPANY

Education . . . is closely associated with change, is its pioneer, is the
never-sleeping agent of revolution, is always fitting men for higher things
and unfitting them for things as they are. Therefore, between institutions
whose very existence depends upon man continuing what he is and true
education, which is one of the instruments for making him something
other than he is, there must always be enmity.

—HERBERT SPENCER, FROM HIS BOOK *SOCIAL STATISTICS* (1851)

To indoctrinate the child early with the prevailing world-view of the
society and class in which he has been born, to enforce conformity in later

life by the thunders of the priest and by the sword of the magistrate has been "the wisdom of our ancestors" at every stage in their progress from savagery to civilization.

—PRESERVED SMITH, FROM HIS BOOK *A HISTORY OF MODERN CULTURE* (1930–1934)

The benefits of education and of useful knowledge, generally diffused through a community, are essential to the preservation of a free government.

—SAM HOUSTON

Wherever is found what is called a paternal government was found a State education. It had been discovered that the best way to insure implicit obedience is to commence tyranny in the nursery.

—BENJAMIN DISRAELI, IN A HOUSE OF COMMONS SPEECH (1874)

Parties and governments may come and go, but the experts stay on forever. Because without them, the system does not work. The machine stops. And *then* where are we?

—THEODORE ROSZAK, FROM HIS BOOK *THE MAKING OF THE COUNTER CULTURE: REFLECTIONS ON THE TECHNOCRATIC SOCIETY AND ITS YOUTHFUL OPPOSITION* (1969)

More and more the specialized knowledge of an expert became the foundation for the power position of the officeholder. Hence a concern of the ruler was how to exploit the special knowledge of experts without having to abdicate in their favor. . . his dominant position.

—MAX WEBER

Teachers have power. We may cripple them by petty economics, by Government regulations, by the foolish criticism of an uniformed press; but their power exists for good or evil.

—WINIFRED HOLTBY, ENGLISH NOVELIST AND JOURNALIST

Public instruction should be the first object of government.

—NAPOLEON BONAPARTE

To separate black children from others of similar age and qualifications solely because of their race generates a feeling of inferiority as to their status in the community that may affect their hearts and minds in a way unlikely ever to be undone.

—EARL WARREN, AS QUOTED IN THE LANDMARK COURT CASE *BROWN V. BOARD OF EDUCATION OF TOPEKA, KANSAS,* 1954

We consider the underlying fallacy of the plaintiff's argument to consist in the assumption that the enforced separation of the two races stamps the colored race with a badge of inferiority. If this be so, it is not by reason of anything found in the act, but solely because the colored race chooses to put that construction upon it.

—HENRY BILLINGS BROWN, AS QUOTED IN THE LANDMARK COURT CASE, *PLESSY V. FERGUSON,* 1896

When will the public cease to insult the teacher's calling with empty flattery? When will men who would never for a moment encourage their own sons to enter the work of the public schools cease to tell us that education is the greatest and noblest of all human callings?

—WILLIAM C. BAGLEY

Brown v. Board helped unite us all, and gave us all great pride knowing we all are truly E Pluribus Unum—One people out of many.

—MIKE ROGERS

The nineteenth century saw the institution of what remains the largest single program for the treatment of childhood—so-called "public schools." Under this colossal program, individuals are placed into treatment groups based on the severity of their condition. For example, those most severely afflicted may be placed in a "kindergarten" program.

—JORDAN W. SMOLLER, FROM *"THE ETIOLOGY OF CHILDHOOD,"*
NETWORKER, MARCH/APRIL 1987

A popular government without popular information, or the means of acquiring it, is but a prologue to a farce or a tragedy, or perhaps both.

—JAMES MADISON

Has there ever been a society which has died of dissent? Several have died of conformity in our lifetime.

—JACOB BRONOWSKI, IN A LECTURE AT MASSACHUSETTS INSTITUTE OF TECHNOLOGY (1953)

Education is the transmission of civilization.

—WILL DURANT

The civilized man has built a coach, but has lost the use of his feet. He is supported on crutches, but lacks so much support of muscle. . . His notebooks impair his memory; his libraries overload his wit; the insurance-office increases the number of accidents . . .

—RALPH WALDO EMERSON, FROM HIS BOOK *SELF-RELIANCE* (1839)

The city is the teacher of the man.

—SIMONIDES

If one race be inferior to the other socially, the Constitution of the United States cannot put them upon the same plane.

—HENRY BILLINGS BROWN

Our progress as a nation can be no swifter than our progress in education.

—JOHN F. KENNEDY

If all the rich and all of the church people should send their children to the public schools they would feel bound to concentrate their money on improving these schools until they met the highest ideals.

—SUSAN B. ANTHONY

When schools flourish, all flourishes.

—MARTIN LUTHER

A university should be a place of light, of liberty, and of learning.

—BENJAMIN DISRAELI

At boarding schools the relaxation of the junior boys is mischief, and of the seniors vice.

—MARY SHELLEY

The idea is to educate, not follow anyone's schedule about when something should be studied.

—RAY DROUILLARD, ON HOMESCHOOLING

A gifted teacher is as rare as a gifted doctor, and makes far less money.

—ANONYMOUS

One father is worth 100 schoolmasters.

—GEORGE HERBERT

The elementary school must assume as its sublime and most solemn responsibility the task of teaching every child in it to read. Any school that does not accomplish this has failed.

—WILLIAM J. BENNETT, FROM "REPORT ON CONDITION OF ELEMENTARY SCHOOLS," THE *NEW YORK TIMES* (1986)

The most admirable of reforms cannot but fall short in practice if teachers of sufficient quality are not available in sufficient quantity. . . . Generally speaking, the more we try to improve our schools, the heavier the teacher's task becomes; and the better our teaching methods, the most difficult they are to apply.

—Jean Piaget

Movie stars and rock musicians, athletes and models aren't heroes, they're celebrities. Heroes abound in public schools, a fact that doesn't make the news. There is no precedent for the level of violence, drugs, broken homes, child abuse, and crime in today's America. Public education didn't create these problems but deals with them every day.

—Frosty Troy, as quoted in the *Oklahoma Observer* (2001)

Murray Cohn has, for twenty-three years, run Brandeis according to his own lights. He believes in cleanliness and order—and the halls of Brandeis are clean and orderly. He believes in homework, especially writing—and the students do it, even if they don't do enough. He believes in publicly praising achievement—and the school's bulletin boards offer congratulations to attendance leaders and the like. What

Cohn and other administrators like him impart to their schools is nothing quantifiable; it is an ethos.

—JAMES TRAUB, AS QUOTED IN *THE GREAT SCHOOL DEBATE: WHICH WAY FOR AMERICAN EDUCATION?* (1985)

A good professor is a bastard perverse enough to think what *he* thinks is important, not what a government thinks is important.

—EDWARD C. BANFIELD, AS QUOTED IN *LIFE* (1967)

There are teachers of French and Spanish, Latin and Greek, who have worked for many years without ever seeing the countries whose spirits they have been endeavored to evoke.

—GILBERT HIGHET, FROM HIS BOOK *THE IMMORTAL PROFESSION* (1976)

Teachers long for respect and autonomy that comes from it. They want the limits of their professional domain clearly outlined and their essential authority within it assured. They want physical, psychological, and economic protection.

—THEODORE R. SIZER, FROM HIS BOOK *PLACES FOR LEARNING, PLACES FOR JOY: SPECULATIONS ON AMERICAN SCHOOL REFORM* (1973)

At a time when we should be opening doors to the future, we are fossilizing a curriculum and kind of teaching that seemed to make sense in the 1950s.

—THOMAS SOBOL, IN HIS CLOSING ADDRESS TO THE SUMMER LAW INSTITUTE AT COLUMBIA UNIVERSITY, 2000

We are being sold a bill of goods when it comes to talking about tougher standards for our schools. The standards movements is pushing teachers and students to focus on memorizing information, then regurgitating fact for high test scores. The shift away from teaching students to be thinkers who can make sense of what they're learning.

—ALFIE KOHN, FROM HIS BOOK *THE CASE AGAINST STANDARDIZED TESTING* (2000)

Restlessness and discontent are the first necessities of progress.

—THOMAS EDISON

———◆———

Education in this country has steadily improved since the systematic study of the science of education was started about 1890. No doubt, it will continue to improve at about the same speed, and schools in the year 2000 will be somewhat better than they are today. The question is, could they be better than that?

—J. LLOYD TRUMP, AS QUOTED IN *THE TEACHER AND THE TAUGHT* (1963)

———◆———

School disruption comes from those children who have given up hope of trying to learn anything.

—ALBERT SHANKER

———◆———

Our earth is degenerated in these latter days; bribery and corruption are common, children no longer obey their parents; and the end of the world is evidently approaching.

—ASSYRIAN CLAY TABLET (2800 B.C.E.)

The public schools are America's children and require the continuing encouragement, nurture, and support of America's people.

—IRA SINGER, PHILOSOPHY PROFESSOR, HOFSTRA UNIVERSITY

Whether you are a middle-class suburbanite, a parent living in the slums of a major city, or a resident of a rural area, your involvement will mean that your child will learn more and do it better in school.

—MELITTA J. CUTRIGHT, FROM HER BOOK *THE NATIONAL PTA TALKS TO PARENTS: HOW TO GET THE BEST EDUCATION FOR YOUR CHILD* (1989)

We have inadvertently designed a system in which being good at what you do as a teacher is not formally rewarded, while being poor at what you do is seldom corrected nor penalized.

—ELLIOT EISNER, AS QUOTED IN THE *NEW YORK TIMES* (1985)

What nobler employment, or more valuable to the state, than that of the man who instructs the rising generation.

—MARCUS TULLIUS CICERO

Parents teach in the toughest school in the world—The School for Making People. You are the board of education, the principal, the classroom teacher, and the janitor.

—VIRGINIA SATIR, AUTHOR AND PSYCHOTHERAPIST, FROM HER BOOK *PEOPLEMAKING* (1972)

We first throw away the Tales along with the Rattles of our Nurses.
Those of the Priest keep their hold a little longer; those of our Governors
the longest of all.

—EDMUND BURKE, FROM HIS BOOK *A VINDICATION OF NATURAL
SOCIETY* (1756)

Do we need conditioned adepts or free-thinking students? Scholastic
fact-factories keep many a pupil too busy to think and educate him in
progressive immaturity. Students are caught in a compulsive school
regimentation which imprints on them dependency and awe of authority.

—JOOST A. M. MEERLOO, FROM "PAVOLVIAN STRATEGY AS A WEAPON
OF MENTICIDE," *AMERICAN JOURNAL OF PSYCHIATRY* (1954)

Every method is used to prove to men that in given political, economic,
and social situations they are bound to be happy, and those who are
unhappy are mad or criminals or monsters.

—ALBERTO MORAVIA, FROM HIS BOOK *MAN AS AN END* (1964)

When you are trained to despise "just what you like" then, of course, you become a much more obedient servant of others—a *good* slave. When you learn not to do "just what you like" then the System loves you.

—ROBERT M. PIRSIG, FROM HIS BOOK *ZEN AND THE ART OF MOTORCYCLE MAINTENANCE: AN INQUIRY INTO VALUES* (1974)

There is no absurdity so palpable but that it may be firmly planted in the human head if you only begin to inculcate it before the age of five, by constantly repeating it with an air of solemnity.

—ARTHUR SCHOPENHAUER, FROM "STUDIES IN PESSIMISM: FURTHER PSYCHOLOGICAL OBSERVATIONS," *ESSAYS OF ARTHUR SCHOPENHAUER* (1851)

Without self-awareness . . . man acts, speaks, studies, reacts mechanically . . . on the basis of "programs" acquired accidentally, unintentionally, mechanically . . . it is therefore not difficult . . . to make him think and do different things from those he had thought and done before. . . . When he is awake, no one can program him: he programs himself.

—E. F. SCHUMACHER, FROM HIS BOOK *A GUIDE FOR THE PERPLEXED* (1977)

The acquisition of knowledge is a duty incumbent on every Muslim, male and female.

—MUHAMMAD

When a youngster like Lincoln sought to educate himself, the immediately available obvious things for him to learn were the Bible, Shakespeare, and Euclid. Was he really worse off than those who try to find their way through the technical smorgasbord of the current school system?

—ALLAN BLOOM, FROM "THE CLEAN SLATE," *THE CLOSING OF THE AMERICAN MIND: HOW HIGHER EDUCATION HAS FAILED DEMOCRACY AND IMPOVERISHED THE SOULS OF TODAY'S STUDENTS* (1987)

The long schooling is a way of keeping the young on ice.

—PAUL GOODMAN, FROM "THE EMPTY SOCIETY," *COMMENTARY* (1966)

The overt teaching was that the finest life is service to God, your family and your state, but the covert teaching, far more subtle and insidious, was somewhat different: ultimately, strength is more important; there is a ruling clique; there is a thing called privilege.

—DAVID HALBERSTAM, ON "*CUIS SERVIARE EST REGNARE*" ("TO SERVE IS TO RULE") THE MOTTO OF GROTON, A PRESTIGIOUS MASSACHUSETTS PREP SCHOOL, FROM HIS BOOK *THE BEST AND THE BRIGHTEST* (1972)

School is about two parts ABCs to fifty parts Where Do I Stand in the Great Pecking Order of Humankind.

—BARBARA KINGSOLVER

You must adjust. . . . This is the imprint in every schoolbook, the invisible message of every blackboard. Our schools have become vast factories for the manufacture of robots.

—ROBERT LINDNER, FROM HIS BOOK *MUST YOU CONFORM?* (1956)

The school system, custodian of print culture, has no place for the rugged individual. It is, indeed, the homogenizing hopper into which we toss our integral tots for processing.

—MARSHALL McLUHAN, FROM "CERVANTES CONFRONTED TYPOGRAPHIC MAN IN THE FIGURE OF DON QUIXOTE," *THE GUTENBERG GALAXY: THE MAKING OF TYPOGRAPHIC MAN* (1962)

Most of our schools are a real jail of captive youth.

—MONTAIGNE, FROM "OF EDUCATION OF CHILDREN," *ESSAYS* (1588)

Virtue consisted in winning: it consisted in being bigger, stronger, handsomer, richer, more popular, more elegant, more unscrupulous than other people—in dominating them, bullying them, making them suffer pain, making them look foolish, getting the better of them in every way.

—GEORGE ORWELL, DESCRIBING THE VALUES OF ST. CYPRIAN'S, THE SCOTTISH BOARDING SCHOOL HE ATTENDED, FROM HIS BOOK *SUCH, SUCH WERE THE JOYS* (1947)

Schools, as they are now regulated, are the hotbeds of vice and folly, and the knowledge of human nature, supposed to be attained there, merely cunning selfishness.

—MARY WOLLSTONECRAFT, FROM HER BOOK *A VINDICATION OF THE RIGHTS OF WOMAN* (1792)

The technology at the leading edge changes so rapidly that you have to keep current after you get out of school. I think probably the most important thing is having good fundamentals.

—GORDON MOORE, FOUNDER OF INTEL

You can't know it all. No matter how smart you are, no matter how comprehensive your education, no matter how wide ranging your experience, there is simply no way to acquire all the wisdom you need to make your business thrive.

—DONALD TRUMP

The schools are a great theater in which we play out the conflicts in the culture.

—DAVID COHEN AND BARBARA NEUFELD

Students learn more when they complete homework that is graded, commented upon, and discussed by their teachers. The teacher's feedback—reinforcing what has been done correctly and re-teaching what has not—is key.

—NANCY PROTHEROE

By the time a man is 35 he knows that the images of the right man, the tough man, the true man which he received in high school do not work in life.

—ROBERT BLY

The schoolteacher is certainly underpaid as a child minder, but ludicrously overpaid as an educator.

—JOHN OSBORNE

A high-school teacher, after all, is a person deputized by the rest of us to explain to the young what sort of world they are living in, and to defend, if possible, the part their elders are playing in it.

—EMILE CAPOUYA

Public schools are the nurseries of all vice and immorality.

—HENRY FIELDING

Part of the American myth is that people who are handed the skin of a dead sheep at graduating time think that it will keep their minds alive forever.

—JOHN MASON BROWN

But, good gracious, you've got to educate him first. You can't expect a boy to be vicious till he's been to a good school.

—SAKI (H. H. MUNRO)

Again and again there comes a time in history when the man who dares to say that two and two make four is punished with death. The schoolteacher is well aware of this.

—ALBERT CAMUS, FROM HIS BOOK *THE PLAGUE* (1948)

Let the children of the rich and poor take their seats together and know of no distinction save that of industry, good conduct, and intellect.

—TOWNSEND HARRIS

To the uneducated, an A is just three sticks.

—A. A. MILNE

I don't want to send them to jail. I want to send them to school.

—ADLAI E. STEVENSON, ON PICKETERS WHO ATTACKED HIM
   IN DALLAS

I see nothing worth living for but the divine virtue which endures
and surrenders all things for truth, duty, and mankind.

—WILLIAM ELLERY CHANNING

A poor surgeon hurts one person at a time. A poor teacher hurts a whole
classroom.

—ERNEST BAYER

The simplest schoolboy is now familiar with truths for which
Archimedes would have sacrificed his life.

—ERNEST RENAN

Many people today don't want honest answers insofar as honest means unpleasant or disturbing. They want a soft answer that turneth away anxiety. They want answers that are, in effect, escapes.

—LOUIS KRONENBERGER, FROM "UNBRAVE NEW WORLD,"
THE CART AND THE HORSE (1964)

We ask a thousand minute questions about the mechanisms and the institutions that surround us: the one question we do not dare to ask is: What is our true nature?

—LEWIS MUMFORD, FROM HIS BOOK *THE CONDUCT OF LIFE* (1951)

Human history becomes more and more a race between education and catastrophe.

—H. G. WELLS

Information is the currency of democracy.

—RALPH NADER

Above all things I hope the education of the common people will be attended to; convinced that on their good sense we may rely with most security for the preservation of a due degree of liberty.

—THOMAS JEFFERSON

The chief cause of human errors is to be found in the prejudices picked up in childhood.

—RENÉ DESCARTES

Those who profess to favor freedom and yet deprecate agitation are men who want crops without plowing the ground.

—FREDERICK DOUGLASS

Respect for the fragility and importance of an individual life is still the first mark of an educated man.

—NORMAN COUSINS

Education breeds confidence. Confidence breeds hope. Hope breeds peace.

—CONFUCIUS

I find, by close observation, that mothers are the levers which move in education. The men talk about it . . . but the women work most for it.

—FRANCES ELLEN WATKINS HARPER, TEACHER, ABOLITIONIST,
AND WRITER

For young black boys looking ahead to a difficult walk in life, the mantra should be education, education, education

—BOB HERBERT, AS QUOTED IN THE *NEW YORK TIMES* (2007)

Almost all education has a political motive: it aims at strengthening some group, national or religious or even social, in the competition with other groups. It is this motive, in the main, which determines the subjects taught, the knowledge offered and the knowledge withheld, and also decides what mental habits the pupils are expected to acquire. Hardly anything is done to foster the inward growth of mind and spirit; in fact, those who have had most education are very often atrophied in their mental and spiritual life.

> —BERTRAND RUSSELL, FROM HIS BOOK *PRINCIPLES OF SOCIAL RECONSTRUCTION* (1916)

Life-long part-time education is the surest way of raising the intellectual and moral level of the masses.

> —ARNOLD J. TOYNBEE, FROM HIS BOOK *THE TOYNBEE-IKEDA DIALOGUE: MAN HIMSELF MUST CHOOSE* (1976)

Education should consist of a series of enchantments, each raising the individual to a higher level of awareness, understanding, and kinship with all living things.

> —ANONYMOUS

There is there moral of all human tales
'Tis but the same rehearsal of the past,

First Freedom, and then Glory—when that fails,
Wealth, vice, corruption—barbarism at last.

—LORD BYRON, FROM HIS BOOK *CHILDE HAROLD'S PILGRIMAGE*
(1812–1818)

Present-day tyranny differs from the old in that the new absolutism must control the mass production of ideas, the spiritual element, or else lose control of the situation.

—CARL G. GUSTAVSON, FROM HIS BOOK *A PREFACE TO HISTORY* (1955)

To make the population love servitude is the task assigned, in present-day totalitarian states, to ministries of propaganda, newspaper editors, and schoolteachers.

—ALDOUS HUXLEY, IN THE FOREWORD TO *BRAVE NEW WORLD* (1932)

Several future presidents are learning from me today; so are the great writers of the next decades, and so are all the so-called ordinary people who will make the decisions in a democracy. I must never forget these same young people could be the thieves and murderers of the future.

—IVAN WELTON FITZWATER

People are the common denominator of progress. So . . . no improvement is possible with unimproved people, and advance is certain when people are liberated and educated.

—JOHN KENNETH GALBRAITH

You cannot hope to build a better world without improving individuals. We all must work for our own improvement, and at the same time, share a general responsibility for all humanity.

—MARIE CURIE

The purpose of education is not to produce more scholars, technicians, and job hunters, but integrated men and women who are free of fear; for only between such human beings can there be enduring peace.

—JIDDU KRISHNAMURTI

The education and empowerment of women throughout the world cannot fail to result in a more caring, tolerant, just, and peaceful life for all.

—Aung San Suu Kyi, Nobel Peace Prize–winning leader of Burma's democracy movement

In free countries, every man is entitled to express his opinions and every other man is entitled not to listen.

—G. Norman Collie

The aim of public education is not to spread enlightenment at all; it is simply to reduce as many individuals as possible to the same safe level, to breed a standard citizenry, to put down dissent and originality.

—H. L. Mencken

If none of us ever read a book that was "dangerous," had a friend who was "different," or joined an organization that advocated "change," we would all be just the kind of people Joe McCarthy wants. Whose fault is that? Not really McCarthy's. He didn't create this situation of fear. He merely exploited it, and rather successfully.

—EDWARD R. MURROW

⟫◆⟪

Parent indifference often rates above low teacher salaries as a cause of dissatisfaction for our nation's teachers.

—MELITTA J. CUTRIGHT, FROM HER BOOK *THE NATIONAL PTA TALKS TO PARENTS: HOW TO GET THE BEST EDUCATION FOR YOUR CHILD* (1989)

⟫◆⟪

If this world were anything near what it should be there would be no more need of a Book Week than there would be of a Society for the Prevention of Cruelty to Children.

—DOROTHY PARKER, AS QUOTED IN *CONSTANT READER* (1928)

⟫◆⟪

No man is an island, entire of itself; every man is a piece of the continent, a part of the main. If a clod be washed away by the sea, Europe is the less, as well as if promontory were, as well as if a manor of thy friend's or of thine own were. Any man's death diminishes me, because I am involved in mankind; and therefore never send to know for whom the bell tolls; it tolls for thee.

—JOHN DONNE

If I were asked . . . to what the singular prosperity and growing strength of Americans ought mainly to be attributed, I should reply: To the superiority of their women.

—ALEXIS DE TOCQUEVILLE

Education, then, beyond all other devices of human origin, is the great equalizer of the conditions of man, the balance-wheel of the social machinery.

—HORACE MANN

A liberally educated person meets new ideas with curiosity and fascination. An illiberally educated person meets new ideas with fear.

—JAMES B. STOCKDALE, NAVAL OFFICER

The American male at the peak of his physical powers and appetites, driving 160 big white horses across the scenes of an increasingly open society, with weekend money in his pocket and with little prior exposure to trouble and tragedy, personifies "an accident going to happen."

—JOHN SLOAN DICKEY, FROM "CONSCIENCE AND THE UNDERGRADUATE," *THE ATLANTIC* (1955)

States and Provinces and curricula around the world track students by age. This practice is so common that we do not think of it as tracking. With few exceptions, a six-year-old must go into first grade even if that six-year-old is not ready or was ready for the grade one year earlier.

—ZALMAN USISKIN, STUDENT OF MATH EDUCATION (1998)

Human nature is not a machine to be built after a model, and set to do exactly the work prescribed for it, but a tree, which requires to grow and develop itself on all sides, according to the tendency of the inward forces which make it a living thing.

—JOHN STUART MILL

Because a thing seems difficult for you, do not think it impossible for anyone to accomplish.

—MARCUS AURELIUS

Expecting something for nothing is the most popular form of hope.

—ARNOLD GLASOW

A remarkable gift, creativity. No other aspect of the human psyche is as powerful. It can exist unused for many years and then, with the right encouragement, creativity can be expressed, improving our lives and the lives of everyone around us.

—C. DIANE EALY, MOTIVATIONAL SPEAKER AND AUTHOR

The world is not interested in what we do for a living. What they are interested in is what we have to offer freely—hope, strength, love, and the power to make a difference!

—SASHA AZEVEDO, ACTRESS

Education is an important element in the struggle for human rights. It is the means to help our children and thereby increase self-respect.

—MALCOLM X

The formation of character in young people is educationally a different task from and a prior task to, the discussion of the great, difficult ethical controversies of the day.

—WILLIAM J. BENNETT, AMERICAN POLITICAL PUNDIT AND FORMER U.S. SECRETARY OF EDUCATION

What should young people do with their lives today? Many things, obviously. But the most daring thing is to create stable communities in which the terrible disease of loneliness can be cured.

—KURT VONNEGUT

In today's knowledge-based economy, what you earn depends on what you learn. Jobs in the information technology sector, for example, pay 85 percent more than the private sector average.

—BILL CLINTON

School is an institution built on the axiom that learning is the result of teaching. And institutional wisdom continues to accept this axiom, despite overwhelming evidence to the contrary.

—IVAN ILLICH, FROM HIS BOOK *DESCHOOLING SOCIETY* (1970)

Today, education is perhaps the most important function of state and local governments. . . . It is the very foundation of good citizenship.

—EARL WARREN, AS QUOTED IN THE LANDMARK COURT CASE *BROWN V. BOARD OF EDUCATION OF TOPEKA, KANSAS* (1954)

Marx, Darwin, and Freud are the three most crashing bores of the Western World. Simplistic popularization of their ideas has thrust our world into a mental straitjacket from which we can only escape by the most anarchic violence.

—WILLIAM GOLDING, AUTHOR OF *LORD OF THE FLIES*

Everything can be taken from a man but one thing; the last of the human freedoms—to choose one's attitude in any given set of circumstances, to choose one's own way.

—VIKTOR FRANKL

Higher education must lead the march back to the fundamentals of human relationships, to the old discovery that is ever new, that man does not live by bread alone.

—JOHN A. HANNAH, FORMER PRESIDENT OF MICHIGAN STATE UNIVERSITY

People should be free to find or make for themselves the kinds of educational experience they want their children to have.

—JOHN HOLT

Unfortunately, the "school" system has been largely ineffective. Not only is the problem a massive tax burden, but it has failed even to slow down the rising incidence of childhood.

—JORDAN W. SMOLLER, FROM "THE ETIOLOGY OF CHILDHOOD," *NETWORKER* (MARCH/APRIL 1987)

We are dealing with the best-educated generation in history. But they've got a brain dressed up with nowhere to go.

—TIMOTHY LEARY

In order to stave off covetousness, greed, and spite, citizens world over must be educated.

—MUSTAFA KEMAL ATATURK, FOUNDER OF THE REPUBLIC OF TURKEY

The bright pupil thus remains democratically fettered to his own age group throughout his school career, and a boy who would be capable of tackling Aeschylus or Dante sits listening to his coeval's attempts to spell out A CAT SAT ON A MAT.

—C. S. Lewis, from "Screwtape Proposes a Toast," *The Screwtape Letters* (1959)

Our duty is to be useful, not according to our desires but according to our powers.

—Henri-Frédéric Amiel

The words *God, Immortality, Duty*—pronounced with terrible earnestness, how inconceivable was the *first*, how unbelievable the *second*, and yet how peremptory and absolute the third.

—George Eliot

It is one of the worst of errors to suppose that there is any other path of safety except that of duty.

—JAMES H. AUGHEY

Do your duty and leave the outcome to the Gods.

—PIERRE CORNEILLE, FROM HIS BOOK *HORACE* (1640)

On an occasion of this kind it becomes more than a moral duty to speak one's mind. It becomes a pleasure.

—OSCAR WILDE, FROM HIS BOOK *THE IMPORTANCE OF BEING EARNEST* (1895)

Take up the White Man's burden—Send forth the best ye breed—
Go, bind your sons to exile
To serve your captives' need.

—RUDYARD KIPLING, FROM HIS POEM "THE WHITE MAN'S BURDEN" (1899)

Do the work that's nearest,
Though it's dull at whiles,
Helping, when we meet them,
Lame dogs over stiles.

—CHARLES KINGSLEY, FROM HIS POEM "THE INVITATION
TO TOM HUGHES" (1956)

Man is saved by love and duty, and by the hope that springs from duty,
or rather from the moral facts of consciousness, as a flower springs
from the soil.

—HENRI-FRÉDÉRIC AMIEL

The latest gospel in this world is, know thy work and do it.

—THOMAS CARLYLE

Consult duty, not events.

—ARTHUR ANNESLEY, FIRST EARL OF ANGLESEY

Do daily and hourly your duty; do it patiently and thoroughly. Do it as it presents itself; do it at the moment, and let it be its own reward. Never mind whether it is known and acknowledged or not, but do not fail to do it.

—JAMES H. AUGHEY

In doing what we ought we deserve no praise, because it is our duty.

—ST. AUGUSTINE

Duty itself is supreme delight when love is the inducement and labor. By such a principle the ignorant are enlightened, the hard-hearted softened, the disobedient reformed, and the faithful encouraged.

—HOSEA BALLOU

Let him who gropes painfully in darkness or uncertain light, and prays vehemently that the dawn may ripen into day, lay this precept well to heart: "Do the duty which lies nearest to thee," which thou knowest to be a duty! Thy second duty will already have become clearer.

—THOMAS CARLYLE

Never to tire, never to grow cold; to be patient, sympathetic, tender; to look for the budding flower and the opening heart; to hope always; like God, to love always—this is duty.

—HENRI-FRÉDÉRIC AMIEL

Our grand business undoubtedly is, not to see what lies dimly at a distance, but to do what lies clearly at hand.

—THOMAS CARLYLE

For men become civilized, not in proportion to their willingness to believe, but in their readiness to doubt.

—H. L. MENCKEN

None should expect to prosper who go out of way of duty.

—James H. Aughey

When a man assumes a public trust, he should consider himself as public property.

—Thomas Jefferson

Duties are ours; events are God's. This removes an infinite burden from the shoulders of a miserable, tempted, dying creature. On this consideration only, can he securely lay down his head, and close his eyes.

—Richard Cecil

What one has to do usually can be done.

—Eleanor Roosevelt

CHAPTER NINE

Between the Lines

It is books that are the key to the wide world; if you can't do anything else, read all that you can.

—JANE HAMILTON

True books will venture, dare you out, whisper secrets, maybe shout across the gloom to you in need, who hanker for a book to read.

—DAVID McCORD

The books that help you the most are those which make you think the most.

—THEODORE PARKER

The man who doesn't read good books has no advantage over the man who can't read them.

—MARK TWAIN

It is easier to buy books than to read them, and easier to read them than to absorb them.

—Sir William Osler

From your parents you learn love and laughter and how to put one foot before the other. But when books are opened you discover you have wings.

—Helen Hayes

Books were my pass to personal freedom. I learned to read at age three, and soon discovered there was a whole world to conquer that went beyond our farm in Mississippi.

—Oprah Winfrey

His mind was fallow. It had lain fallow all his life so far and the abstract thought of the books was concerned, and it was ripe for sowing. It had never been jaded by study, and it bit hold of the knowledge in the books with sharp teeth that would not let go.

—JACK LONDON, FROM HIS BOOK *MARTIN EDEN*

I have often wondered about two things: First, why high-school kids almost invariably hate the books they are assigned to read by their English teachers, and second, why English teachers almost invariably hate the books their students read in their spare time.

—STEPHEN KING, FROM "WHAT STEPHEN KING DOES FOR LOVE,"
SEVENTEEN (1990)

Great books conserve time.

—HOLBROOK JACKSON, FROM HIS BOOK *MAXIMS OF BOOKS AND READING* (1934)

Read not Books alone, but Man also; and chiefly thyself.

—THOMAS FULLER

I am old-fashioned and romantic enough to believe that many children, given the right circumstances, are natural readers until this instinct is destroyed by the media. It may be an illusion to believe that the magical connection of solitary children to the best books can endure, but such a relationship does go so long a way back that it will not easily expire.

—HAROLD BLOOM, IN *SHORT STORIES AND POEMS FOR EXCEPTIONALLY INTELLIGENT CHILDREN* (2001)

Reading, in contrast to sitting before the screen, is not a purely passive exercise. The child, particularly one who reads a book dealing with real life, has nothing before it but the hieroglyphics of the printed page. Imagination must do the rest; and imagination is called upon to do it.

—GEORGE F. KENNAN, IN "AMERICAN ADDICTIONS," *NEW OXFORD REVIEW* (1993)

I cannot live without books.

—THOMAS JEFFERSON

The books I have read were composed by generations of fathers and sons, mothers and daughters, teacher and disciples. I am the sum total of their experiences and so are you.

—ELIE WIESEL

It is sense-experience that serves as a foundation for the reason of the intelligence; our first teachers in natural philosophy are our feet, hands, and eyes. To substitute books for them does not teach us to reason, it teaches us to use the reason of others, rather than our own; it teaches us to believe much and know little.

—JEAN-JACQUES ROUSSEAU, FROM HIS BOOK *ÉMILE; OR, TREATISE ON EDUCATION* (1762)

Some books are to be tasted, others to be swallowed, and some few to be chewed and digested.

—FRANCIS BACON

I know what I should love to do—to build a study; to write, and to think of nothing else. I want to bury myself in a den of books. I want to saturate myself with the elements of which they are made, and breathe their atmosphere until I am of it. Not a bookworm, being which is to give off no utterances; but a man in the world of writing—one with a pen that shall stop men to listen to it, whether they wish to or not.

—Lew Wallace, American writer and soldier

He who studies books alone will know how things ought to be, and he who studies men will know how they are.

—Charles Caleb Colton

We read books to find out who we are. What other people, real or imaginary, do and think and feel is an essential guide to our understanding of what we ourselves are and may become.

—Ursula K. Le Guin

Without books the development of civilization would have been impossible. They are the engines of change, windows of the world, lighthouses erect in the sea of time. They are companions, teachers, magicians, bankers of the treasures of the mind. Books are humanity in print.

—BARBARA TUCHMAN

Life-transforming ideas have always come to me through books.

—"BELL HOOKS"

My first book was the book that changed my life.

—STEPHEN AMBROSE

This paperback is very interesting, but I find it will never replace a hardcover book—it makes a very poor doorstop.

—ALFRED HITCHCOCK

There's a certain kind of conversation you have from time to time at parties in New York about a new book . . . The conversation goes around and around various literary criticisms, and by the time it moves on one thing is clear: No one read the book; we just read the reviews.

—ANNA QUINDLEN

There is no mistaking a real book when one meets it. It is like falling in love.

—CHRISTOPHER MORLEY

Don't join the book burners. Don't think you're going to conceal faults by concealing evidence that they ever existed. Don't be afraid to go in your library and read every book.

—DWIGHT D. EISENHOWER

Properly, we should read for power. Man reading should be man intensely alive. The book should be a ball of light in one's hand.

—EZRA POUND

I think it is good that books still exist, but they do make me sleepy.

—FRANK ZAPPA

I find television very educating. Every time somebody turns on the set, I go into the other room and read a book.

—GROUCHO MARX

The love of learning, the sequestered nooks,
And all the sweet serenity of books.

—HENRY WADSWORTH LONGFELLOW, FROM HIS POEM "MORITURI SALUTAMUS" (1875)

Do give books—religious or otherwise—for Christmas. They're never fattening, seldom sinful, and permanently personal.

—LENORE HERSHEY

When I step into this library, I cannot understand why I ever step out of it.

—Marie de Sevigne

There is no such thing as a moral or an immoral book. Books are well written or badly written.

—Oscar Wilde, from the Preface to his book *The Picture of Dorian Gray* (1891)

Be as careful of the books you read, as of the company you keep; for your habits and character will be as much influenced by the former as by the latter.

—Paxton Hood

The multitude of books is making us ignorant.

—Voltaire

Knowing I lov'd my books, he furnish'd me
From mine own library with volumes that
I prize above my dukedom.

—WILLIAM SHAKESPEARE, FROM *THE TEMPEST*

Some books are undeservedly forgotten, none are undeservedly remembered.

—W. H. AUDEN

I suggest that the only books that influence us are those for which we are ready, and which have gone a little further down our particular path than we have gone ourselves.

—E. M. FORSTER

Choose your friends like your books, few but choice.

—AMERICAN PROVERB

It had been startling and disappointing to me to find out that story books had been written by people, that books were not natural wonders, coming of themselves like grass.

—Eudora Welty

Imagine a survivor of a failed civilization with only a tattered book on aromatherapy for guidance in arresting a cholera epidemic. Yet, such a book would more likely be found amid the debris than a comprehensible medical text.

—James Lovelock, environmentalist and scientist

Anyone who says they have only one life to live must not know how to read a book.

—Anonymous

Today's public figures can no longer write their own speeches or books, and there is some evidence that they can't read them either.

—Gore Vidal

A book of quotations . . . can never be complete.

—ROBERT M. HAMILTON

Read an hour every day in your chosen field. This works out to about one book per week, fifty books per year, and will guarantee your success.

—BRIAN TRACY, MOTIVATIONAL COACH AND AUTHOR

Read something positive every night and listen to something helpful every morning.

—TOM HOPKINS, MOTIVATIONAL SPEAKER

I always read the last page of a book first so that if I die before I finish I'll know how it turned out.

—NORA EPHRON

It is only by introducing the young to great literature, drama and music, and to the excitement of great science that we open to them the possibilities that lie within the human spirit—enable them to see visions and dream dreams.

—Eric Anderson

To encourage literature and the arts is a duty which every good citizen owes to his country.

—George Washington

You don't have to burn books to destroy a culture. Just get people to stop reading them.

—Ray Bradbury

So please, oh PLEASE, we beg, we pray, Go throw your TV set away, And in its place you can install, A lovely bookshelf on the wall.

—Roald Dahl, from his book *Charlie and the Chocolate Factory* (1964)

Reading aloud with children is known to be the single most important activity for building the knowledge and skills they will eventually require for learning to read.

—MARILYN JAGER ADAMS

There are many little ways to enlarge your child's world. Love of books is the best of all.

—JACQUELINE KENNEDY ONASSIS

No entertainment is so cheap as reading, nor any pleasure so lasting. She will not want new fashions nor regret the loss of expensive diversions or variety of company if she can be amused with an author in her closet.

—LADY MONTAGU, PROVIDING ADVICE ON RAISING HER
GRANDDAUGHTER, 1752

The more that you read, the more things you will know. The more you learn, the more places you'll go.

> —THEODOR "DR. SEUSS" GEISEL, FROM HIS BOOK *I CAN READ WITH MY EYES SHUT!*

The ability to read awoke inside me some long dormant craving to be mentally alive.

> —MALCOLM X, FROM *THE AUTOBIOGRAPHY OF MALCOLM X* (1964)

A book must be the ax for the frozen sea within us.

> —FRANZ KAFKA

To learn to read is to light a fire; every syllable that is spelled out is a spark.

> —VICTOR HUGO, FROM *LES MISÉRABLES* (1862)

Oh, magic hour, when a child first knows she can read printed words!

—BETTY SMITH, FROM HER BOOK *A TREE GROWS IN BROOKLYN* (1943)

⎯⎯◈⎯⎯

I have always imagined that paradise will be a kind of library.

—JORGE LUIS BORGES

⎯⎯◈⎯⎯

Once you learn to read, you will be forever free.

—FREDERICK DOUGLASS

⎯⎯◈⎯⎯

Babies are born with the instinct to speak, the way spiders are born with the instinct to spin webs. You don't need to train babies to speak; they just do. But reading is different.

—STEVEN PINKER

⎯⎯◈⎯⎯

The good of a book lies in its being read. A book is made up of signs that speak of other signs, which in their turn speak of things.

—UMBERTO ECO, FROM HIS BOOK *THE NAME OF THE ROSE*

Generally speaking, men are influenced by books which clarify their own thought, which express their own notions well, or which suggest to them ideas which their minds are already predisposed to accept.

—CARL LOTUS BECKER, AMERICAN HISTORIAN

It's an insane tragedy that 700,000 people get a diploma each year and can't read the damned diploma.

—WILLIAM E. BROCK, FORMER U.S. SENATOR

Were we to choose our leaders on the basis of their reading experience and not their political programs, there would be much less grief on earth.

—JOSEPH BRODSKY, RUSSIAN POET AND NOBEL PRIZE–WINNER

Believe nothing, no matter where you read it, or who said it, no matter if I have said it, unless it agrees with your own reason and your own common sense.

—BUDDHA

I still find each day too short for all the thoughts I want to think, all the walks I want to take, all the books I want to read, and all the friends I want to see.

—JOHN BURROUGHS, AMERICAN NATURALIST AND ESSAYIST

I sometimes think of what future historians will say of us. A single sentence will suffice for modern man: he fornicated and read the papers.

—ALBERT CAMUS

Most of today's books have an air of having been written in one day from books read the night before.

—NICOLAS CHAMFORT

Each time we re-read a book we get more out of it because we put more into it; a different person is reading it, and therefore it is a different book.

—MURIEL CLARK

Politicians should read science fiction, not westerns and detective stories.

—ARTHUR C. CLARKE

Imagine a school with children that can read or write, but with teachers who cannot, and you have a metaphor of the Information Age in which we live.

—PETER COCHRANE, FUTURIST AND STRATEGIST FOR TECHNOLOGY-
DRIVEN BUSINESSES

Every man has one thing he can do better than anyone else—and usually it's reading his own handwriting.

—G. NORMAN COLLIE

The biggest critics of my books are people who never read them.

—JACKIE COLLINS

Literature is the art of writing something that will be read twice.

—CYRIL CONNOLLY

Associate with the noblest people you can find; read the best books;
live with the mighty. But learn to be happy alone. Rely upon your own
energies, and so do not wait for, or depend on other people.

—THOMAS DAVIDSON

When you read a classic you do not see in the book more than you did
before. You see more in you than there was before.

—CLIFTON PAUL FADIMAN, AMERICAN EDITOR AND LITERARY CRITIC

Johnny couldn't read . . . for the simple reason that nobody ever showed him how.

—RUDOLF FRANZ FLESCH

Today a reader, tomorrow a leader.

—W. FUSSELMAN, ART CRITIC

We live at the level of our language. Whatever we can articulate we can imagine or explore. All you have to do to educate a child is leave him alone and teach him to read. The rest is brainwashing.

—ELLEN GILCHRIST

The greatest gift is a passion for reading. It is cheap, it consoles, it distracts, it excites, it gives you knowledge of the world and experience of a wide kind. It is a moral illumination.

—ELIZABETH HARDWICK

Books give not wisdom where none was before, But where some is, there reading makes it more.

—SIR JOHN HARINGTON, INVENTOR OF THE FIRST MODERN FLUSH TOILET

If we wish to know the force of human genius we should read Shakespeare. If we wish to see the insignificance of human learning we may study his commentators.

—WILLIAM HAZLITT

To limit the press is to insult a nation; to prohibit reading of certain books is to declare the inhabitants to be either fools or slaves.

—CLAUDE ADRIEN HELVETIUS

Do your bit to save humanity from lapsing back into barbarity by reading all the novels you can.

—RICHARD HUGHES

You are the same today that you are going to be in five years from now except for two things: the people with whom you associate and the books you read.

—CHARLES JONES

When I read great literature, great drama, speeches, or sermons, I feel that the human mind has not achieved anything greater than the ability to share feelings and thoughts through language.

—JAMES EARL JONES

If the book we are reading does not wake us, as with a fist hammering on our skulls, then why do we read it?

—FRANZ KAFKA

Until I feared I would lose it, I never loved to read. One does not love breathing.

—HARPER LEE

To read means to borrow; to create out of one's readings is paying off one's debts.

—GEORG CHRISTOPHER LICHTENBERG

People everywhere confuse what they read in newspapers with news.

—A. J. LIEBLING

Without question, reading has been the foundation of whatever success I've had in my life.

—HUGH MCCOLL, JR., BANKER AND ENTREPRENEUR

Reading transports me. I can go anywhere and never leave my chair. It lets me shake hands with new ideas.

—ROLFE NEILL, FORMER PUBLISHER OF *THE CHARLOTTE OBSERVER*

This will never be a civilized country until we expend more money for books than we do for chewing gum.

—Elbert Hubbard

To read without reflecting is like eating without digesting.

—Edmund Burke

A good book on your shelf is a friend that turns its back on you and remains a friend.

—Anonymous

To acquire the habit of reading is to construct for yourself a refuge from almost all the miseries of life.

—W. Somerset Maugham

A book is a garden, an orchard, a storehouse, a party, a company by the way, a counsellor, a multitude of counsellors.

—HENRY WARD BEECHER

People say life is the thing, but I prefer reading.

—LOGAN PEARSALL SMITH (1865–1946)

Books worth reading are worth re-reading.

—HOLBROOK JACKSON

What refuge is there for the victim who is oppressed with the feeling that there are a thousand new books he ought to read, while life is only long enough for him to attempt a hundred?

—OLIVER WENDELL HOLMES, SR.

To read a writer is for me not merely to get an idea of what he says, but to go off with him, and travel in his company.

—ANDRÉ GIDE

Reading furnishes the mind only with the materials of knowledge; it is thinking that makes what we read ours.

—JOHN LOCKE

I have lost all sense of home, having moved about so much. It means to me now—only that place where the books are kept.

—JOHN STEINBECK

A fondness for reading changes the inevitable dull hours of our life into exquisite hours of delight.

—BARON DE MONTESQUIEU

I would rather be a poor man in a garret with plenty of books than a king who did not love reading.

—THOMAS B. MACAULAY, POLITICIAN AND POET

Books worth reading are worth reading twice; and what is most important of all, the masterpieces of literature are worth reading a thousand times.

—JOHN MORLEY, BRITISH STATESMAN

I love to lose myself in other men's minds.
When I am not walking, I am reading;
I cannot sit and think. Books think for me.

—GEORG CHRISTOPH LICHTENBERG

All good books are alike in that they are truer than if they really happened and after you are finished reading one you feel that it all happened to you and after which it all belongs to you.

—ERNEST HEMINGWAY

All of the glory of the world would be buried in oblivion, unless God had provided mortals with the remedy of books.

—RICHARD DE BURY, ENGLISH WRITER AND CLERGYMAN

He has only half learned the art of reading who has not added to it the even more refined accomplishments of skipping and skimming.

—ARTHUR BALFOUR

If a book is worth reading at all, it is worth reading more than once. Suspense is the lowest of excitants, designed to take your breath away when the brain and heart crave to linger in nobler enjoyment. Suspense drags you on; appreciation causes you to linger.

—WILLIAM GERHARDIE, BRITISH NOVELIST AND PLAYWRIGHT

Nothing links man to man like the frequent passage from hand to hand of a good book.

—WALTER SICKERT, ENGLISH PAINTER

The fact of knowing how to read is nothing, the whole point is knowing what to read.

—JACQUES ELLUL

The habit of reading is the only enjoyment in which there is no alloy; it lasts when all other pleasures fade.

—ANTHONY TROLLOPE

The possession of a book becomes a substitute for reading it.

—ANTHONY BURGESS

The responsibility of a dictionary is to record a language, not set its style.

—PHILIP BABCOCK GOVE, AMERICAN LEXICOGRAPHER

To finish [a book] is both a relief and a release from an extraordinarily pleasant prison.

—ROBERT BURCHFIELD

What is reading but a silent conversation?

—WALTER SAVAGE LANDOR

Sartor Resartus is simply unreadable, and for me that always sort of spoils a book.

—HARRY S. TRUMAN

You should read it, though there is much that is skip-worthy.

—HERBERT ASQUITH

The greatest masterpiece in literature is only a dictionary out of order.

—JEAN COCTEAU

The central theme of the novel is that they were glad to see each other.

—GERTRUDE STEIN

The most technologically efficient machine that man has ever invented is the book.

—NORTHROP FRYE

Just the knowledge that a good book is awaiting one at the end of a long day makes that day happier.

—KATHLEEN NORRIS

Laws die, books never.

—EDWARD BULWER-LYTTON

A good book is the precious life-blood of a master spirit, embalmed and treasured up on purpose to a life beyond life.

—JOHN MILTON

Any book which is at all important should be re-read immediately.

—ARTHUR SCHOPENHAUER

A dictionary should be descriptive, not prescriptive.

—PHILLIP BABCOCK GOVE

Book lovers never go to bed alone.

—ANONYMOUS

The first book of the nation is the dictionary of its language.

—CONSTANTIN FRANÇOIS DE CHASSEBŒUF, COMTE DE VOLNEY

A novel is a mirror carried along a main road.

—STENDHAL

I read part of it all the way through.

—SAM GOLDWYN

⬥

A successful book cannot afford to be more than ten percent new.

—MARSHALL MCLUHAN

⬥

A good book has no ending.

—R. D. CUMMING

⬥

What a sense of security in an old book which time has criticized for us!

—JAMES RUSSELL LOWELL

⬥

Books think for me.

—CHARLES LAMB

⬥

Does it afflict you to find your books wearing out? I mean literally . . . the mortality of all inanimate things is terrible to me, but that of books most of all.

—WILLIAM DEAN HOWELLS

One man is as good as another until he has written a book.

—BENJAMIN JOWETT

If a book is worth reading, it is worth buying.

—JOHN RUSKIN

Where is human nature so weak as in the bookstore?

—HENRY WARD BEECHER

I am a part of all I have read.

—JOHN KIERAN

⎯⎯◆⎯⎯

Reading is the work of the alert mind, is demanding, and under ideal conditions produces finally a sort of ecstasy. This gives the experience of reading a sublimity and power unequalled by any other form of communication.

—E. B. WHITE

⎯⎯◆⎯⎯

To me the charm of an encyclopedia is that it knows—and I needn't.

—FRANCIS YEATS-BROWN

⎯⎯◆⎯⎯

A good title is the title of a successful book.

—RAYMOND CHANDLER

⎯⎯◆⎯⎯

Reading, like prayer, remains one of our few private acts.

—WILLIAM JOVANOVICH

Dylan

My education was the liberty I had to read indiscriminately and all the time, with my eyes hanging out.

—DYLAN THOMAS

A publisher is somebody looking for someone who has something to say.

—LORNE PIERCE

There are perhaps no days of our childhood we lived so fully as those we believe we left without having lived them: those we spent with a favorite book.

—MARCEL PROUST

If you would understand your own age, read the works of fiction produced in it. People in disguise speak freely.

—ARTHUR HELPS

Camerado, this is no book.
Who touches this, touches a man.

—WALT WHITMAN

A book is like a garden carried in the pocket.

—CHINESE PROVERB

The walls of books around him, dense with the past, formed a kind of insulation against the present world and its disasters.

—ROSS MACDONALD

There are still a few of us booklovers around despite the awful warnings of Marshall McLuhan with his TV era and his pending farewell to Gutenberg.

—FRANK DAVIES

If I had read as other men, I should have known no more than they.

—THOMAS HOBBES

Deep-versed in books
And shallow in himself.

—JOHN MILTON

When I get a little money, I buy books and if any is left, I buy food and clothes.

—ERASMUS

The reading of all good books is like a conversation with the finest people of past centuries.

—René Descartes

⟫◆⟪

The oldest books are only just out to those who have not read them.

—Samuel Butler

⟫◆⟪

In five minutes the earth would be a desert, and you cling to books.

—Elias Canetti

⟫◆⟪

What one knows best is . . . what one has learned not from books but as a result of books, through the reflections to which they have given rise.

—Nicolas Chamfort

⟫◆⟪

The diffusion of these silent teachers, books, through the whole community, is to work greater effects than artillery, machinery, and legislation. Its peaceful agency is to supersede stormy revolutions.

—WILLIAM ELLERY CHANNING

The easiest books are generally the best, for whatever author is obscure and difficult in his own language certainly does not think clearly.

—LORD CHESTERFIELD, IN A LETTER TO HIS SON (FEBRUARY 1750)

The dearest ones of time, the strongest friends of the soul—BOOKS.

—EMILY DICKINSON

One always tends to overpraise a long book, because one has got through it.

—E. M. FORSTER

Learning hath gained most by those books . . . which the printers have lost.

  —THOMAS FULLER, FROM HIS BOOK *THE HOLY STATE AND THE PROFANE STATE* (1642)

Everything comes t' him who waits but a loaned book.

  —KIN HUBBARD, FROM HIS BOOK *ABE MARTIN'S PRIMER* (1914)

If we are imprisoned in ourselves, books provide us with the means of escape. If we have run too far away from ourselves, books show us the way back.

  —HOLBROOK JACKSON, FROM HIS BOOK *MAXIMS OF BOOKS AND READING* (1934)

Some men are born only to suck out the poison of books.

  —BEN JONSON

Books are a narcotic.

—FRANZ KAFKA

———✦———

Shortchange your education now and you may be short of change the rest of your life.

—ANONYMOUS

———✦———

Books which are no books . . .
I confess that it moves my spleen to see these *things in books' clothing*.

—CHARLES LAMB

———✦———

I have a low opinion of books; they are but piles of stones set up to show coming travelers where other minds have been. . . . One day's exposure to mountains is better than cartloads of books.

—JOHN MUIR

———✦———

You can't tell a book by its movie.

—LOUIS A. SAFIAN

———◆◆◆———

What really knocks me out is a book that, when you're all done reading
it, you wish the author that wrote it was a terrific friend of yours and
you could call him up on the phone whenever you like it. That doesn't
happen much though.

—J. D. SALINGER, FROM HIS BOOK *THE CATCHER IN THE RYE* (1951)

———◆◆◆———

Books are good enough in their own way, but they are a mighty bloodless
substitute for life.

—ROBERT LOUIS STEVENSON, FROM "AN APOLOGY FOR IDLERS,"
    VIRGINIBUS PUERISQUE (1881)

———◆◆◆———

One sure window into a person's soul is his reading list.

—MARY B. W. TABOR, FROM "BOOK NOTES," *THE NEW YORK
    TIMES* (1995)

———◆◆◆———

No one has stepped twice into the same river. But did anyway ever step twice into the same book?

—MARINA TSVETAEVA, FROM HER BOOK *PUSHKIN AND PUGACHEV* (1937)

The books that the world calls immoral are books that show the world its own shame.

—OSCAR WILDE, FROM HIS BOOK *THE PICTURE OF DORIAN GRAY* (1891)

Of making books there is no end, and much study is a weariness of the flesh.

—ECCLESIASTES 12:12

You can't judge a book by its cover.

—AMERICAN PROVERB

Beware of the man of one book.

—ITALIAN PROVERB

Any teacher can study books. But books do not necessarily bring wisdom, nor that human insight essential to consummate teaching skills.

—BLISS PERRY

How to tell students what to look for without telling them what to see is the dilemma of teaching.

—LASCELLES ABERCROMBIE

Books can not be killed by fire. People die, but books never die. No man and no force can take from the world the books that embody man's eternal fight against tyranny . . . In this war, we know, books are weapons.

—FRANKLIN DELANO ROOSEVELT, IN A "MESSAGE TO THE BOOKSELLERS OF AMERICA," MAY 6, 1942

The principle of procrastinated rape is said to be the ruling one in all the great best-sellers.

—V. S. PRITCHETT, FROM HIS BOOK *THE LIVING NOVEL* (1946)

This is not a book to be tossed aside lightly. It should be thrown with great force.

—DOROTHY PARKER, AS QUOTED IN R. E. DRENNAN'S *WIT'S END* (1973)

Book—what they make a movie out of for television.

—LEONARD LOUIS LEVINSON

Books say: she did this because. Life says: she did this. Books are where things are explained to you; life is where things aren't. . . . Books make sense of life. The only problem is that the lives they make sense of are other people's lives, never your own.

—JULIAN BARNES, FROM HIS BOOK *FLAUBERT'S PARROT* (1984)

What literature can and should do is change the people who teach the people who don't read the books.

—A. S. BYATT

Literature is mostly about having sex and not much about having children. Life is the other way around.

—DAVID LODGE, FROM HIS BOOK *THE BRITISH MUSEUM IS FALLING DOWN* (1965)

This will never be a civilized country until we expend more money for books than we do for chewing gum.

—ELBERT HUBBARD

A library is thought in cold storage.

—VISCOUNT HERBERT SAMUEL

One teacher is better than two books.

—GERMAN PROVERB

<hr>

The greatest university of all is a collection of books.

—THOMAS CARLYLE

<hr>

I hate books. They only teach us to talk about things we know nothing about.

—JEAN-JACQUES ROUSSEAU

<hr>

The reading or non-reading a book—will never keep down a single petticoat.

—LORD BYRON, IN A LETTER TO RICHARD HOPPNER (1819)

Your *borrowers of books*—those mutilators of collections, spoilers of the symmetry of shelves, and creators of odd volumes.

—CHARLES LAMB, FROM HIS BOOK *THE ESSAYS OF ELIA* (1823)

A good book is the best of friends, the same to-day and for ever.

—MARTIN TUPPER, FROM HIS BOOK *PROVERBIAL PHILOSOPHY* (1838)

No furniture so charming as books.

—SYDNEY SMITH

Books are made not like children but like pyramids . . . and they're just as useless! And they stay in the desert! . . . Jackals piss at their foot and the bourgeois climb up on them.

—GUSTAVE FLAUBERT, IN A LETTER TO ERNEST FEYDEAU (1857)

"What is the use of a book," thought Alice, "without pictures or conversations?"

—LEWIS CARROLL, FROM HIS BOOK *ALICE'S ADVENTURES IN WONDERLAND* (1865)

There is no such thing as a moral or immoral book. Books are well written, or badly written.

—OSCAR WILDE, FROM HIS BOOK *THE PICTURE OF DORIAN GRAY* (1891)

Classic. A book which people praise and don't read.

—MARK TWAIN, FROM HIS BOOK *FOLLOWING THE EQUATOR* (1897)

All books are either dreams or swords,
You can cut, or you can drug, with words.

—AMY LOWELL, FROM HER POEM "SWORD BLADES AND POPPY SEED" (1914)

Beware you be not swallowed up in books: an ounce of love is worth a pound of knowledge.

—JOHN WESLEY, IN A LETTER TO JOSEPH BENSON, 1768

Real education should consist of drawing the goodness and the best out of our own students. What better books can there be than the book of humanity?

—CÉSAR CHÁVEZ

We shouldn't teach great books; we should teach a love of reading.

—B. F. SKINNER

When you sell a man a book you don't sell him just twelve ounces of paper and ink and glue—you sell him a whole new life.

—CHRISTOPHER MORLEY, FROM HIS BOOK *PARNASSUS ON WHEELS* (1917)

Poetry is so vital to us until school spoils it.

—RUSSELL BAKER, AMERICAN PULITZER PRIZE–WINNING WRITER

Reading maketh a full man, conference a ready man, and writing an exact man.

—FRANCIS BACON

My advice to kids who want to become authors and to kids who just want to write well just for fun is to read. I think that we really learn how to write by reading.

—JOANNA COLE, AUTHOR OF *THE MAGIC SCHOOL BUS* SERIES

Reading well makes children more interesting both to themselves and others, a process in which they will develop a sense of being separate and distinct selves.

—HAROLD BLOOM, IN *SHORT STORIES AND POEMS FOR EXCEPTIONALLY INTELLIGENT CHILDREN* (2001)

I would be most content if my children grew up to be the kind of people who think decorating consists mostly of building enough bookshelves.

—ANNA QUINDLEN, 1992 PULITZER PRIZE–WINNING JOURNALIST AND AUTHOR

I believe—not empirically, alas, but only theoretically—that for someone who has read a lot of Dickens to shoot his like in the name of an idea is harder than for someone who has read no Dickens.

—JOSEPH BRODSKY, RUSSIAN POET AND NOBEL PRIZE–WINNER

Education no doubt can be suggested in the classroom; but education happens in the library.

—JOHN V. FLEMING, PROFESSOR AT PRINCETON UNIVERSITY

A man's library is a kind of harem.

—RALPH WALDO EMERSON

A book is a gift you can open again and again.

—GARRISON KEILLOR

Learning is acquired by reading books; but the much more necessary learning, the knowledge of the world, is only to be acquired by reading man, and studying all the various editions of them.

—LORD CHESTERFIELD

Teaching reading IS rocket science.

—LOUISA MOATS

The one man who should never attempt an explanation of a poem is its author. If the poem can be improved by its author's explanations it never should have been published, and if the poem cannot be improved by its author's explanations the explanations are scarcely worth reading.

—ARCHIBALD MACLEISH, AMERICAN WRITER AND LIBRARIAN OF CONGRESS

We should get into the habit of reading inspirational books, looking
at inspirational pictures, hearing inspirational music, associating with
inspirational friends.

—ALFRED A. MONTAPERT

The best of my education has come from the public library . . . my tuition
fee is a bus fare and once in a while, five cents a day for an overdue
book. You don't need to know very much to start with, if you know the
way to the public library.

—LESLEY CONGER

Reading is to the mind, what exercise is to the body.

—SIR RICHARD STEELE

Literature is news that stays news.

—EZRA POUND, FROM HIS BOOK *ABC OF READING* (1934)

How many a man has dated a new era in his life from the reading of a book! The book exists for us, perchance, that will explain our miracles and reveal new ones.

—HENRY DAVID THOREAU, FROM HIS BOOK *WALDEN; OR LIFE IN THE WOODS* (1854)

Education begins by teaching children to read and ends by making most of them hate reading.

—HOLBROOK JACKSON, SUPREME COURT ASSOCIATE JUSTICE

The whole world opened to me when I learned to read.

—MARY McLEOD BETHUNE, EDUCATOR BORN TO FORMER SLAVE

I am what the librarians have made me with a little assistance from a professor of Greek and a few poets.

—BERNARD KEBLE SANDWELL, NEWSPAPER WRITER AND EDITOR

Education . . . has produced a vast population able to read but unable to distinguish what is worth reading.

—G. M. TREVELYAN, FROM HIS BOOK *ENGLISH SOCIAL HISTORY* (1942)

As good almost kill a man as kill a good book.

—JOHN MILTON, FROM HIS BOOK *AREOPAGITICA* (1644)

I drew men's faces on my copy-books,
Scrawled them within the antiphony's marge,
Joined legs and arms to the long music-notes,
Found nose and eyes and chins for A's and B's,
And made a string of pictures of the world,
Betwixt the ins and outs of verb and noun,
On the wall, the bench, the door. The monks looked black.
"Nay," quoth the Prior, "Turn him out, d'ye say?
In no wise. Lose a crow and catch a lark.

—ROBERT BROWNING, FROM HIS POEM "FRA LIPPO LIPPI"

What we become depends on what we read after all the professors have finished with us.

—THOMAS CARLYLE

Read not to contradict and confute, nor to believe and take for granted . . . but to weigh and consider.

—FRANCIS BACON

How many writers are there . . . who, breaking up their subject into details, destroy its life, and defraud us of the whole by their anxiety about the parts.

—JOHN HENRY CARDINAL NEWMAN

It is not often that we use language correctly; usually we use it incorrectly, though we understand each other's meaning.

—ST. AUGUSTINE

The limits of your language are the limits of your world.

—LUDWIG WITTGENSTEIN

When you stack up the years we are allowed against all there is to read, time is very short indeed.

—STEPHEN KING, FROM "WHAT STEPHEN KING DOES FOR LOVE," *SEVENTEEN* (1990)

Master books, but do not let them master you. Read to live, not live to read.

—EDWARD BULWER-LYTTON

I decided that adventure was the best way to learn about writing.

—LLOYD ALEXANDER

I needed to be made to feel that there was real, permanent happiness in tranquil contemplation. Wordsworth taught me this, not only without turning away from, but with a greatly increased interest in the common feelings and common destiny of human beings.

—JOHN STUART MILL, FROM *AUTOBIOGRAPHY* (1873)

Out of the Books thou readest, extract what thou likest; and then single out some Particular from the rest for that Day's Meditation.

—THOMAS FULLER

The secret to speed-reading is moving your lips faster.

—CHARLES SCHULZ

So much has already been written about everything that you can't find out anything about it.

—JAMES THURBER

Instead of Man Thinking, we have the bookworm

  —RALPH WALDO EMERSON, FROM HIS BOOK *THE AMERICAN SCHOLAR SELF-RELIANCE COMPENSATION* (1837)

Employ your time in improving yourself by other men's writings, so that you shall gain easily what others have labored hard for.

  —SOCRATES

Oh, do let me go on. I want to see how it ends.

  —OSCAR WILDE, UPON BEING TOLD HE COULD STOP TRANSLATING A BIBLE PASSAGE FROM GREEK DURING HIS ORAL EXAM AT OXFORD

Let a scholar all Earth's volumes carry,
He will be but a walking dictionary.

  —GEORGE CHAPMAN, FROM HIS POEM "THE TEARS OF PEACE" (1609)

C-l-e-a-n, clean, verb active, to make bright bright, to scour, W-i-n, win, d-e-r, der winder, a casement. When the boy knows this out of the book, he goes and does it.

—CHARLES DICKENS, FROM HIS BOOK *NICHOLAS NICKELBY* (1839)

Whilst others have been at the balloo, I have been at my book, and am now past the craggy paths of study, and come to flowery plains of honor and reputation.

—BEN JONSON, FROM HIS BOOK *VOLPONE* (1606)

CHAPTER TEN

Nuts and Bolts

There is no Royal Road to Geometry.

—Euclid

Mathematics is the Queen of the Sciences.

—Carl Friedrich Gauss

The most important questions in life are, for the most part, really only problems of probability.

—Pierre Simon de La Place

Perfect numbers, like perfect men, are very rare.

—René Descartes

Five out of four people have trouble with fractions.

—STEVEN WRIGHT, COMEDIAN AND ACTOR

Algebra is generous; she often gives more than is asked of her.

—D'ALEMBERT

There is no branch of mathematics, however abstract, which may not someday be applied to the phenomena of the real world.

—NICOLAI LOBACHEVSKY

Logic is the anatomy of thought.

—JOHN LOCKE

I tell them if they will occupy themselves with the study of mathematics, they will find in it the best remedy against the lusts of the flesh.

—THOMAS MANN

The mathematical rules of the universe are visible to men in the form of beauty.

—JOHN MICHEL

It is easier to square a circle than to get round a mathematician.

—DE MORGAN

The union of the mathematician with the poet, fervor with measure, passion with correctness, this surely is the ideal.

—WILLIAM JAMES

We have to reinvent the wheel every once in a while, not because we need a lot of wheels; but because we need a lot of inventors.

—BRUCE JOYCE

It is impossible to be a mathematician without being a poet in soul.

—SOPHIA KOVALEVSKAYA

All the effects of nature are only mathematical results of a small number of immutable laws.

—PIERRE SIMON DE LA PLACE

Music is the pleasure the human mind experiences from counting without being aware that it is counting.

—LEIBNIZ

The essence of mathematics is not to make simple things complicated, but to make complicated things simple.

—S. GUDDER

The value of a problem is not so much coming up with the answer as in the ideas and attempted ideas it forces on the would be solver.

—I. N. HERSTEIN

The infinite! No other question has ever moved so profoundly the spirit of man.

—DAVID HILBERT

The object of mathematics is the honor of the human spirit.

—CARL JACOBI

One person's constant is another person's variable.

—SUSAN GERHART

Mathematics is the gate and key to the sciences.

—ROGER BACON

Logic is invincible, because in order to combat logic it is necessary to use logic.

—PIERRE BOATROUX

The advancement and perfection of mathematics are intimately connected with the prosperity of the state.

—NAPOLEON BONAPARTE

There is geometry in the humming of the string.

—PYTHAGORAS

What would life be without arithmetic but a scene of horrors?

—SYDNEY SMITH

A mathematician who is not also something of a poet will never be a complete mathematician.

—KARL WEIERSTRASS

Mathematics is the science of definiteness, the necessary vocabulary of those who know.

—W. J. WHITE

I must study politics and war that my sons may have liberty to study mathematics and philosophy.

—JOHN ADAMS

⎯⎯◆⎯⎯

Medicine makes people ill, mathematics makes them sad, and theology makes them sinful.

—MARTIN LUTHER

⎯⎯◆⎯⎯

There are two ways to do great mathematics. The first is to be smarter than everybody else. The second way is to be stupider than everybody else—but persistent.

—RAOUL BOTT

⎯⎯◆⎯⎯

Mathematics is the life of the gods.

—NOVALIS (FRIEDRICH VON HARDENBERG)

⎯⎯◆⎯⎯

Mathematics is the science of what is clear by itself.

—Carl Jacobi

All great theorems were discovered after midnight.

—Adrian Mathesis

Life is good for only two things: discovering mathematics and teaching mathematics.

—Simeon Poisson

It is the duty of all teachers, and of teachers of mathematics in particular, to expose their students to problems much more than to facts.

—Paul Halmos

God exists since mathematics is consistent and the devil exists since we cannot prove the consistency.

—MORRIS KLINE

Calculus is the most powerful weapon of thought yet devised by the wit of man.

—W. B. SMITH

Numbers constitute the only universal language.

—NATHANAEL WEST

I never got a pass mark in math. . . . Just imagine—mathematicians now use my prints to illustrate their books.

—M. C. ESCHER

The title which I most covet is that of teacher. The writing of a research paper and the teaching of freshman calculus, and everything in between, falls under this rubric. Happy is the person who comes to understand something and then gets to explain it.

—MARSHALL COHEN

Mathematical knowledge adds vigor to the mind, frees it from prejudice, credulity, and superstition.

—JOHN ARBUTHNOT

I am persuaded that this method for calculating the volume of a sphere will be of no little service to mathematics. For I foresee that once it is understood and established, it will be used to discover other theorems which have not yet occurred to me, by other mathematicians, now living or yet unborn.

—ARCHIMEDES

Some mathematician, I believe, has said that true pleasure lies not in the discovery of truth, but in the search for it.

—LEO TOLSTOY

In the fall of 1972 President Nixon announced that the rate of increase of inflation was decreasing. This was the first time a sitting president used the third derivative to advance his case for reelection.

—HUGO ROSSI

The real danger is not that computers will begin to think like men, but that men will begin to think like computers.

—SYDNEY J. HARRIS

Millions saw the apple fall, but Newton asked why.

—BERNARD BARUCH

Home computers are being called upon to perform many new functions, including the consumption of homework formerly eaten by the dog.

—DOUG LARSON

A math student's best friend is BOB (the Back Of the Book), but remember that BOB doesn't come to school on test days.

—JOSH FOLB

I advise my students to listen carefully the moment they decide to take no more mathematics courses. They might be able to hear the sound of closing doors.

—JAMES CABALLERO

Science and art sometimes can touch one another, like two of the jigsaw puzzle which is our human life, and that contact may be made across the borderline between the two respective domains.

—M. C. ESCHER

In real life, I assure you, there is no such thing as algebra.

—FRAN LEBOWITZ

The most exciting phrase to hear in science, the one that heralds new discoveries, is not "Eureka!" (I've found it!), but "That's funny..."

—ISAAC ASIMOV

Calculus rendered thousand-year-old questions immediately transparent. Calculus is truly amazing. But, how many students who take the course as freshmen look up and say, "Wow! That's amazing!"? How often, math faculty members, have your students had that experience? I mean, the stuff just sort of goes by. No passion, no soul.

—URI TREISMAN, PROFESSOR OF MATHEMATICS

In an age when science is essential to our safety and to our economic welfare, it might be argued that a shortage of science teachers, and of scientists, is a clear and present danger to the nation.

—JAMES R. KILLIAN, AS QUOTED IN *THE TEACHER AND THE TAUGHT* (1963)

The best teachers I ever had were science teachers . . . thus my chosen profession! They were great because they loved their subject matter as much as I did and they inspired me to pursue my questions, curiosities, and interests. They were active, lifelong learners and that rubbed off on me.

—JIM GARDINEER, SCIENCE TEACHER FROM MAHOPAC, NEW YORK

Direct the attention of your pupil to the phenomena of nature, and you will soon awaken his curiosity; but to keep that curiosity alive, you must be in no haste to satisfy it: he should not learn but invent the sciences.

—JEAN-JACQUES ROUSSEAU

That is the essence of science: ask an impertinent question, and you are on the way to a pertinent answer.

—JACOB BRONOWSKI, FROM HIS BOOK *THE ASCENT OF MAN* (1973)

To me it seems that those sciences are vain and full of error which are not born of experience, mother of all certainty, first hand experience which in its origins, or means, or end has passed through one of the five senses.

—LEONARDO DA VINCI

The inertia of humanity has never yielded, save under the impulsion of genius. In a word, science demands a twofold effort, that of a few men to find some new thing and that of all the others to adapt themselves to it.

—HENRI BERGSON

The distinctive feature of the regime of experts lies in the fact that, while possessing ample power to coerce, it prefers to charm conformity from us by exploiting our deep-seated commitment to the scientific world-view and by manipulating the securities and creature comforts of the industrial affluence which science has given us.

—THEODORE ROSZAK, FROM HIS BOOK *THE MAKING OF THE COUNTER CULTURE: REFLECTIONS ON THE TECHNOCRATIC SOCIETY AND ITS YOUTHFUL OPPOSITION* (1969)

Science is organized knowledge. Wisdom is organized life.

—IMMANUEL KANT

There is a single light of science, and to brighten it anywhere is to brighten it everywhere.

—ISAAC ASIMOV

Every science has for its basis a system of principles as fixed and unalterable as those by which the universe is regulated and governed. Man cannot make principles; he can only discover them.

—THOMAS PAINE

Math treats all people equally. Especially when you're in a hard class with all boys, when nobody's cheering you on from the sidelines, when it's not "cool" to be smart, math is a nice thing to have. When nothing else makes sense, math reaches an answer.

—REBECCA L. EISENBERG, FROM "GIRLS NEED MATH," *THE EXAMINER* (OCTOBER 19, 1997)

It has been my experience that competency in mathematics, both in numerical manipulations and in understanding its conceptual foundations, enhances a person's ability to handle the more ambiguous and qualitative relationships that dominate our day-to-day financial decision-making.

—ALAN GREENSPAN

The key to solving problems is not through the heart, not by one's schematic mind, nor by a person's points of view; it is through Mathematics!

—VIRGIN LIONS

The good Christian should beware the mathematician and all those who make empty prophecies. The danger already exists that the mathematicians have made a covenant with the devil to darken the spirit and to confine man in the bonds of hell.

—St. Augustine

Once upon a time, America sheltered an Einstein, went to the moon, and gave the world the laser, the electronic computer, nylons, television, and the cure for polio. Today, we are in the process, albeit unwittingly, of abandoning this leadership role.

—Leon M. Lederman, Nobel Prize–winner in Physics

A high-school girl, seated next to a famous astronomer at a dinner party, struck up a conversation with him by asking: "What do you do for a living?" "I study astronomy," he replied. "Really?" said the teenager, wide-eyed, "I finished astronomy last year."

—James Keller, in *Three Minutes* (1950)

We save a boy's soul at the same time we are saving his algebra.

—GEORGE ST. JOHN

———⊰•⊱———

Mathematics is a more powerful instrument of knowledge than any other that has been bequeathed to us by human agency.

—RENÉ DESCARTES

———⊰•⊱———

It should be possible to explain the laws of physics to a barmaid.

—ALBERT EINSTEIN

———⊰•⊱———

I have an infamously low capacity for visualizing relationships, which made the study of geometry and all subjects derived from it impossible for me.

—SIGMUND FREUD

———⊰•⊱———

If I were again beginning my studies, I would follow the advice of Plato and start with mathematics.

—GALILEO GALILEI

I cannot join the space program and restart my life as an astronaut, but this opportunity to connect my abilities as an educator with my interests in history and space is a unique opportunity to fulfill my early fantasies.

—CHRISTA MCAULIFFE, TEACHER KILLED ON *CHALLENGER* SPACE
SHUTTLE

Had silicon been a gas, I would have been a major-general by now.

—JAMES MCNEIL WHISTLER, ON HAVING BEEN FOUND "DEFICIENT IN
CHEMISTRY" IN A WEST POINT EXAMINATION, FROM *THE LIFE OF
JAMES MCNEIL WHISTLER* (1908)

Statistics means never having to say you're certain.

—ANONYMOUS

42.7% of all statistics are made up on the spot.

—STEVEN WRIGHT, COMEDIAN AND ACTOR

History not used is nothing, for all intellectual life is action, like practical life, and if you don't use the stuff—well, it might as well be dead.

—ARNOLD J. TOYNBEE

If history were taught in the form of stories, it would never be forgotten.

—RUDYARD KIPLING

I never read history for the story itself as a story. The only thing interesting to me was the principles to be evolved from, and illustrated by, the facts.

—SAMUEL TAYLOR COLERIDGE, IN *TABLE TALK* (1835)

Truth, naked unblushing truth, the first virtue of more serious history.

—EDWARD GIBBON, FROM HIS BOOK *THE DECLINE AND FALL OF THE
ROMAN EMPIRE* (1776–1778)

The wrong way to teach history would be to show that there's only one perspective and only one history.

—JONATHAN WENN, 2001 DISNEY TEACHER OF THE YEAR, FROM
ROOSEVELT MIDDLE SCHOOL IN GLENDALE, NEW YORK

American history is longer, larger, more various, more beautiful, and more terrible than anything anyone has ever said about it.

—JAMES BALDWIN, FROM HIS ARTICLE "A TALK TO TEACHERS" (1963)

History, real solemn history, I cannot be interested in. I read it a little as a duty, but it tells me nothing that does not either vex or weary me. The quarrels of popes and kings, with wars and pestilence in every page; the men so good for nothing and hardly any women at all.

—JANE AUSTEN

Any written history inevitably reflects the thought of the author in his time and cultural setting.

—CHARLES A. BEARD, FROM "WRITTEN HISTORY AS AN ACT OF FAITH," *AMERICAN HISTORICAL REVIEW* (1934)

History, n. An account mostly false, of events mostly unimportant, which are brought about by rulers mostly knaves, and soldiers mostly fools.

—AMBROSE BIERCE, FROM HIS BOOK *THE DEVIL'S DICTIONARY* (1911)

History is the record of what one age finds worthy of note in another.

—JACOB BURCKHARDT

The main work of the historian is not to record, but to evaluate; for, if he does not evaluate, how can he know what is worth recording?

—EDWARD HALLETT CARR, FROM HIS BOOK *WHAT IS HISTORY?* (1961)

Tyrants seem willing to allow the crimes of their predecessors to be transmitted to posterity, to divert attention from the horror that they themselves inspire. In fact there is no longer any way to console the people except by teaching them that their forebears were as wretched as they are, or more so.

—NICOLAS CHAMFORT, FROM HIS BOOK *MAXIMS AND THOUGHTS* (1796)

Historians . . . are the guardians of mankind's collective memory.

—PIETER GEYL, FROM HIS BOOK *DEBATES WITH HISTORIANS* (1955)

History . . . is, indeed, little more than the register of the crimes, follies, and misfortunes of mankind.

—EDWARD GIBBON, FROM HIS WORK *THE DECLINE AND FALL OF THE ROMAN EMPIRE* (1776–1778)

History repeats itself. Historians repeat each other.

—PHILIP GUEDALLA, FROM HIS BOOK *SUPERS AND SUPERMEN* (1920)

History is not contained in thick books but lives in our very blood.

—CARL JUNG, FROM HIS BOOK *CIVILIZATION IN TRANSITION* (1964)

The time is not come for impartial history. If the truth were told just now, it would not be credited.

—ROBERT E. LEE

A sound rule of historical evidence is that while assertions should be treated with critical doubt, admissions are likely to be reliable.

—B. H. LIDDELL HART

Few learn much from history who do not bring much with them to its study.

—JOHN STUART MILL, FROM HIS BOOK *THE SUBJECTION OF WOMEN* (1869)

1. Whom the gods destroy, they first make mad with power.
2. The mills of God grind slowly, yet they grind exceedingly small.
3. The bee fertilizes the flower it robs.
4. When it is dark enough, you can see all the stars.

—CHARLES A. BEARD, HISTORIAN, WHEN ASKED IF HE COULD
SUMMARIZE THE LESSONS OF HISTORY IN A SHORT BOOK (HE SAID HE
COULD DO IT IN FOUR SENTENCES)

I love studying Ancient History and seeing how empires rise and fall, sowing the seeds of their own destruction.

—MARTIN SCORSESE

During the Depression, or back when we were fighting Hitler, people didn't have time to sue a company if the coffee was too hot. There were urgent, pressing problems. If you think you have it tough, read history books.

—BILL MAHER

Today our knowledge of the past is increasing at an unprecedented rate, and this at both ends of its ever lengthening vista. The archaeologists are making history by exhuming buried and forgotten civilizations as fast as the politicians are making it by taking new action for contemporary historians to study.

—Arnold J. Toynbee, as quoted in *The Teacher and the Taught* (1963)

History is Philosophy teaching by examples.

—Thucydides

History is a vast early warning system.

—Norman Cousins

The concept of history implies the scholar and the reader. Without a generation of civilized people to study history, to preserve its records, to absorb its lessons and relate them to its own problems, history, too, would lose its meaning.

—GEORGE F. KENNAN

What the historian is called on to investigate is what lies behind the act; and to this the conscious thought of motive of the individual actor may be quite irrelevant.

—EDWARD HALLETT CARR, FROM HIS BOOK *WHAT IS HISTORY?* (1961)

CHAPTER ELEVEN

Fundamental Elements

Thought: an idea in transition.

—Pythagoras

One thought fills immensity.

—William Blake

We think too small. Like the frog at the bottom of the well. He thinks the sky is only as big as the top of the well. If he surfaced, he would have an entirely different view.

—Mao Tse-Tung

Thought is the strongest thing we have. Work done by true and profound thought—that is a real force.

—Albert Schweitzer

Anything one man can imagine, other men can make real.

—JULES VERNE

Dream lofty dreams, and as you dream, so shall you become. Your Vision is the promise of what you shall one day be. Your Ideal is the prophecy of what you shall at last unveil.

—JAMES ALLEN

If you can dream it, you can do it.

—WALT DISNEY

Whether you think you can or think you can't—you are right.

—HENRY FORD

I have the unlimited capacity to not know what can't be done.

—Dr. Larry Lezotte

⟨⟨◆⟩⟩

What was once thought can never be unthought.

—Friedrich Dürrenmatt

⟨⟨◆⟩⟩

There are two distinct classes of what are called thoughts: those that we produce in ourselves by reflection and the act of thinking and those that bolt into the mind of their own accord.

—Thomas Paine

⟨⟨◆⟩⟩

I have great belief in the fact that whenever there is chaos, it creates wonderful thinking. I consider chaos a gift.

—Septima Poinsette Clark, American educator and civil rights activist

⟨⟨◆⟩⟩

The thoughts that come often unsought, and, as it were, drop into the mind, are commonly the most valuable of any we have.

—JOHN LOCKE

To be conscious that we are perceiving and thinking is to be conscious of our own existence.

—ARISTOTLE

I think therefore I am.

—RENÉ DESCARTES, FROM HIS BOOK *DISCOURSE ON METHOD* (1637)

They can because they think they can.

—VIRGIL

Our life is shaped by our mind; we become what we think. Suffering follows an evil thought as the wheels of a cart follow the oxen that draws it.
Our life is shaped by our mind; we become what we think. Joy follows a pure thought like a shadow that never leaves.

—Buddha

Great minds have purposes; others have wishes. Little minds are tamed and subdued by misfortune; but great minds rise above them.

—Washington Irving

Inspiration is the impact of a fact on a well-prepared mind.

—Louis Pasteur

Nurture your minds with great thoughts. To believe in the heroic makes heroes.

—BENJAMIN DISRAELI

Thinking is a momentary dismissal of irrelevancies.

—BUCKMINSTER FULLER

One must live the way one thinks or end up thinking the way one lives.

—PAUL BOURGET

Language is the dress of thought.

—SAMUEL JOHNSON

But words are things, and a small drop of ink
Falling like dew upon a thought, produces
That which makes thousands, perhaps millions, think.

—Sir Aubrey De Vere, Irish poet

Language is the close-fitting dress of Thought.

—R. C. Trench, Anglican archbishop and poet

Folks that blurt out just what they think wouldn't be so bad
if they thought.

—Kin Hubbard

Some people say it is better to appear foolish than open your mouth and
remove all doubt. I say if it is already thought then you have nothing to lose.

—Dane Helmers

I'm not trying to be something that I'm not. I'm just trying to be myself and talk about what I know, and admit what I don't know.

—ANDERSON COOPER

When you open your mouth to speak, you reveal a great deal. The words you use and the way you speak are like a blueprint of who you are deep inside.

—ROBERT K. DELLENBACH, MORMON LEADER

The less men think, the more they talk.

—BARON DE MONTESQUIEU

Every man who says frankly and fully what he thinks is doing a public service.

—LESLIE STEPHEN

Words without thoughts never to heaven go.

—WILLIAM SHAKESPEARE

Many a time I have wanted to stop talking and find out what I really believed.

—WALTER LIPPMANN

Speaking without thinking is shooting without taking aim.

—SPANISH PROVERB

Men use thought only to justify their wrongdoings, and speech only to conceal their thoughts.

> —VOLTAIRE

The purpose of a liberal education is to make one's mind a pleasant place to spend one's leisure.

> —ANONYMOUS

Thought is the labor of the intellect; reverie is its pleasure.

> —VICTOR HUGO

What I'm concerned about is the people who don't dwell on the meaninglessness of their lives, or the meaningfulness of it—who just pursue mindless entertainment.

> —MICHAEL K. HOOKER, AS QUOTED IN THE *CHRISTIAN SCIENCE MONITOR* (1986)

The only big ideas I've ever had have come from daydreaming, but modern life keeps people from daydreaming. Every moment of the day your mind is being occupied, controlled, by someone else—at school, at work, watching television.

—PAUL MACCREADY

Man's mind, once stretched by a new idea, never regains its original dimensions.

—OLIVER WENDELL HOLMES

You are searching for the magic key that will unlock the door to the source of power; and yet you have the key in your own hands, and you may make use of it the moment you learn to control your thoughts.

—NAPOLEON HILL

Knowing others is intelligence; knowing yourself is true wisdom.
Mastering others is strength; mastering yourself is true power.

—LAO-TZU

It is not worth an intelligent man's time to be in the majority.
By definition, there are already enough people to do that.

—G. H. HARDY, ENGLISH MATHEMATICIAN

Knowledge is power. Unfortunate dupes of this saying will keep on
reading, ambitiously, till they have stunned their native initiative,
and made their thoughts weak.

—CLARENCE DAY

In order to improve the mind, we ought less to learn than to contemplate.

—RENÉ DESCARTES

To arrive at the simplest truth requires years of contemplation.

—ISAAC NEWTON

Three minutes' thought would suffice to find this out; but thought is irksome and three minutes is a long time.

—A. E. HOUSEMAN

The extra calories needed for one hour of intense mental effort would be completely met by eating one oyster cracker or one half of a salted peanut.

–FRANCIS C. BENEDICT

We shall succeed only so far as we continue that most distasteful of all activity, the intolerable labor of thought.

—LEARNED HAND

When you appeal to the highest level of thinking, you get the highest level of performance.

—JACK STACK

When thought becomes excessively painful, action is the finest remedy.

—SALMAN RUSHDIE

There is no expedient to which a man will not go to avoid the labor of thinking.

—THOMAS EDISON

Action springs not from thought, but from a readiness for responsibility.

—DIETRICH BONHOEFFER, GERMAN THEOLOGIAN

Think like a man of action, act like a man of thought.

—HENRI BERGSON

Strength of mind is exercise, not rest.

—ALEXANDER POPE

Difficulties, by bracing the mind to overcome them, assist cheerfulness, as exercise assists digestion.

—CHRISTIAN NESTELL BOVEE

A man of action forced into a state of thought is unhappy until he can get out of it.

—JOHN GALSWORTHY

A man is not idle because he is absorbed in thought. There is a visible labor and there is an invisible labor.

—Victor Hugo

We bring forth weeds when our quick minds lie still.

—William Shakespeare

Curiosity is one of the most permanent and certain characteristics of a vigorous mind.

—Samuel Johnson

Learning without thought is labor lost; thought without learning is perilous.

—Confucius

Delightful task! To rear the tender thought,
To teach the young idea how to shoot.

—JAMES THOMSON

In a child's lunchbox, a mother's thoughts.

—JAPANESE PROVERB

I am beginning to suspect all elaborate and special systems of education. They seem to me to be built up on the supposition that every child is a kind of idiot who must be taught to think.

—ANNE SULLIVAN, TUTOR TO HELEN KELLER

He has to be taught to think, to understand, to integrate, to prove. He has to be taught the essentials of the knowledge discovered in the past—and he has to be equipped to acquire further knowledge by his own effort.

—AYN RAND

The aim of education should be to teach us rather how to think, than what to think, rather to improve our minds, so as to enable us to think for ourselves, than to load the memory with the thoughts of other men.

—JAMES BEATTIE

Think wrongly, if you please, but in all cases think for yourself.

—DORIS LESSING

Where all think alike, no one thinks very much.

—WALTER LIPPMANN

To think is to differ.

—CLARENCE DARROW

There are two ways to slide easily through life: to believe everything or to doubt everything. Both ways save us from thinking.

—ALFRED KORZYBSKI

Obvious thinking commonly leads to wrong judgments and wrong conclusions.

—HUMPHREY B. NEIL

New opinions are always suspected, and usually opposed, without any other reason but because they are not already common.

—JOHN LOCKE

It is easy to spot an informed man—his opinions are just like your own.

—MIGUEL DE UNAMUNO, SPANISH WRITER AND PHILOSOPHER

An amazing thing, the human brain. Capable of understanding incredibly complex and intricate concepts. Yet at times unable to recognize the obvious and simple.

—JAY ABRAHAM

Sometimes I'm confused by what I think is really obvious. But what I think is really obvious obviously isn't obvious.

—MICHAEL STIPE, SINGER OF ROCK BAND R.E.M.

What one doesn't understand one doesn't possess.

—JOHANN WOLFGANG VON GOETHE, FROM HIS BOOK *ART AND ANTIQUITY* (1821)

An object in possession seldom contains the same charm that it had in pursuit.

—PLINY THE YOUNGER

We find it hard to believe that other people's thoughts are as silly as our own, but they probably are.

—JAMES HARVEY ROBINSON

Thinking is like loving or dying—each of us must do it for himself.

—JOSIAH ROYCE

The efficient man is the man who thinks for himself, and is capable of thinking hard and long.

—CHARLES W. ELIOT, FORMER PRESIDENT OF HARVARD UNIVERSITY

A great many people mistake opinions for thoughts.

—HERBERT PROCHNOW, AMERICAN BANKING EXECUTIVE AND AUTHOR

The fundamental fact about the Greek was that he had to use his mind. The ancient priests had said, "Thus far and no farther. We set the limits of thought." The Greek said, "All things are to be examined and called into question. There are no limits set on thought."

—EDITH HAMILTON

If you don't think, you will sink.

—V. VENKATACHALM

Data, data, everywhere, but not a thought to think.

—THEODORE ROSZAK

It is possible to store the mind with a million facts and still be entirely uneducated.

—ALEC BOURNE

Facts do not interest me much. Facts are for accountants. Truth creates illumination.

—WERNER HERZOG

Facts in books, statistics in encyclopedias, the ability to use them in men's heads.

—FOGG BRACKELL

Unobstructed access to facts can produce unlimited good only if it is matched by the desire and ability to find out what they mean and where they lead.

—NORMAN COUSINS

In the spider-web of facts, many a truth is strangled.

—PAUL ELDRIDGE

Man is a slow, sloppy, and brilliant thinker; the machine is fast, accurate, and stupid.

—WILLIAM M. KELLY

Thought is born of failure.

—LANCELOT LAW WHYTE

As surgeons keep their instruments and knives always at hand for cases requiring immediate treatment, so shouldst thou have thy thoughts ready to understand things divine and human, remembering in thy every act, even the smallest, how close is the bond that unites the two.

—MARCUS AURELIUS

Intellect distinguishes between the possible and the impossible; reason distinguishes between the sensible and the senseless. Even the possible can be senseless.

—MAX BORN

Intelligence is derived from two words—*inter* and *legere*—inter meaning "between" and legere meaning "to choose." An intelligent person, therefore, is one who has learned "to choose between." He knows that good is better than evil . . . and that truth has more virtue than ignorance.

—J. Martin Klotsche

Do not judge my intelligence by the answers I give, but instead by the questions I ask.

—Mark McGranaghan

Questions are creative acts of intelligence.

—Frank Kingdon

We are faced with the paradoxical fact that education has become one of the chief obstacles to intelligence and freedom of thought.

—Bertrand A. Russell

Many highly intelligent people are poor thinkers. Many people of average intelligence are skilled thinkers. The power of a car is separate from the way the car is driven.

—EDWARD DE BONO

It has always seemed strange to me that in our endless discussions about education so little stress is laid on the pleasure of becoming an educated person, the enormous interest it adds to life. To be able to be caught up into the world of thought—that is to be educated.

—EDITH HAMILTON

Intelligence is quickness in seeing things as they are.

—GEORGE SANTAYANA

The test of a first-rate intelligence is the ability to hold two opposed ideas in the mind at the same time, and still retain the ability to function.

One should, for example, be able to see that things are hopeless and yet be determined to make them otherwise.

—F. Scott Fitzgerald, from "The Crack-Up," *Esquire* (February 1936)

He who learns but does not think is lost! He who thinks but does not learn is in great danger.

—Confucius

Man is ready to die for an idea, provided that idea is not quite clear to him.

—Paul Eldridge

Nothing contributes so much to tranquilize the mind as a steady purpose—a point to which the soul may fix its intellectual eye.

—Mary Shelley

Intelligence alone, without wisdom and empathy for suffering, is hollow.

—JOHN G. STOESSINGER, FROM HIS BOOK *WHY NATIONS GO TO WAR* (1974)

<hr>

Intelligent people are allus on th' unpop'lar side of anything.

—KIN HUBBARD, FROM HIS BOOK *ABE MARTIN HOSS SENSE AND NONSENSE* (1926)

<hr>

A warrior of light who trusts too much in his intelligence will end up underestimating the power of his opponent.

—PAULO COELHO

<hr>

Of work comes knowledge, of knowledge comes fruitful work; of the union of knowledge and work comes the development of intelligence.

—VINOBA BHAVE, FROM THE PRELUDE TO *THOUGHTS ON EDUCATION* (1964)

<hr>

Knowledge itself is power.

—FRANCIS BACON, FROM "*DE HAERESIBUS*," *MEDITATIONES SACRAE* (1597)

Knowledge is pleasure as well as power.

—WILLIAM HAZLITT, FROM "ON IMITATION," *THE ROUND TABLE* (1817)

Somewhere, something incredible is waiting to be known.

—CARL SAGAN

In spiritual matters, knowledge is dependent upon being; as we are, so we know.

—ALDOUS HUXLEY

We are here and now. Further than that, all knowledge is moonshine.

—H. L. MENCKEN

Knowledge is seeing the oneness of the Self with God.

—SRIMAD BHAGAVATAM

The knowledge of sin is the beginning of salvation.

—EPICURUS

When you eat of the fruit of the tree your eyes will be opened, and you will be like God, knowing good and evil.

—GENESIS 2:17, IN REFERENCE TO "THE TREE OF THE KNOWLEDGE OF GOOD AND EVIL"

Knowledge is the true organ of sight, not the eyes.

—Panchatantra, originally a canonical collection of Sanskrit and Pali (Buddhist) animal fables in verse and prose (c. 200 b.c.e.)

The real voyage of discovery consists not in seeking new landscapes but in having new eyes.

—Marcel Proust

All our knowledge has its origins in our perceptions.

—Leonardo da Vinci

We have a hunger of the mind which asks for knowledge of all around us, and the more we gain, the more is our desire; the more we see, the more we are capable of seeing.

—Maria Mitchell

Knowledge is the eye of desire and can become the pilot of the soul.

—WILL DURANT

Knowledge without conscience is but the ruin of the soul.

—RABELAIS, FROM HIS BOOK *GARGANTUA AND PANTAGRUEL* (1532–1552)

And what, Socrates, is the food of the soul? Surely, I said, knowledge is the food of the soul.

—PLATO, FROM HIS BOOK *PROTAGORAS* (380 B.C.E.)

I imagine, therefore I belong and am free.

—LAWRENCE DURRELL

Imagination will often carry us to worlds that never were. But without it we go nowhere.

—CARL SAGAN

Imagination . . . its limits are only those of the mind itself.

—ROD SERLING

The sorcery and charm of imagination, and the power it gives to the individual to transform his world into a new world of order and delight, makes it one of the most treasured of all human capacities.

—FRANK BARRON

Imagination disposes of everything; it creates beauty, justice, and happiness, which are everything in this world.

—BLAISE PASCAL

What a glorious gift is imagination, and what satisfaction it affords!

> —THOMAS MANN, FROM HIS BOOK *CONFESSIONS OF FELIX KRULL,*
> *CONFIDENCE MAN* (1954)

I believe that imagination is stronger than knowledge—
That myth is more potent than history.
I believe that dreams are more powerful than facts—
That hope always triumphs over experience—
That laughter is the cure for grief.
And I believe that love is stronger than death.

> —ROBERT FULGHUM, ESSAYIST AND AUTHOR OF *ALL I REALLY NEED*
> *TO KNOW I LEARNED IN KINDERGARTEN* (1988)

Nothing is more powerful and liberating than knowledge.

> —WILLIAM H. GRAY III, FORMER CONGRESSMAN AND EXECUTIVE
> OF THE UNITED NEGRO COLLEGE FUND

Every great advance in natural knowledge has involved the absolute rejection of authority.

—Thomas Huxley

Resisting conformity and developing some small eccentricities are among the steps to independence and self-confidence.

—A. L. McGinnis

Knowledge is the antidote to fear.

—Ralph Waldo Emerson

Know the enemy and know yourself; in a hundred battles you will never peril.

—Sun Tzu

If you would perfect your body, guard your mind.

—JAMES ALLEN

The mind is more vulnerable than the stomach, because it can be poisoned without feeling immediate pain.

—HELEN MACINNES

More than those who hate you, more than all your enemies, an undisciplined mind does greater harm.

—BUDDHA

The more you know, the less sure you are.

—VOLTAIRE

Sometimes, we just don't know enough about what we are trying to achieve.

—STUART WILDE

———◆———

He who does not know one thing knows another.

—KENYAN PROVERB

———◆———

It is one thing to know one thing and another thing to know another thing.

—A. R. AMMONS

———◆———

When you know a thing, to hold that you know it and when you do not know a thing, to allow that you do not know it—this is knowledge.

—CONFUCIUS

———◆———

Wonder is the desire for knowledge.

—St. Thomas Aquinas

———◆———

As I learned in later life, one passes insensibly from thoughtless certainties to the knowledge that little if anything is certain.

—Paula Fox, from her book *A Servant's Tale*

———◆———

I alone know that I know nothing.

—Democritus

———◆———

As knowledge increases, wonder deepens.

—Charles Morgan

———◆———

Wonder, rather than doubt, is the root of knowledge.

—ABRAHAM JOSHUA HESCHEL, FROM HIS BOOK *MAN IS NOT ALONE* (1951)

The possession of knowledge does not kill the sense of wonder and mystery. There is always more mystery.

—ANAÏS NIN

As we acquire more knowledge, things do not become more comprehensible, but more mysterious.

—ALBERT SCHWEITZER

Be curious always, for knowledge will not acquire you. You must acquire it.

—SUDIE BACK

If it be urged that some men have such weak intellects that it is not possible for them to acquire knowledge, I answer that it is scarcely possible to find a mirror so dulled that it will not reflect images of some kind, or for a tablet to have such a rough surface that nothing can be inscribed on it.

—JOHN AMOS COMENIUS

People go into exile for want of knowledge.

—ISAIAH 5:13

Our knowledge is a little island in a great ocean of non-knowledge.

—ISAAC BASHEVIS SINGER, IN AN INTERVIEW WITH RICHARD BURGIN IN *THE NEW YORK TIMES MAGAZINE* (DECEMBER 3, 1978)

We're drowning in information and starving for knowledge.

—RUTHERFORD ROGERS

You don't drown by falling in the water. You drown by staying there.

—ANONYMOUS

You can swim all day in the Sea of Knowledge and still come out completely dry. Most people do.

—NORMAN JUSTER, AUTHOR OF *THE PHANTOM TOLLBOOTH* (1988)

Some students drink at the fountain of knowledge. Others just gargle.

—E. C. McKENZIE, AUTHOR OF FOURTEEN BOOKS, INCLUDING *MIXED NUTS*

In your thirst for knowledge, be sure not to drown in all the information.

—ANTHONY J. D'ANGELO, FROM HIS BOOK *THE COLLEGE BLUE BOOK* (1995)

Knowledge is a sacred cow, and my problem will be how we can milk her while keeping clear of her horns.

—ALBERT SZENT-GYÖRGYI, FROM "TEACHING AND EXPANDING KNOWLEDGE," *SCIENCE* (1964)

All our knowledge merely helps us to die a more painful death than animals that know nothing.

—MAURICE MAETERLINCK, BELGIAN NOBEL LAUREATE

If we value the pursuit of knowledge, we must be free to follow wherever that search may lead us.

—ADLAI E. STEVENSON, IN A SPEECH AT THE UNIVERSITY OF WISCONSIN, MADISON, 1952

Gold miners mine gold. As a student, mine knowledge.

—IBRAHIM HENA

If we would have new knowledge, we must get a whole world of new questions.

—Susanne K. Langer

Seek knowledge from the cradle to the grave.

—Muhammad

You don't have to be great to start, but you have to start to be great.

—Zig Ziglar

You have to think big to be big.

—Claude M. Bristol

As your body grows bigger
Your mind must flower
It's great to learn
'Cause knowledge is power.

> —TOM YOHE, FROM ABC'S SATURDAY MORNING PUBLIC-SERVICE
> CAMPAIGN, "SCHOOLHOUSE ROCK"

Knowledge is a comfortable and necessary retreat and shelter for us in
an advanced age; and if we do not plant it while young, it will give us
no shade when we grow old.

> —LORD CHESTERFIELD

A complacent satisfaction with present knowledge is the chief bar to the
pursuit of knowledge.

> —B. H. LIDDELL HART, FROM HIS BOOK *THE GHOST OF NAPOLEON* (1933)

Knowledge is not simply another commodity. On the contrary. Knowledge is never used up. It increases by the diffusion and grows by the dispersion.

—DANIEL J. BOORSTIN, TO THE HOUSE APPROPRIATIONS SUBCOMMITTEE, AS QUOTED IN THE *NEW YORK TIMES* (1986)

Knowledge rests on knowledge; what is new is meaningful because it departs slightly from what was known before.

—ROBERT OPPENHEIMER

It is good to rub and polish our brains against that of others.

—MICHEL DE MONTAIGNE

Depend on it there comes a time when for every addition of knowledge you forget something that you knew before. It is of the highest importance, therefore, not to have useless facts elbowing out the useful ones.

—SIR ARTHUR CONAN DOYLE, FROM HIS BOOK *A STUDY IN SCARLET* (1888)

Our minds thus grow in spots; and like grease spots, the spots spread. But we let them spread as little as possible: we keep unaltered as much of our old knowledge, as many of our old prejudices and beliefs, as we can.

—JAMES TRUSLOW ADAMS

In the practical use of our intellect, forgetting is as important as remembering.

—WILLIAM JAMES

The difficulty lies, not in the new ideas, but in escaping the old ones, which ramify, for those brought up as most of us have been, into every corner of our minds.

—JOHN MAYNARD KEYNES

If there is anything more dangerous to the life of the mind than having no independent commitment to ideas, it is having an excess of commitment to some special and constricting idea.

—RICHARD HOFSTADTER

The best way to have a good idea is to have lots of ideas.

—LINUS PAULING

Any piece of knowledge I acquire today has a value at this moment exactly proportioned to my skill to deal with it. Tomorrow, when I know more, I recall that piece of knowledge and use it better.

—MARK VAN DOREN

I must be vigilant every day, lest I lose one fragile opportunity to improve tomorrow.

—Ivan Welton Fitzwater

⎯⬦⎯

The power of concentration is the only key to the treasure-house of knowledge.

—Swami Vivekananda

⎯⬦⎯

If a man empties his purse into his head, no man can take it away from him. An investment in knowledge always pays the best interest.

—Benjamin Franklin

⎯⬦⎯

One must spend time in gathering knowledge to give it out richly.

—Edward C. Steadman

⎯⬦⎯

Knowledge Is Money.

—JOHN R. HAYES, ARTICLE TITLE, *FORBES* (FEBRUARY 13, 1995)

If money is your hope for independence you will never have it. The only real security that a man will have in this world is a reserve of knowledge, experience, and ability.

—HENRY FORD

Knowledge . . . serves as a wealth and force multiplier. It can be used to augment the available force or wealth, or alternately, to reduce the amount needed to achieve any given purpose. In either case, it increases efficiency, permitting one to spend fewer power "chips" in any showdown.

—ALVIN TOFFLER, FROM HIS BOOK *POWERSHIFT: KNOWLEDGE, WEALTH, AND VIOLENCE AT THE EDGE OF THE 21ST CENTURY* (1990)

Your earning ability today is largely dependent upon your knowledge, skill, and your ability to combine that knowledge and skill in such a way that you contribute value for which customers are going to pay.

—BRIAN TRACY, MOTIVATIONAL COACH AND AUTHOR

———⟫◆⟪———

That we can comprehend the little we know already is mind-boggling in itself.

—TOM GATES

———⟫◆⟪———

Knowledge is of no value unless you put it into practice.

—ANTON CHEKHOV

———⟫◆⟪———

We are what we repeatedly do. Excellence, then, is not an act, but a habit.

—ARISTOTLE

———⟫◆⟪———

Knowledge generation really only occurs in teams where people engage in doing meaningful work.

—PAUL SENGE, AUTHOR OF *THE DANCE OF CHANGE* (1999)

The difference between a successful person and others is not a lack of strength, not a lack of knowledge, but rather in a lack of will.

—VINCE LOMBARDI

In the fields of observation, chance favors only the prepared mind.

—LOUIS PASTEUR

The great end of life is not knowledge but action.

—THOMAS HUXLEY

Let no one be deluded that a knowledge of the path can substitute for putting one foot in front of the other.

—MARY C. RICHARDS

It is a great nuisance that knowledge can be acquired only by hard work.

—W. SOMERSET MAUGHAM

Knowledge must come through action; you can have no test which is not fanciful, save by trial.

—SOPHOCLES

Knowledge of the universe would somehow be . . . defective were no practical results to follow.

—CICERO

Action is the proper Fruit of Knowledge.

—THOMAS FULLER

⸺◆⸺

You have first an instinct, then an opinion, then a knowledge, as the plant has root, bud, and fruit.

—RALPH WALDO EMERSON

⸺◆⸺

Practice, knowledge, again practice, and again knowledge. This form repeats itself in endless cycles, and with each cycle the content of practice and knowledge rises to a higher level.

—MAO TSE-TUNG

⸺◆⸺

The secret of joy in work is contained in one word—excellence. To know how to do something well is to enjoy it.

—PEARL S. BUCK, FROM HER BOOK *THE JOY OF CHILDREN* (1964)

⸺◆⸺

I have come to believe that the whole world is an enigma, a harmless
enigma that is made terrible by our own mad attempt to interpret it
as though it had an underlying truth.

—UMBERTO ECO

How dreadful knowledge of the truth can be
When there's no help in truth!

—SOPHOCLES

If what you seek is Truth, there is one thing you must have above all else
. . . an unremitting readiness to admit you may be wrong.

—ANTHONY DE MELLO

No man's knowledge here can go beyond his experience.

—JOHN LOCKE, FROM *AN ESSAY CONCERNING HUMAN
UNDERSTANDING* (1690)

Knowledge is haunted by the ghost of past opinion.

—ANONYMOUS

If a little knowledge is dangerous, where is the man who has so much as to be out of danger?

—THOMAS HUXLEY, FROM HIS STUDY "ON ELEMENTARY INSTRUCTION IN PHYSIOLOGY" (1877)

Know or listen to those who know.

—BALTASAR GRACIÁN

Most of our positive knowledge has passed through a filter devised to eliminate those aspects of experience that reveal autonomous and purposeful activities, not characteristic of purely physical systems.

—LEWIS MUMFORD

The only Fence against the World is a thorough Knowledge of it.

—JOHN LOCKE, FROM HIS BOOK *SOME THOUGHTS CONCERNING EDUCATION AND OF THE CONDUCT OF THE UNDERSTANDING* (1693)

An Indian has his knowledge for use, and it only appears in use. Most white men that we know have theirs for talking purposes.

—RALPH WALDO EMERSON

The Red Indian acquires the swiftness and agility which make him a successful hunter, by the actual pursuit of animals.

—HERBERT SPENCER

To know that we know what we know, and that we do not know what we do not know, that is true knowledge.

—CONFUCIUS

I respect faith, but doubt is what gets you an education.

—WILSON MIZNER, AS QUOTED BY ALVA JOHNSTON IN *THE LEGENDARY MIZNERS* (1953)

———

A belief constantly inculcated during the early years of life, while the brain is impressible, appears to acquire almost the nature of an instinct; and the very essence of an instinct is that it is followed independently of reason.

—CHARLES DARWIN, FROM HIS BOOK *THE DESCENT OF MAN AND SELECTION IN RELATION TO SEX* (1874)

———

You can't convince a believer of anything; for their belief is not based on evidence, it's based on a deep-seated need to believe.

—CARL SAGAN

———

Begin challenging your own assumptions. Your assumptions are your windows on the world. Scrub them off every once in awhile, or the light won't come in.

—ALAN ALDA

Blessed are the hearts that can bend; they shall never be broken.

—ALBERT CAMUS

Bodily exercise, when compulsory, does no harm to the body; but knowledge which is acquired under compulsion obtains no hold on the mind.

—PLATO

As long as the acquisition of knowledge is rendered habitually repugnant, so long will there be a prevailing tendency to discontinue it when free from the coercion of parents and masters.

—HERBERT SPENCER

The acquisition of knowledge for which no use can be found is a sure method of driving a man to revolt.

—GUSTAVE LE BON, FROM HIS BOOK *THE CROWD* (1895)

Acquire knowledge. It enables its possessor to distinguish right from wrong; it lights the way to Heaven; it is our friend in the desert, our society in solitude, our companion when friendless; it guides us to happiness; it sustains us in misery; it is an ornament among friends and an armor against enemies.

—MUHAMMAD

We know of our own knowledge that we are human beings, and, as such, imperfect. But we are bathed by the communications industry in a ceaseless tide of inhuman, impossible perfection.

—MARGARET HALSEY

Someday, in the distant future, our grandchildren's grandchildren will develop a new equivalent of our classrooms. They will spend many hours in front of boxes with fires glowing within. May they have the wisdom to know the difference between light and knowledge.

—PLATO

A strong argument that men's knowledge antedates their birth is the fact that mere children, in studying difficult subjects, so quickly lay hold upon innumerable things that they seem not to be . . . learning . . . for the first time, but to be recalling.

—CICERO

The aim of education is the knowledge, not of facts, but of values.

—WILLIAM RALPH INGE

Those who have the answer have misunderstood the question.

—ANONYMOUS

Knowledge—that is, education in its true sense—is our best protection against unreasoning prejudice and panic-making fear, whether engendered by special interest, illiberal minorities, or panic-stricken leaders.

—FRANKLIN DELANO ROOSEVELT

Knowledge is the best eraser in the world for disharmony, distrust, despair, and the endless physical deficiencies of man.

—ORLANDO A. BATTISTA

Some men covet knowledge out of a natural curiosity and inquisitive temper; some to entertain the mind with variety and delight; some for ornament and reputation; some for victory and contention; many for lucre and a livelihood; and but few for employing the Divine gift of reason to the use and benefit of mankind.

—FRANCIS BACON, FROM HIS BOOK *ADVANCEMENT OF LEARNING* (1605)

We owe almost all our knowledge not to those who have agreed, but to those who have differed.

—CHARLES CALEB COLTON

Knowledge is of two kinds. We know a subject ourselves, or we know where we can find information upon it.

—SAMUEL JOHNSON

Research, as the college student will come to know it, is relatively thorough investigation, primarily in libraries, of a properly limited topic, and presentation of the results of this investigation in a carefully organized and documented paper of some length.

—CECIL B. WILLIAMS AND ALAN H. STEVENSON

There is no other source of knowledge but the intellectual manipulation of carefully verified observations—in fact, what is called research . . . and no knowledge can be obtained from revelation, intuition, or inspiration.

—SIGMUND FREUD, FROM HIS BOOK *NEW INTRODUCTORY LECTURES IN PSYCHOANALYSIS* (1933)

What is research, but a blind date with knowledge?

—WILL HENRY

A love affair with knowledge will never end in heartbreak.

—MICHAEL GARRETT MARINO

True knowledge leads to love.

—WILLIAM WORDSWORTH, FROM HIS POEM "LINES LEFT UPON A SEAT IN A YEW-TREE" (1798)

Love looks not with the eyes, but with the mind;
And therefore is winged Cupid painted blind.

—WILLIAM SHAKESPEARE

Life is indeed darkness save when there is urge,
And all urge is blind save when there is knowledge,
And all knowledge is vain save when there is work,
And all work is empty save when there is love.

—KHALIL GIBRAN, FROM HIS BOOK THE PROPHET (1923)

An age is called Dark not because the light fails to shine, but because people refuse to see it.

—JAMES A. MICHENER

We think much less than what we know. We know much less than what we love. We love much less than what there is. And to this precise extent, we are much less than what we are.

—R. D. LAING

A loving heart is the beginning of all Knowledge.

—ANONYMOUS

Go to your bosom: Knock there, and ask your heart what it doth know.

—WILLIAM SHAKESPEARE

As our knowledge is converted to wisdom, the door to opportunity is unlocked.

—BARBARA W. WINDER

Knowledge speaks, but wisdom listens.

—JIMI HENDRIX

—⬦—

The biggest difficulty with mankind today is that our knowledge has increased so much faster than our wisdom.

—FRANK WHITMORE

—⬦—

Philosophy I have I digested,
The whole of Law and Medicine,
From each its secrets I have wrested,
Theology, alas, thrown in.
Poor fool, with all this sweated lore,
I stand no wiser than I was before.

—JOHANN WOLFGANG VON GOETHE, FROM HIS BOOK
   FAUST (1808–1832)

—⬦—

Knowledge is the measure of the man. By how much we know, so much we are.

—RALPH WALDO EMERSON, AS QUOTED IN *THE COMPLETE WORKS OF RALPH WALDO EMERSON* (1893)

Desire is a treasure map. Knowledge is the treasure chest. Wisdom is the jewel. Yet without action they all stay buried. Hope is the pillar that holds up the world.

—PLINY THE ELDER

If facts are the seeds that later produce knowledge and wisdom, then the emotions and the impressions of the senses are the fertile soil in which the seeds must grow.

—RACHEL CARSON, AMERICAN MARINE BIOLOGIST AND AUTHOR OF *SILENT SPRING*

Knowledge is learning something every day. Wisdom is letting go of something every day.

—ANONYMOUS

In much wisdom is much grief; and he that increaseth knowledge increaseth sorrow.

—ECCLESIASTES 1:18

Knowledge is a process of piling up facts; wisdom lies in their simplification.

—MARTIN LUTHER KING, JR.

We can be Knowledgeable with other men's knowledge, but we cannot be wise with other men's wisdom.

—MICHEL DE MONTAIGNE

Knowledge comes, but wisdom lingers.

—ALFRED LORD TENNYSON

These days people seek knowledge, not wisdom. Knowledge is of the past, wisdom is of the future.

—VERNON COOPER

The beginning of wisdom is to call things by their rightful names.

—THOMAS JEFFERSON

Wisdom begins at the end.

—DANIEL WEBSTER

It is good even for old men to learn wisdom.

—AESCHYLUS, FROM *FRAGMENTS*

The wisdom of the wise and the experience of the ages are perpetuated in quotations.

—BENJAMIN DISRAELI

Lessons of wisdom have the most power over us when they capture the heart through the groundwork of a story, which engages the passions.

—LAURENCE STERNE

So teach us to number our days, that we may apply our hearts unto wisdom.

—PSALMS 90:12

There is a wisdom of the head, and . . . a wisdom of the heart.

—CHARLES DICKENS

Never does nature say one thing and wisdom another.

—JUVENAL, FROM HIS BOOK *THE SATIRES*

Do not seek to follow in the footsteps of the wise. Seek what they sought.

—MATSUO BASHO

There are two things to aim at in life; first to get what you want, and after that to enjoy it. Only the wisest of mankind has achieved the second.

—LOGAN PEARSALL SMITH

We don't receive wisdom; we must discover it for ourselves after a journey that no one can take us or spare us.

—MARCEL PROUST

A gauge for wisdom: the growth of wisdom may be gauged exactly by the diminution of ill-temper.

—FRIEDRICH NIETZSCHE

The awakened sages call a person wise when all his undertakings are free from anxiety about results.

—KRISHNA

Good people are good because they've come to wisdom through failure.

—WILLIAM SAROYAN

The art of being wise is the art of knowing what to overlook.

—WILLIAM JAMES

Wisdom is as the moon rises, perceptible not in progress but in result.

—CHINESE PROVERB

Nurture your minds with great thoughts, for you will never go any higher than you think.

—BENJAMIN DISRAELI

The road to wisdom? Well, it's plain and simple to express: Err and err and err again but less and less and less.

—PIET HEIN

Along with success comes a reputation for wisdom.

—EURIPIDES

———✦———

In seeking wisdom, the first step is silence, the second listening, the third remembering, the fourth practicing, the fifth—teaching others.

—IBN GABIROL

———✦———

It is more easy to be wise for others than for ourselves.

—FRANÇOIS DUC DE LA ROCHEFOUCAULD

———✦———

Wisdom is the reward you get for a lifetime of listening when you'd have preferred to talk.

—DOUG LARSON

———✦———

Wisdom doesn't necessarily come with age. Sometimes age just shows up all by itself.

—TOM WILSON

He who devotes sixteen hours a day to hard study may become at sixty as wise as he thought himself at twenty.

—MARY WILSON LITTLE

A man begins cutting his wisdom teeth the first time he bites off more than he can chew.

—HERB CAEN

Wisdom is knowing what to do next; virtue is doing it.

—DAVID STARR JORDAN, FROM HIS BOOK *THE PHILOSOPHY OF DESPAIR*

Wisdom is the quality that keeps you from getting into situations where you need it.

—Doug Larson

Wisdom is always an overmatch for strength.

—Phaedrus

Wisdom is ofttimes nearer when we stoop than when we soar.

—William Wordsworth

He dares to be a fool, and that is the first step in the direction of wisdom.

—James Gibbons Huneker

If you don't know, ask. You will be a fool for the moment, but a wise man for the rest of your life.

—LUCIUS A. SENECA

The whole problem with the world is that fools and fanatics are always so certain of themselves, and wiser people so full of doubts.

—BERTRAND RUSSELL

A man should never be ashamed to own he has been wrong, which is but saying in other words that he is wiser today than he was yesterday.

—ALEXANDER POPE

I find four great classes of students: The dumb who stay dumb. The dumb who become wise. The wise who go dumb. The wise who remain wise.

—MARTIN H. FISCHER, SCIENTIST

It is a sign of strength, not of weakness, to admit that you don't know all the answers.

—JOHN P. LOUGBRANE

It is better to ask some of the questions than know all the answers.

—JAMES THURBER

The way a question is put can often predetermine an answer.

—HENRY KISSINGER

The question of a wise man is half the answer.

—IBN GABIROL

When we have arrived at the question, the answer is already near.

—RALPH WALDO EMERSON

Never answer a question before it's asked.

—PROVERB

Gentlemen, I am ready for the questions to my answers.

—CHARLES DE GAULLE, ADDRESSING REPORTERS AT A NEWS CONFERENCE.

To be uncertain is to be uncomfortable, but to be certain is to be ridiculous.

—CHINESE PROVERB

There aren't any embarrassing questions—just embarrassing answers.

—CARL T. ROWAN, JR., FROM "TALK OF THE TOWN," THE *NEW YORKER* (DECEMBER 7, 1963)

A wise man can see more from the bottom of a well than a fool can from a mountaintop.

—ANONYMOUS

Wise men learn more from fools than fools from wise men.

—PROVERB

What is of value and wisdom to one man is nonsense to another.

—HERMANN HESSE

The fool doth think he is wise, but the wise man knows himself to be a fool.

—WILLIAM SHAKESPEARE

Even a fool, when he holdeth his peace, is counted wise: and he that shutteth his lips is esteemed a man of understanding.

—PROVERBS 17:28

Be wiser than other people if you can; but do not tell them so.

—LORD CHESTERFIELD

The wise man does at once what the fool does finally.

—BALTASAR GRACIÁN

It is best for the wise man not to seem wise.

—AESCHYLUS, FROM HIS BOOK *PROMETHEUS BOUND* (430 B.C.E.)

It requires wisdom to understand wisdom: the music is nothing if the audience is deaf.

—WALTER LIPPMANN

A note of music gains significance from the silence on either side.

—ANN MORROW LINDBERGH

Wisdom outweighs any wealth.

—SOPHOCLES

The most valuable piece of real estate you own is the six inches between your ears.

—JODIE VICTOR

There is great treasure there behind our skull and this is true about all of us. This little treasure has great, great powers, and I would say we only have learned a very, very small part of what it can do.

—ISAAC BASHEVIS SINGER

A man is rich in proportion to the number of things he can afford to let alone.

—HENRY DAVID THOREAU

If wisdom and diamonds grew on the same tree we could soon tell how much men loved wisdom.

—LEMUEL K. WASHBURN, AS QUOTED IN *IS THE BIBLE WORTH READING AND OTHER ESSAYS* (1911)

How can you be a sage if you're pretty? You can't get your wizard papers without wrinkles.

—Bill Veeck

I believe that all wisdom consists in caring immensely for a few right things, and not caring a straw about the rest.

—John Buchan

It is easier to find a score of men wise enough to discover the truth than to find one intrepid enough, in the face of opposition, to stand up for it.

—A. A. Hodge

Common-sense in an uncommon degree is what the world calls wisdom.

—Samuel Taylor Coleridge

Learning passes for wisdom among those who want both.

—WILLIAM TEMPLE

The highest wisdom is continual cheerfulness; such a state, like the region above the moon, is always clear and serene.

—MICHEL DE MONTAIGNE

Life is a festival only to the wise.

—RALPH WALDO EMERSON

So irresistible is the transformative power of enlightenment that your life seems to be shifted into a new dimension, opened to new and unsuspected possibilities.

—EUGEN HERRIGEL, FROM "ENLIGHTENMENT, REBIRTH, BUDDHA NATURE," *THE METHOD OF ZEN* (1960)

Before enlightenment, chop wood, carry water. After enlightenment, chop wood, carry water.

—Zen Proverb

Enlightenment is becoming conscious of the Unconscious.

—D. T. Suzuki, Japanese Zen master, from "The Education of an Amphibian," *Tomorrow and Tomorrow and Tomorrow* (1956)

The enlightened ones are neither attached to nor detached from their senses and thoughts.

—Huang-Po

Enlighten the people generally, and tyranny and oppression of body and mind will vanish like evil spirits at the dawn of day.

—Thomas Jefferson, in a letter to Dupont de Nemours (1816)

What you think is an illusion created by your glands, your emotions, and . . . by the content of your stomach. That gray matter you're so proud of it like a mirror in an amusement park which transmits to you nothing but distorted signals from reality forever beyond your grasp.

—AYN RAND

The most dangerous of all falsehoods is a slightly distorted truth.

—GEORG CHRISTOPH LICHTENBERG

The opposite of a correct statement is a false statement. But the opposite of a profound truth may well be another profound truth.

—NIELS BOHR

The most formidable weapon against errors of every kind is reason.

—THOMAS PAINE

I have one request: may I never use my reason against truth.

—ELIE WIESEL

How often have I said to you that when you have eliminated the impossible, whatever remains, however improbable, must be the truth?

—SIR ARTHUR CONAN DOYLE

Man has such a predilection for systems and abstract deductions that he is ready to distort the truth intentionally, he is ready to deny the evidence of his senses only to justify his logic.

—FYODOR DOSTOYEVSKY

Love truth, but pardon error.

—VOLTAIRE

CHAPTER TWELVE

Extremes of Intelligence

Sixty years ago I knew everything; now I know nothing; education is a progressive discovery of our own ignorance.

—WILL DURANT

If knowledge can create problems, it is not through ignorance that we can solve them.

—ISAAC ASIMOV

The greatest obstacle to discovering the shape of the earth, the continents, and the ocean was not ignorance but the illusion of knowledge.

—DANIEL J. BOORSTIN, FROM HIS BOOK *THE DISCOVERERS: A HISTORY OF MAN'S SEARCH TO KNOW HIS WORLD AND HIMSELF* (1985)

Awareness need never remain superficial in an educated man, whereas unawareness is certain to be ignorance probably compounded by arrogance.

—NATIONAL CONFERENCE ON HIGHER EDUCATION, 1964

If ignorance is bliss, there should be more happy people.

—VICTOR COUSINS

Ignorance is not innocence but sin.

—ROBERT BROWNING, FROM HIS BOOK *THE INN ALBUM* (1875)

Where ignorance is bliss,
'Tis folly to be wise.

—THOMAS GRAY, FROM HIS BOOK *ODE ON A DISTANT PROSPECT OF ETON COLLEGE* (1747)

There is no sin greater than ignorance.

—RUDYARD KIPLING

At present we educate people only up to the point where they can earn a living and marry; then education ceases altogether, as though a complete mental outfit had been acquired. . . . Vast numbers of men and women thus spend their entire lives in complete ignorance of the most important things.

—CARL JUNG, FROM HIS ESSAY "CHILD DEVELOPMENT AND EDUCATION" (1928)

A seeming ignorance is very often a most necessary part of worldly knowledge.

—LORD CHESTERFIELD, IN A LETTER TO HIS SON (1753)

The ignorant man is dead while alive.

—ALI

Ignorance of the world leaves one at the mercy of its malice.

—WILLIAM HAZLITT, FROM "ON THE DISADVANTAGES OF INTELLECTUAL SUPERIORITY," *TABLE TALK* (1822)

Being ignorant is not so much a Shame,
as being unwilling to learn.

>   —BENJAMIN FRANKLIN, FROM *POOR RICHARD'S ALMANAC*
>   (OCTOBER 1755)

Between true Science and erroneous Doctrines, Ignorance is in the middle.

>   —THOMAS HOBBES, FROM HIS BOOK *LEVIATHAN* (1651)

We don't know because we don't want to know.

>   —ALDOUS HUXLEY, FROM HIS BOOK *ENDS AND MEANS: AN INQUIRY INTO
>   THE NATURE OF IDEALS AND INTO THE METHODS EMPLOYED FOR THEIR
>   REALIZATION* (1937)

There is no slavery but ignorance.

>   —ROBERT GREEN INGERSOLL

I seemed to have gained nothing in trying to educate myself unless it was to discover more and more fully how ignorant I was.

—RENÉ DESCARTES, FROM HIS BOOK *DISCOURSE ON METHOD* (1637)

Real knowledge is to know the extent of one's ignorance.

—CONFUCIUS

To be ignorant of one's ignorance is the malady of the ignorant.

—AMOS BRONSON ALCOTT

You always admire what you really don't understand.

—BLAISE PASCAL

The greatest obstacle to discovery is not ignorance—it is the illusion of knowledge.

—DANIEL BOORSTIN

Blessed is the man who, having nothing to stay, abstains from giving us worthy evidence of the fact.

—GEORGE ELIOT

I believe that ignorance is the root of all evil. And that no one knows the truth.

—MOLLY IVINS

Ignorance is preferable to error, and he is less remote from the truth who believes nothing than he who believes what is wrong.

—THOMAS JEFFERSON

A great deal of intelligence can be invested in ignorance.

—SAUL BELLOW

It is impossible to defeat an ignorant man in argument.

—WILLIAM G. MCADOO, FORMER U.S. SENATOR AND SECRETARY
OF THE TREASURY

A little learning is a dangerous thing, but a lot of ignorance is just as bad.

—BOB EDWARDS

The trouble with people is not that they don't know but that they know so much that ain't so.

—JOSH BILLINGS

Some folks are wise and some are otherwise.

—TOBIAS SMOLLETT

Ignorance is a right! Education is eroding one of the few democratic freedoms remaining to us.

—CHRISTOPHER ANDREA

It's innocence when it charms us, ignorance when it doesn't.

—MIGNON MCLAUGHLIN, FROM HER BOOK *THE SECOND NEUROTIC'S NOTEBOOK* (1966)

Bigotry is the disease of ignorance, of morbid minds; enthusiasm of the free and buoyant. Education and free discussion are the antidotes of both.

—THOMAS JEFFERSON

Prejudice is the child of ignorance.

—WILLIAM HAZLITT

Admission of ignorance is often the first step in our education.

—STEPHEN COVEY, AUTHOR OF *THE SEVEN HABITS OF HIGHLY SUCCESSFUL PEOPLE* (2004)

Reason obeys itself; and ignorance submits to whatever is dictated to it.

—THOMAS PAINE

Ignorance more frequently begets confidence than does knowledge.

—CHARLES DARWIN

The essence of knowledge is, having it, to apply it; not having it,
to confess your ignorance.

—CONFUCIUS

There is that indescribable freshness and unconsciousness about
an illiterate person that humbles and mocks the power of the noblest
expressive genius.

—WALT WHITMAN

Constant effort and frequent mistakes are the stepping stones of genius.

—ELBERT HUBBARD

A man of genius inspires us with a boundless confidence in our own
powers.

—RALPH WALDO EMERSON

We love most of all to see a genius wearing a martyr's crown.

—WILHELM LANGE-EICHBAUM, FROM HIS BOOK *THE PROBLEM OF GENIUS* (1931)

Someone who has completely lost his way in a forest, but strives with uncommon energy to get out of it in whatever direction, sometimes discovers a new, unknown way: this is how geniuses come into being, who are then praised for their originality.

—FRIEDRICH NIETZSCHE

We are tied down, all our days for the greater part of our days, to the commonplace. That is where with great thinkers, great literature helps. In their company we are still in the ordinary world, but it is the ordinary world transfigured and seen through the eyes of wisdom and genius. And some of their vision becomes our own.

—SIR RICHARD LIVINGSTONE

Great minds discuss ideas, mediocre minds discuss events, small minds discuss personalities.

—ELEANOR ROOSEVELT

When a true genius appears in the world, you may know him by this sign, that the dunces are all in confederacy against him.

—JONATHAN SWIFT

Mediocrity knows nothing higher than itself; but talent instantly recognizes genius.

—ARTHUR CONAN DOYLE, FROM HIS BOOK *THE VALLEY OF FEAR* (1914)

The difference between genius and stupidity is that genius has its limits.

—ANONYMOUS

Always to see the general in the particular is the very foundation of genius.

—ARTHUR SCHOPENHAUER, FROM HIS BOOK *PARERGA AND PARALIPOMENA* (1851)

Genius is one percent inspiration, ninety-nine percent perspiration.

—THOMAS A. EDISON

Susceptibility to the highest forces is the highest genius.

—HENRY ADAMS, FROM HIS BOOK *THE EDUCATION OF HENRY ADAMS* (1907)

No great genius has ever existed without some touch of madness.

—ARISTOTLE

I have known no man of genius who had not to pay, in some affliction or defect either physical or spiritual, for what the gods had given him.

    —MAX BEERBOHM, FROM "NO. 2, THE PINES," *AND EVEN NOW* (1920)

Genius defies all anticipation.

    —HENRI BERGSON

Since when was genius found respectable?

    —ELIZABETH BARRETT BROWNING, FROM HER BOOK *AURORA LEIGH* (1857)

Genius knows both love and hates, but not as we know them, for it will fly to help its bitterest foe or attack its dearest friend in the interests of the art it serves.

    —SAMUEL BUTLER, FROM HIS BOOK *THE NOTE-BOOKS OF SAMUEL BUTLER* (1907)

A good plan itself, this comes not of its own accord; it is the fruit of genius (which means transcendent capacity of taking trouble, first of all).

—THOMAS CARLYLE, FROM HIS BOOK *HISTORY OF FREDERICK II OF PRUSSIA* (1865)

———

The sum total of excellence is good sense and method. When these have passed into the instinctive readiness of habit, when the well revolves to rapidly that we cannot see it revolve at all, then we call the combination genius.

—SAMUEL TAYLOR COLERIDGE

———

The individuals who seem to us most outstanding, who are honored with the name of genius, are those who have proposed to enact the fate of all humanity in their personal existences.

—SIMONE DE BEAUVOIR, FROM HER BOOK *THE SECOND SEX* (1950)

———

Time, place, and action, may with pains be wrought;
But genius must be born, and never can be taught.

—JOHN DRYDEN, FROM HIS POEM "TO MY DEAR FRIEND
MR. CONGREVE, ON HIS COMEDY CALL'D THE DOUBLE-DEALER"
(1693)

———◆———

The words of genius have a wider meaning than the thought that
prompted them.

—GEORGE ELIOT, FROM HER BOOK *ADAM BEDE* (1859)

———◆———

Every man of genius sees the world at a different angle from his fellows,
and there is his tragedy.

—HAVELOCK ELLIS, FROM HIS BOOK *THE DANCE OF LIFE* (1923)

———◆———

In every work of genius we recognize our own rejected thoughts.

—RALPH WALDO EMERSON, FROM HIS BOOK *SELF-RELIANCE* (1839)

———◆———

High original genius is always ridiculed on its first appearance; most of all by those who have won themselves the highest reputation in working on the established lines. Genius only commands recognition when it has created the taste which is to appreciate it.

—JAMES ANTHONY FROUDE, FROM HIS BOOK *THOMAS CARLYLE: A HISTORY OF THE FIRST FORTY YEARS, 1795–1835* (1882)

The genius is especially inspired with the good spirit of recognizing quickly what is useful to him.

—JOHANN WOLFGANG VON GOETHE, FROM HIS BOOK *WILHELM MEISTER'S TRAVELS* (1829)

An occasional genius, by extremely dexterous and willful actions, may achieve a historical mutation.

—CARL. G. GUSTAVSON, FROM HIS BOOK *A PREFACE TO HISTORY* (1955)

Genius is an infinite capacity for giving pains.

  —DON HEROLD

Genius is an infinite capacity for giving pains.

What distinguishes the genius and the madman decisively and fundamentally is the success of their efforts.

  —ALFRED HOCK, FROM HIS BOOK *REASON AND GENIUS: STUDIES IN THEIR ORIGIN* (1960)

Genius: the ability to act wisely without precedent—the power to do the right thing for the first time. A capacity for evading hard work.

  —ELBERT HUBBARD, FROM HIS BOOK *THE ROYALCROFT DICTIONARY CONCOCTED BY ALI BABA AND THE BUNCH ON RAINY DAYS* (1914)

Not every "man" fits every "hour." . . . A given genius may come either too early or too late. Peter the Hermit would now be sent to a lunatic asylum. John Stuart Mill in the tenth century would have lived and died unknown.

—WILLIAM JAMES, FROM HIS ESSAY "GREAT MEN
AND THEIR ENVIRONMENT" (1880)

A man of genius makes no mistakes. His errors are volitional and are the portals of discovery.

—JAMES JOYCE, FROM HIS BOOK *ULYSSES* (1922)

Is genius in spite of this psychopathic component, or because of it?

—ERNST KRETSCHMER, FROM HIS BOOK *THE PSYCHOLOGY OF MEN
OF GENIUS* (1931)

The genius must seem to us one capable of doing that which we ourselves cannot do.

—WILHELM LANGE-EICHBAUM, FROM HIS BOOK *THE PROBLEM
OF GENIUS* (1931)

The man who early on regards himself as a genius is lost.

—GEORG CHRISTOPH LICHTENBERG, FROM HIS BOOK *APHORISMS* (1806)

Genius, being essentially original and a lover of originality, is the natural enemy of traditions and conservatism: he is the born revolutionary, the precursor and the most active pioneer of revolutions.

—CESARE LOMBROSO

The inarticulate message of his contemporaries simply becomes articulate in someone, and behold a genius.

—EVERETT DEAN MARTIN, FROM HIS BOOK *THE BEHAVIOR OF CROWDS: A PSYCHOLOGICAL STUDY* (1920)

Genius, all over the world, stands hand in hand, and one shock of recognition runs the whole circle round.

—HERMAN MELVILLE

Genius can only breathe freely in an atmosphere of freedom. Persons of Genius are, more individual than any other people—less capable, consequently, of fitting themselves, without hurtful compression, into any of the small number of molds which society provides in order to save its members the trouble of forming their own character.

—JOHN STUART MILL, FROM HIS BOOK *ON LIBERTY* (1859)

A people which is becoming conscious of its dangers produces a genius.

—FRIEDRICH NIETZSCHE

When a true genius appears in the world, you may know him by this sign, that the dunces are all in confederacy against him.

—JONATHAN SWIFT

The persecution of genius fosters its influence.

—TACITUS

Thousands of geniuses live and die undiscovered—either by themselves or by others.

—Mark Twain

Genius is another name for the perfection of human nature; for genius is not a fact, but an ideal. It is nothing less than the possession of all the powers and impulses of humanity, in their greatest possible strength and most harmonious combination.

—Edwin Percy Whipple, from his book *Literature and Life* (1849)

Genius creates the combinations which assure its success.

—Anonymous

This is the nature of genius, to be able to grasp the knowable even when no one else recognizes that it is present.

—Deepak Chopra

Genius . . . has been defined as a supreme capacity for taking trouble. It might be more fitly described as a supreme capacity for getting its possessors into pains of all kinds, and keeping them therein so long as the genius remains.

—SAMUEL BUTLER, FROM *THE NOTE-BOOKS OF SAMUEL BUTLER* (1907)

The word "genius" isn't applicable in football. A genius is a guy like Norman Einstein.

—JOE THEISMAN, NFL QUARTERBACK AND FOOTBALL ANALYST

The principal mark of genius is not perfection but originality, the opening of new frontiers.

—ARTHUR KOESTLER

One is not born a genius: one becomes a genius.

—SIMONE DE BEAUVOIR, FROM HER BOOK *THE SECOND SEX* (1950)

To be conscious that you are ignorant is a great step to knowledge.

   —BENJAMIN DISRAELI

Genius . . . means little more than the faculty to perceiving in an unhabitual way.

   —WILLIAM JAMES, FROM HIS BOOK *THE PRINCIPLES OF PSYCHOLOGY*
    (1890)

Geniuses, it has been said, serve the human race. Often enough they do; but, first of all, the genius serves himself.

   —WILHELM LANGE-EICHBAUM, FROM HIS BOOK *THE PROBLEM*
    OF GENIUS (1931)

Genius at first is little more than a great capacity for receiving discipline.

   —GEORGE ELIOT, FROM HER BOOK *DANIEL DERONDA* (1876)

Every soul is potentially Genius, if not arrested.

—RALPH WALDO EMERSON

I am not ashamed to confess that I am ignorant of what I do not know.

—MARCUS CICERO

We can get over being poor, but it takes longer to get over being ignorant.

—JANE SEQUICHIE HIFLER

Every man has a right to be wrong in his opinions, but no man has a right to be wrong in facts.

—BERNARD BARUCH, FROM HIS BOOK *BARUCH: MY OWN STORY* (1996)

Nothing has more retarded the advancement of learning than the disposition of vulgar minds to ridicule and vilify what they cannot comprehend.

—SAMUEL JOHNSON

There are some people that if they don't know, you can't tell 'em.

—LOUIS ARMSTRONG

The dumbest people I know are those who know it all.

—MALCOLM FORBES

The first step towards knowledge is to know that we are ignorant.

—RICHARD CECIL

One part of knowledge consists in being ignorant of such things as are not worthy to be known.

—CRATES OF THEBES, CONSIDERED THE FOUNDER OF GREEK COMEDY

If we become increasingly humble about how little we know, we may be more eager to search.

—JOHN TEMPLETON

There is no squabbling so violent as that between people who accepted an idea yesterday and those who will accept the same idea tomorrow.

—CHRISTOPHER MORLEY

The eye sees only what the mind is prepared to comprehend.

—HENRI BERGSON

If the blind lead the blind, both shall fall into the ditch.

—MATTHEW 15:14

———⟫⬧⟪———

An expert is a man who has made all the mistakes which can be made, in a narrow field.

—NIELS BOHR

———⟫⬧⟪———

An expert is one who knows more and more about less and less.

—NICHOLAS MURRAY BUTLER

———⟫⬧⟪———

The function of an expert is not to be more right than others, but to be wrong for more sophisticated reasons.

—DAVID BUTLER

———⟫⬧⟪———

Everyone is a reactionary on the subject he is expert about.

—Conquest's Law, from John O'Sullivan's article "1861 and
All That," *National Review* (May 14, 1990)

If you consult enough experts, you can confirm any opinion.

—Hiram's Law, as quoted by Arthur Bloch in his book *Murphy's
Law: Book Three* (1982)

The expert has his constituency—those who have a vested interest in
commonly held opinions; elaborating and defining its consensus at
a high level has, after all, made him an expert.

—Henry Kissinger, from his book *American Foreign Policy* (1969)

A man who knows no one thing intimately has no views worth hearing
on things in general.

—Charles Horton Cooley, from his book *Human Nature
and Social Order* (1922)

There is a tradition of men become experts simply by being put in positions that require expertise.

> —MICHAEL LEWIS, FROM "BEYOND ECONOMICS, BEYOND POLITICS, BEYOND ACCOUNTABILITY," *WORTH* (MAY 1995)

We have not overthrown the divine right of kings to fall down for the divine right of experts.

> —HAROLD MACMILLAN, BRITISH PRIME MINISTER, IN A SPEECH (1950)

Expertise can always be hired.

> —GEORGE REEDY, FROM HIS BOOK *THE TWILIGHT OF THE PRESIDENCY* (1970)

Expert, n. A modern seer, often self-styled, whose pronouncements are received as if emanating from an oracle. A "recognized expert" is one whose pronouncements are closest to conventional wisdom.

—EDMUND H. VOLKART, FROM HIS BOOK *THE ANGEL'S DICTIONARY: A MODERN TRIBUTE TO AMBROSE BIERCE* (1986)

An expert is a man who has stopped thinking—he knows.

—FRANK LLOYD WRIGHT

Experts are never right or wrong; they win or lose. Right and wrong are decided by proof; winning and losing are decided by who is doing the talking or talks the loudest, has the last, latest, or only word, and is quoted by reporters.

—M. A. ZEIDNER, FROM "EXPERTS: A DEFINITION," *QUARTERLY REVIEW OF DOUBLESPEAK* (OCTOBER 1988)

The more experts agree among themselves, the less likely they are to be right.

—ANONYMOUS

⟶◆⟵

I have found further that my own personhood has educatable value. When I don't have to know all the answers, I seem to have more answers than before when I tried to be the expert.

—ANONYMOUS TEACHER, QUOTED BY EVERETT SHOSTROM IN *MAN, THE MANIPULATOR* (1968)

⟶◆⟵

Be careful to leave your sons well instructed rather than rich, for the hopes of the instructed are better than the wealth of the ignoratn.

—EPICTETUS

⟶◆⟵

Not to know is bad; not to wish to know is worse.

—AFRICAN PROVERB

Anyone and everyone cannot be a guru. A huge timber floats on the water and can carry animals as well. But a piece of worthless wood sinks, if a man sits on it, and drowns him.

—*THE GOSPEL OF SRI RAMAKRISHNA* (1942)

Those who think they know it all are very annoying to those who do.

—SHEETZ'S RUMINATION

Success is not a matter of luck or genius. Success is the outcome of adequate preparation and indomitable determination.

—AMOS BRONSON ALCOTT

A long habit of not thinking a thing wrong gives it a superficial appearance of being right.

—THOMAS PAINE

Make something your specialty. Life is a very uncertain affair. Knowing a little about 500 things won't do us much good. We must be able to do something well, that our work will be needed and valuable.

—THOMAS CARLYLE

The same man cannot be skilled in everything, each has his own special excellence.

—EURIPIDES

Everyone is ignorant, only on different subjects.

—WILL ROGERS

An excellent plumber is infinitely more admirable than an incompetent philosopher.

—JOHN W. GARDNER

———⋙◆⋘———

It iz better tew know nothing than two know what ain't so.

—JOHN BILLINGS, FROM "SOLLUM THOUGHTS," EVERYBODY'S FRIEND (1874)

———⋙◆⋘———

Opposites are not contradictory but complementary.

—NIELS BOHR

———⋙◆⋘———

CHAPTER THIRTEEN

The Funny Side of Teaching

A little inaccuracy sometimes saves tons of explanation.

—SAKI (H. H. MUNRO), SCOTTISH AUTHOR

Blessed are they who have nothing to say, and who cannot be persuaded to say it.

—JAMES RUSSELL LOWELL

Trouble is, kids feel they have to shock their elders, and each generation grows up into something harder to shock.

—CAL CRAIG

The first half of our lives is ruined by our parents and the second half by our children.

—CLARENCE DARROW

Nature makes boys and girls lovely to look upon so they can be tolerated until they acquire some sense.

—WILLIAM LYON PHELPS

Blessed are the young, for they shall inherit the national debt.

—HERBERT HOOVER

One of the disadvantages of having children is that they eventually get old enough to give you presents they make at school.

—ROBERT BYRNE

If it weren't for the last minute nothing would get done.

—ANONYMOUS

What is algebra, exactly? Is it those three-cornered things?

—J. M. BARRIE

———◈———

Bad spellers of the world, untie.

—GRAFITTO

———◈———

People who think they know everything are very irritating to those of us who do.

—ANONYMOUS

———◈———

Learning to dislike children at an early age saves a lot of aggravation later in life.

—ROBERT BYRNE

———◈———

Lucy: If you're not beguiling by age twelve, forget it.

—CHARLES SCHULZ

When you are eight years old, nothing is any of your business.

—LENNY BRUCE

We adults have learned how to disguise our terrible character, but children, well, they are like grotesque drawings of *us*. They should be neither seen nor heard, and no one must make another one.

—GORE VIDAL

I never met a kid I liked.

—W. C. FIELDS

Aristotle was famous for knowing everything. He taught that the brain exists merely to cool the blood and is not involved in the process of thinking. This is true only of certain persons.

—WILL CUPPY

Charlie Brown: Some days are like being in the "ten items or less" line behind a dozen people who don't understand the new math.

—CHARLES SCHULZ

I'm bilingual. I speak English and educationese.

—SHIRLEY HUFSTEDLER

Educating a beautiful woman is like pouring honey into a fine Swiss watch: everything stops.

—KURT VONNEGUT

I didn't know the facts of life until I was seventeen. My father never talked about his work.

—MARTIN FREUD

What Peter tells you about Paul tells you more about Peter than it does about Paul.

—ANONYMOUS

It has been estimated that well over half of all Americans alive today have experienced childhood directly (Seuss, 1983). In fact, the actual numbers are probably much higher, since these data are based on self-reports which may be subject to social desirability biases and retrospective distortions.

—JORDAN W. SMOLLER, FROM "THE ETIOLOGY OF CHILDHOOD," NETWORKER (MARCH/APRIL 1987)

He couldn't get into Harvard even if he had the dean's wife at gunpoint.

—DAVE BARRY

College is the best time of your life. When else are your parents going to spend several thousand dollars a year just for you to go to a strange town and get drunk every night?

—DAVID WOOD

It's strange how few of the world's great problems are solved by people who remember their algebra.

—HERBERT PROCHNOW, AMERICAN BANKING EXECUTIVE AND AUTHOR

My husband managed to cram four years of college into five.

—JUDY HAMPTON

Everyone is in awe of the lion tamer in a cage with half a dozen lions—everyone but a school bus driver.

—ANONYMOUS

It was going all wrong at my college interview until I nonchalantly asked, "Do you need any large donations for new buildings?"

—TODD ANDERSON

Passing the SAT: My personal theory is that it has to do with how much money you send them in the mail. I think the amounts they tell you to send are actually just suggested minimum donations—if you get my drift.

—DAVE BARRY

A kindergarten teacher is a woman who knows how to make little things count.

—ANONYMOUS

I used to keep my college roommate from reading my personal mail by hiding it in her textbooks.

—JOAN WELSH

We didn't feel so good when we took our son to college and saw a sign on the liquor store—Back to School Sale.

—BRIAN MORGAN

I went to a high school that was so dangerous, the school newspaper had an obituary column.

—ROCKY RAY

"Do you think your boy will forget all he learned in college?"
"I hope so. He can't make a living drinking."

—LARRY WILDE

You'll have to excuse me if I cry. I've been a little teary-eyed all week; the sadness, the joy . . . the fact that I'm off my parents' payroll.

—MELISSA AMERNICK, IN HER GRADUATION SPEECH.

I was dropped from New York University because of bad marks. I was a film major.

—WOODY ALLEN, IN AN INTERVIEW IN *ROLLING STONE* (1987)

You can always tell a Harvard man, but you can't tell him much.

—JAMES BARNES

I was a modest, good-humored boy. It was Oxford that has made me insufferable.

—MAX BEERBOHM

They have professors of all the languages of the principle beasts and birds.

> —SAMUEL BUTLER, ON HIS UTOPIAN UNIVERSITY, FROM *THE NOTE-BOOKS OF SAMUEL BUTLER* (1907)

These kids are smart. But I'd rather take a python to bed than hire one.

> —NED DEWEY, ON RECENT BUSINESS SCHOOL GRADUATES BRUCE NUSSBAUM AND ALEX BEAM, FROM "REMAKING HARVARD B-SCHOOL," *BUSINESS WEEK* (MARCH 24, 1986)

Remember that a kick in the ass is a step forward.

> —ANONYMOUS

I was thrown out of college for cheating on the metaphysics exam; I looked into the soul of the boy next to me.

> —WOODY ALLEN

Political history is far too criminal a subject to be a fit thing to teach children.

—W. H. AUDEN

Outside of a dog, a book is man's best friend. Inside of a dog, it's too dark to read.

—GROUCHO MARX

It is no wonder that people are so horrible when they start life as children.

—KINGSLEY AMIS

How to Raise Your I.Q. by Eating Gifted Children

—LEWIS B. FRUMKES, BOOK TITLE (1983)

Humorists always sit at the children's table.

—WOODY ALLEN

———————

Princeton sent me a rejection letter so elegantly worded that I still think of myself as an alumnus.

—NEWT GINGRICH, IN *NEWSWEEK* (JANUARY 9, 1995)

———————

Often, when I am reading a good book, I stop and thank my teacher. That is, I used to, until she got an unlisted number.

—ANONYMOUS

———————

Sex education may be a good idea in the schools, but I don't believe the kids should be given homework.

—BILL COSBY

You must learn from the mistakes of others. You can't possibly live long enough to make them all yourself.

—SAM LEVINSON

Before we work on artificial intelligence why don't we do something about natural stupidity?

—STEVE POLYAK

You can be sincere and still be stupid.

—CHARLES F. KETTERING

Your ignorance cramps my conversation.

—ANTHONY HOPE

A university professor set an examination question in which he asked what is the difference between ignorance and apathy. The professor had to give an A+ to a student who answered: I don't know and I don't care.

—RICHARD PRATT, IN *PACIFIC COMPUTER WEEKLY* (JULY 20, 1990)

As we read the school reports on our children, we realize a sense of relief that can rise to delight that—thank Heaven—nobody is reporting in this fashion on us.

—JOHN BOYNTON PRIESTLEY

Many public school children seem to know only two dates—1492 and Fourth of July, and as a rule they don't know what happened on either occasion.

—MARK TWAIN

I took a test in Existentialism. I left all the answers blank and got 100.

—WOODY ALLEN

———◆———

I don't have to attend every argument I'm invited to

—ANONYMOUS

———◆———

In our school you were searched for guns and knifes on the way in and if you didn't have any, they gave you some.

—EMO PHILIPS

———◆———

My school days were the happiest days of my life, which should give you some indication of the misery I've endured over the past twenty-five years.

—PAUL MERTON

———◆———

A lot of fellows nowadays have a B.A., M.D. or Ph.D. Unfortunately, they don't have a J.O.B.

—FATS DOMINO

You go to school, you get a master's degree, you study Shakespeare, and you wind up being famous for plastic glasses.

—SALLY JESSY RAPHAEL

The only reason I always try to meet and know the parents better is because it helps me to forgive their children.

—LOUIS JOHANNOT, AS QUOTED IN *LIFE* (1965)

Why are there five syllables in the word "monosyllabic"? And how come "abbreviated" is such a long word?

—STEVEN WRIGHT

If the teacher said on the report card, *This kid is a total and hopeless jackass who may have trouble learning his zip code,* then the parent wouldn't be teased by the possibility of scholastic success.

—BILL COSBY, FROM HIS BOOK *FATHERHOOD* (1987)

Young people are more hopeful at a certain age than adults, but I suspect that's glandular.

—GORE VIDAL

Education seems to be in America the only commodity of which the customer tries to get as little as he can for his money.

—MAX FORMAN, SPECIAL EDUCATION CONSULTANT, CALIFORNIA DEPT. OF EDUCATION

Television commercials are educational. They teach you how stupid advertisers think you are.

—ANONYMOUS

Coach Spencer taught in the upbeat, vibrant manner of a coach and was energetic in a way that made you pay attention. He also related moments in history to quotes from movies like *The Blues Brothers*. Classic!

—JEREMY HOGERSON, MAMARONECK HIGH SCHOOL CLASS OF 1990

SUGGESTED BUMPER STICKER: We Are the Proud Parents of a Child Whose Self-Esteem Is Sufficient that He Doesn't Need Us Advertising His Minor Scholastic Achievement on the Bumper of Our Car.

—GEORGE CARLIN, FROM HIS BOOK *NAPALM & SILLY PUTTY* (2001)

We're going to have the best-educated American people in the world.

—DAN QUAYLE

If people did not do silly things, nothing intelligent would ever get done.

— LUDWIG WITTGENSTEIN

The sound that best describes teaching is the sound of a car being driven by someone just learning how to drive a stick shift. It's getting somewhere, but nowhere quickly, and there are a lot of stops and starts in between.

—MARGARET STRUHAR, ENGLISH TEACHER IN YORKTOWN HEIGHTS, NEW YORK

Few statements on quality education deal with teachers' needs in day-to-day school operation. Teachers, apparently, are taken for granted as part of the classroom scenery, like desks, chairs, and books.

—J. LLOYD TRUMP, AS QUOTED IN *THE TEACHER AND THE TAUGHT* (1963)

If you promise not to believe everything your child says happens at school, I'll promise not to believe everything he says happens at home.

—A NOTE TO STUDENTS' PARENTS FROM AN ENGLISH SCHOOLMASTER, AS QUOTED IN THE *WALL STREET JOURNAL* (1985)

Why doesn't glue stick to the inside of the bottle?

—STEVEN WRIGHT

———>•<———

When you think about it, attention deficit disorder makes a lot of sense. In this country there isn't a lot worth paying attention to.

—GEORGE CARLIN, FROM HIS BOOK *NAPALM & SILLY PUTTY* (2001)

———>•<———

Childhood is a syndrome which has only recently begun to receive serious attention from clinicians. . . . As early as the eighth century, the Persian historian Kidnom made reference to "short, noisy creatures," who may well have been what we now call "children." The treatment of children, however, was unknown until this century.

—JORDAN W. SMOLLER, FROM "THE ETIOLOGY OF CHILDHOOD," *NETWORKER* (MARCH/APRIL 1987)

———>•<———

Parents may tell
But never teach

Unless they practice
What they preach.

—ANONYMOUS

If nobody said anything unless he knew what he was talking about, a
ghastly hush would descent upon the earth.

—SIR ALAN HERBERT

If there were no schools to take the children away from home part of the
time, the insane asylum would be filled with mothers.

—EDGAR W. HOWE

The vanity of teaching often tempteth a man to forget he is a blockhead.

—GEORGE SAVILE, MARQUIS OF HALIFAX

Whose cruel idea was it for the word "lisp" to have an "s" in it?

—STEVEN WRIGHT

In the first place God made idiots. This was for practice. Then He made School Boards.

—MARK TWAIN

Smartness runs in my family. When I went to school I was so smart my teacher was in my class for five years.

—GRACIE ALLEN

The mark of a true MBA is that he is often wrong but seldom in doubt.

—ROBERT BUZZELL

How is it that little children are so intelligent and men so stupid? It must be education that does it.

—ALEXANDRE DUMAS

I think the world is run by C students.

—AL MCGUIRE

When asked to spell Mississippi the boy asked, "The river or the state?"

—ANONYMOUS

It is bad enough to see young fools, but worse to see old fools.

—BRIGHAM YOUNG

He was so learned that he could name a horse in nine languages; so ignorant that he bought a cow to ride on.

—BENJAMIN FRANKLIN, FROM *POOR RICHARD'S ALMANAC* (1758)

Teaching for tests creates learnoids.

—ALAN SCOTT WINSTON, AUTHOR OF *FOR THE LOVE OF TEACHING*

Compromise is fine for people who aren't as right as me.

—ESMÉ RAJI CODELL, FROM HER BOOK *EDUCATING ESMÉ* (1999)

As for helping me in the outside world, the Convent taught me only that if you spit on a pencil eraser, it will erase ink.

—DOROTHY PARKER, ON PAROCHIAL SCHOOL, WHICH SHE ATTENDED UNTIL SHE WAS ASKED TO LEAVE AT AGE THIRTEEN

I was gratified to be able to answer promptly. I said I didn't know.

—MARK TWAIN

————⇒◆⇐————

Start a program for gifted children, and every parent demands that his child be enrolled.

—THOMAS BAILEY, AS QUOTED IN THE *WALL STREET JOURNAL* (1961)

————⇒◆⇐————

To be loose with grammar is to be loose with the worst woman in the world.

—OTIS C. EDWARDS, IN A LECTURE AT NASHOTAH HOUSE EPISCOPAL SEMINARY, 1966

————⇒◆⇐————

Ignorant people in preppy clothes are more dangerous to America than oil embargoes.

—V. S. NAIPAUL, AFTER A YEAR OF TEACHING AT WESLEYAN UNIVERSITY, AS QUOTED IN *TIME* (1979)

————⇒◆⇐————

The University of Miami is not a campus with visible school spirit, just visible tan lines.

—LISA BIRNBACH, FROM *LISA BIRNBACH'S COLLEGE BOOK* (1984)

Minerva House . . . was a "finishing establishment for young ladies," where some twenty girls of the ages from thirteen to nineteen inclusive, acquired a smattering of everything and a knowledge of nothing.

—CHARLES DICKENS, FROM HIS BOOK *SKETCHES OF BOZ* (1835)

For God's sake give me a young man who has brains enough to make a fool of himself!

—ROBERT LOUIS STEVENSON, FROM HIS BOOK *CRABBED AGE AND YOUTH* (1881)

Winter is the time for study, you know, and the colder it is the most studious we are.

—HENRY DAVID THOREAU, IN A LETTER TO SOPHIA THOREAU, 1847

Wit is educated insolence.

—ARISTOTLE

Microscopes and telescopes really confuse our minds.

—JOHANN WOLFGANG VON GOETHE, FROM HIS BOOK *REFLECTIONS IN THE SPIRIT OF THE TRAVELERS* (1829)

A fellow declaring he's no fool usually has his suspicions.

—WILSON MIZNER

Never try to teach a pig to sing . . . it wastes your time and annoys the pig.

—ANONYMOUS

Adorable children are considered to be the general property of the human race. Rude children belong to their mothers.

—JUDITH MARTIN, FROM HER BOOK *MISS MANNERS' GUIDE TO REARING PERFECT CHILDREN* (1993)

All good qualities in a child are the result of environment, while all the bad ones are the result of poor heredity on the side of the other parent.

—ELINOR GOULDING SMITH, FROM HER BOOK *THE COMPLETE BOOK OF ABSOLUTELY PERFECT BABY AND CHILD CARE* (1957)

All mothers think their children are oaks, but the world never lacks for cabbages.

—ROBERTSON DAVIES

As the youngsters grow attached to their teachers and classmates, they can finally say goodbye to their mothers without re-enacting the death scene from *Camille*.

—SUE MITTENTHAL, IN *THE NEW YORK TIMES* (SEPTEMBER 6, 1984)

Being constantly with the children was like wearing a pair of shoes that were expensive and too small. She couldn't bear to throw them out, but they gave her blisters.

—BERYL BAINBRIDGE, FROM HER BOOK *INJURY TIME* (1978)

BS is just what it stands for, an MS is More of the Same, and a Ph.D. is Piled Higher and Deeper.

—BOBBY KNIGHT

Our bombs are smarter than the average high school student. At least they can find Kuwait.

—A. WHITNEY BROWN

❦

Whenever you asked him how he was doing in school, he always said, "No problem." And his answer made sense: there was no problem, no confusion about how he was doing. He had failed everything; and what he hadn't failed, he hadn't taken yet.

—BILL COSBY, FROM HIS BOOK *FATHERHOOD* (1987)

❦

But there are advantages to being elected President. The day after I was elected, I had my high school grades classified Top Secret.

—RONALD REAGAN

❦

There is no crisis to which academics will not respond with a seminar.

—ANONYMOUS

❦

I expect you'll be becoming a schoolmaster, sir. That's what most of the gentlemen does, sir, that gets sent down for indecent behavior.

—EVELYN WAUGH

There are three good reasons to be a teacher—June, July, and August.

—ANONYMOUS

If I were asked to enumerate ten educational stupidities, the giving of grades would head the list. . . . If I can't give a child a better reason for studying than a grade on a report card, I ought to lock my desk and go home and stay there.

—DOROTHY DE ZOUCHE, MISSOURI TEACHER, IN A 1945 ARTICLE

I think, therefore, I am. I think.

—GEORGE CARLIN, FROM HIS BOOK *NAPALM & SILLY PUTTY* (2001)

In America the young are always ready to give to those who are older than themselves the full benefits of their inexperience.

—OSCAR WILDE, FROM "THE AMERICAN INVASION," *COURT AND SOCIETY REVIEW* (1887)

Praise does wonders for our sense of hearing.

—ARNOLD H. GLASOW

If you're so smart, how come you ain't rich?

—AMERICAN PROVERB

Of course there's a lot of knowledge in universities: the freshmen bring a little in; the seniors don't take much away, so knowledge sort of accumulates.

—ABBOTT LAWRENCE LOWELL, AMERICAN EDUCATOR AND FORMER HARVARD UNIVERSITY PRESIDENT

Life is tough. It's tougher if you're stupid.

—JOHN WAYNE

Sometimes the majority only means that all the fools are on the same side.

—ANONYMOUS

It's like being grounded for eighteen years.

—NEW YORK CITY BOARD OF EDUCATION POSTER, WARNING AGAINST TEEN PREGNANCY, 1986

It's not their fault they're slugs.

—THE MACOMBER SISTERS

His test scores, for general aptitude, showed that he wasn't very apt at anything; he was no natural. This came as no surprise to Garp, who shared with his mother a belief that nothing came naturally.

—JOHN IRVING, FROM HIS BOOK *THE WORLD ACCORDING TO GARP* (1978)

Equality is not when a female Einstein gets promoted to assistant professor. Equality is when a female schlemiel moves ahead as fast as a male schlemiel.

—EWALD B. NYQUIST, AS QUOTED IN THE *NEW YORK TIMES* (1975)

A schoolmaster should have an atmosphere of awe, and walk wonderingly, as if he was amazed at being himself.

—NEWTON D. BAKER

When a teacher calls a boy by his entire name, it means trouble.

—MARK TWAIN

The dawn of legibility in his handwriting has revealed his utter inability to spell.

—Ian Hay

Better that a girl has beauty than brains, because boys see better than they think.

—Anonymous

An Englishman thinks seated; a Frenchman, standing; an American, pacing; an Irishman, afterward.

—Austin O'Malley

I'm not going to buy my kids an encyclopedia. Let them walk to school like I did.

—Yogi Berra

If I had more time, I would have written a shorter letter.

—MARCUS CICERO

CHAPTER FOURTEEN

Finding Inspiration

Education's purpose is to replace an empty mind with an open one.

—MALCOLM S. FORBES

A young branch takes on all the bends that one gives it.

—CHINESE PROVERB

No bubble is so iridescent or floats longer than that blown by the successful teacher.

—SIR WILLIAM OSLER

There are three things to remember when teaching: know your stuff; know whom you are stuffing; and then stuff them elegantly.

—LOLA MAY

It's not what is poured into a student that counts, but what is planted.

—LINDA CONWAY

Education is not the filling of a bucket, but the lighting of a fire.

—W. B. YEATS

School is where you go between when your parents can't take you and industry can't take you.

—JOHN UPDIKE

A mind is a fire to be kindled, not a vessel to be filled.

—PLUTARCH

Teaching is leaving a vestige of one self in the development of another. And surely the student is a bank where you can deposit your most precious treasures.

—EUGENE P. BERTIN

Education is not merely a means for earning a living or an instrument for the acquisition of wealth. It is an initiation into life of spirit, a training of the human soul in the pursuit of truth and the practice of virtue.

—VIJAYA LAKSHMI PANDIT

In large states public education will always be mediocre, for the same reason that in large kitchens the cooking is usually bad.

—FRIEDRICH NIETZSCHE

Anyone can steer the ship when the sea is calm.

—PUBLILIUS SYRUS

Education is a companion which no future can depress, no crime can destroy, no enemy can alienate it and no nepotism can enslave.

—Ropo Oguntimehin

It is among the commonplaces of education that we often first cut off the living root and then try to replace its natural functions by artificial means. Thus we suppress the child's curiosity and then when he lacks a natural interest in learning he is offered special coaching for his scholastic difficulties.

—Alice Duer Miller

Good schools, like good societies and good families, celebrate and cherish diversity.

—Deborah Meier, considered a founder of the modern small schools movement

Thought flows in terms of stories—stories about events, stories about people, and stories about intentions and achievements. The best teachers are the best storytellers. We learn in the form of stories.

—FRANK SMITH

The wise adapt themselves to circumstances, as water molds itself to the pitcher.

—CHINESE PROVERB

He who wrestles with us strengthens our nerves and sharpens our skills.

—EDWARD BURKE

The shell must be cracked apart if what is in it is to come out, for if you want the kernel you must break the shell.

—JOHANNES ECKHART

The key to everything is patience. You get the chicken by hatching the egg—not by smashing it.

—ELLEN GLASGOW

You cannot shake hands with a clenched fist.

—INDIRA GANDHI

An idea can turn to dust or magic, depending on the talent that rubs against it.

—BILL BERNBACH

Grade school is the snooze button on the clock radio of life.

—JOHN ROGERS

The roots of education are bitter, but the fruit is sweet.

—ARISTOTLE

The ink of the scholar is more sacred than the blood of the martyr.

—MUHAMMAD

All the world is a laboratory to the inquiring mind.

—MARTIN H. FISCHER

Sit down before fact as a little child, be prepared to give up every conceived notion, follow humbly wherever and whatever abysses nature leads, or you will learn nothing.

—THOMAS HUXLEY

The larger the island of knowledge, the longer the shoreline of wonder.

—Ralph M. Sockman

Give me a fruitful error any time, full of seeds, bursting with its own corrections. You can keep your sterile truth for yourself.

—Vilfredo Pareto

Good timber does not grow with ease; the stronger the wind, the stronger the trees.

—J. Willard Marriott

A handful of good life is better than a bushel of learning.

—George Herbert

Stupidity consists in wanting to reach conclusions. We are a thread, and we want to know the whole cloth.

—GUSTAVE FLAUBERT

We cannot live only for ourselves. A thousand fibers connect us with our fellow men; and among those fibers, as sympathetic threads, our actions run as causes, and they come back to us as effects.

—HERMAN MELVILLE

What makes the desert so beautiful is that somewhere it hides a well.

—ANTOINE DE SAINT-EXUPÉRY

One doesn't discover new lands without consenting to lose sight of the shore for a very long time.

—ANDRÉ GIDE

I could always drop people from a helicopter into Lake Pontchartrain and see how many drown. But what we do is start from the shore and teach them how to swim.

—J. W. CARMICHAEL, ON TEACHING COLLEGE PREPARATORY COURSES, AS QUOTED IN THE *NEW YORK TIMES* (MARCH 28, 1990)

An empty book is like an infant's soul, in which anything may be written. It is capable of all things, but containeth nothing.

—THOMAS TRAHERNE, FROM HIS BOOK *CENTURIES OF MEDITATIONS*

I consider a human soul without education like marble in a quarry, which shows none of its inherent beauties until the skill of the polisher sketches out the colors, makes the surface shine, and discovers every ornamental cloud, spot, and vein that runs through it.

—JOSEPH ADDISON

Education is a better safeguard of liberty than a standing army.

—EDWARD EVERETT, WHIG PARTY POLITICIAN

It is not the answer that enlightens, but the question.

—EUGENE IONESCO DECOUVERTES

He who opens a school door, closes a prison.

—VICTOR HUGO

If the teacher be corrupt, the world will be corrupt.

—PERSIAN PROVERB

What sculpture is to a block of marble, education is to the soul.

—JOSEPH ADDISON, AS QUOTED IN *SPECTATOR* (1711)

To define is to destroy, to suggest is to create.

—STÉPHANE MALLARMÉ

A scholar without practice is a tree without fruit.

—SA'DI, FROM HIS BOOK *THE GULISTAN, OR ROSE GARDEN* (1258)

Every child's life is like a piece of paper on which every person leaves a mark.

—CHINESE PROVERB

You don't have to be tall to see the moon.

—AFRICAN PROVERB

A man's mind may be likened to a garden, which may be intelligently cultivated or allowed to run wild; but whether cultivated or neglected, it must, and will bring forth. If no useful seeds are put into it, then an abundance of useless weed-seeds will fall therein, and will continue to produce their kind.

—JAMES ALLEN

Skill and confidence are an unconquered army.

—GEORGE HERBERT

To climb steep hills requires a slow pace at first.

—WILLIAM SHAKESPEARE

Shallow brooks are noisy. Deep rivers flow in silent majesty.

—ANONYMOUS

⟫⬥⟪

The nail that sticks out is hammered down.

—JAPANESE PROVERB

⟫⬥⟪

Those who can't beat the ass beat the saddle.

—ROMAN PROVERB

⟫⬥⟪

Bad herdsmen ruin their flocks.

—HOMER

⟫⬥⟪

Challenge of the day: Find something good in everyone.

—Anonymous

Ⅸ

I have gathered a posie of other men's flowers and only the thread that bonds them is my own.

—Michel Montaigne

Ⅸ

Even the clearest water appears opaque at great depth.

—Anonymous

Ⅸ

The fragrance always stays in the hand that gives the rose.

—Hada Bejar

Ⅸ

Keep on sowing your seed, for you never know which will grow—perhaps it all will.

—ECCLESIASTES 11:6

Don't judge each day by the harvest you reap, but by the seeds you plant.

—ROBERT LOUIS STEVENSON

Talent builds itself in stillness, character in the stream of the world.

—JOHANN WOLFGANG VON GOETHE

Teaching your child a trade is better than giving him a thousand ounces of gold.

—CHINESE PROVERB

All growth is a leap in the dark.

—HENRY MILLER

———◆———

You must have an aim, a vision, a goal. For the man sailing through life with no destination or "port of call," every wind is the wrong wind.

—TRACY BRINKMANN

———◆———

You must not only aim right, but draw the bow with all your might.

—HENRY DAVID THOREAU

———◆———

As an irrigator guides water to his fields, as an archer aims an arrow, as a carpenter carves wood, the wise shape their lives.

—BUDDHA

———◆———

Iron rusts from disuse; stagnant water loses its purity and in cold weather becomes frozen; even so does inaction sap the vigor of the mind.

—LEONARDO DA VINCI

No great thing is created suddenly, any more than a bunch of grapes or a fig. If you tell me that you desire a fig, I answer you that there must be time. Let it first blossom, then bear fruit, then ripen.

—EPICTETUS

What the caterpillar calls the end, the rest of the world calls a butterfly.

—LAO-TZU

There is no need for temples; no need for complicated philosophy. Our own brain, our own heart is our temple; the philosophy is kindness.

—TENZIN GYATSO, THE FOURTEENTH DALAI LAMA

Men are born soft and supple; dead, they are stiff and hard. Plants are born tender and pliant; dead, they are brittle and dry. Thus whoever is stiff and inflexible is a disciple of death. Whoever is soft and yielding is a disciple of life. The hard and stiff will be broken. The soft and supple will prevail.

—LAO-TZU

Some men rob you with a six gun; others with a fountain pen.

—WOODY GUTHRIE

The price of your hat isn't the measure of your brain.

—AMERICAN PROVERB

A man should keep his little brain attic stocked with all the furniture that he is likely to use, and the rest he can put away in the lumber room of his library, where he can get it if he wants it.

—SIR ARTHUR CONAN DOYLE, FROM "THE FIVE ORANGE PIPS,"
THE ADVENTURES OF SHERLOCK HOLMES (1892)

A library may be very large; but if it is in disorder, it is not so useful as one that is small but well arranged. In the same way, a many may have a great mass of knowledge, but if he has not worked it up by thinking it over for himself, it has much less value than a far smaller amount which he has thoroughly pondered.

—ARTHUR SCHOPENHAUER, FROM "THE ART OF LITERATURE: ON
THINKING FOR ONE'S SELF," *ESSAYS OF ARTHUR SCHOPENHAUER* (1851)

If you plan for a year, plant a seed. If for ten years, plant a tree. If for a hundred years, teach the people. When you sow a seed once, you will reap a single harvest. When you teach the people, you will reap a hundred harvests.

—KUAN CHUNG

The potential of the average person is like a huge ocean unsailed, a new continent unexplored, a world of possibilities waiting to be released and channeled toward some great good.

—BRIAN TRACY

If you want to build a ship, don't drum up people together to collect wood and don't assign them tasks and work, but rather teach them to long for the sea.

—ANTOINE DE SAINT-EXUPÉRY

If the only tool you have is a hammer, you tend to see every problem as a nail.

—ABRAHAM MASLOW

By viewing the old we learn the new.

—CHINESE PROVERB

He ketched a frog one day and took him home and said he cal'lated to education him; and so he never done nothing for three months but set in his back yard and learn that frog to jump. . . . He'd give him a little punch behind, and the next minute you'd see that frog whirling in the air like a doughnut. . . . Smiley said all a frog wanted was education, and he could do most anything—and I believe him.

> —MARK TWAIN, FROM HIS BOOK *THE NOTORIOUS JUMPING FROG OF CALAVERAS COUNTY* (1875)

You can't pick cherries with your back to the tree.

> —J. P. MORGAN

No bird soars too high,
If he soars with his own wings.

> —WILLIAM BLAKE

Simply being different isn't wrong. Don't try to be a duckling if you're born to be a swan.

—ANONYMOUS

The great pilot can sail even when his canvas is rent.

—LUCIUS A. SENECA

Whatever you are, be a good one.

—ABRAHAM LINCOLN

THOSE QUOTED

A

Aames, Willie
Abel, Lenni
Abercrombie, Lascelles
Abraham, Jay
Adams, Abigail
Adams, Douglas
Adams, Franklin P.
Adams, Henry
Adams, James Truslow
Adams, John
Adams, Marilyn Jager
Addams, Jane
Addison, Joseph
Adelman, Kenneth
Adler, Mortimer J.
Aeschylus
Aesop
Albers, Josef
Albom, Mitch
Alcott, Amos Bronson
Alda, Alan
Aldrich, Thomas Bailey
Alexander, Lloyd
Alexander, Mary Ann
Aldiss, Brian
Ali, Muhammad
Allen, Gracie
Allen, James
Allen, Robert G.
Allen, Woody
Allin, William
Ambrose, Stephen
Amernick, Melissa
Amiel, Henri-Frédéric
Amis, Kingsley
Ammons, A. R.
Anderson, Eric
Anderson, Sherwood
Anderson, Todd
Andrea, Christopher
Angelou, Maya
Anisthenes
Annesley, Arthur

Anouilh, Jean
Anthony, Susan B.
Antisthenes
Antrim, Minna
Aps, Jerold W.
Arbuthnot, John
Archambault, Reginald D.
Archimedes
Arendt, Hannah
Aretino, Pietro
Argento, Dario
Aristotle
Armstrong, Louis
Ascham, Roger
Ashe, Arthur
Ashton-Warner, Sylvia
Asimov, Isaac
Astor, Nancy
Asquith, Herbert
Ataturk, Mustafa Kemal
Auden, W. H.
Aughey, James H.
Aurelius, Marcus
Austen, Jane
Avila, Carol
Ayres, William
Azevedo, Sasha

B

Bacall, Aaron
Bach, Richard
Bacon, Francis
Bacon, Roger
Back, Sudie
Baer, Allison L.
Bagehot, Walter
Bagley, Desmond
Bagley, William C.
Bailey, Thomas
Bainbridge, Beryl
Baker, Howard
Baker, Newton D.
Baker, Russell
Bakst, Leon

Baldwin, James
Balfour, Arthur
Ballard, M. Russell
Ballou, Hosea
Banfield, Edward C.
Bangs, Lester
Bankhead, Tallulah
Banks-Lee, Camille
Barbauld, Anna Laetitia
Barber, Benjamin
Barnes, Henry
Barnes, James
Barnes, Julian
Barrie, J. M.
Barron, Frank
Barry, Dave
Barrymore, Ethel
Baruch, Bernard
Barzun, Jacques
Batten, Joe
Basho, Matsuo
Bayer, Ernest
Beard, Charles A.
Beattie, Bill
Beattie, James
Beatty, Cameron
Becker, Carl Lotus
Bedford, Clay P.
Beecher, Henry Ward
Beerbohm, Max
Bejar, Hada
Belcher, Gerald
Bellow, Saul
Benedict, Francis C.
Benevento, Mike
Bennett, Alan
Bennett, Dan
Bennis, Warren G.
Bennett, William J.
Benson, A. C.
Bergson, Henri
Berlioz, Louis Hector
Berman, Louis A.
Bernbach, Bill
Bernard, Claude

Clarke, John
Cleaver, Eldridge
Clemenceau, Georges
Clinton, Bill
Clyde, R. D.
Cochrane, Peter
Cocteau, Jean
Codell, Esmé Raji
Coelho, Paulo
Cohen, David
Cohen, Marshall
Cole, Joanna
Coleridge, Samuel Taylor
Colette
Collie, G. Norman
Collier, Robert
Collins, Marva
Colorose, Barbara
Colton, Charles Caleb
Combs, Arthur
Coménius, Jan Amos
Commager, Henry Steele
Conant, James B.
Condorcet
Confucius
Conger, Lesley
Connors, Jimmy
Conroy, Pat
Conway, Linda
Conwell, Russell H.
Cooley, Charles Horton
Coolidge, Calvin
Cooney, Joan Ganz
Cooper, Anderson
Cooper, Vernon
Corneille, Pierre
Counts, George S.
Cousins, Norman
Covey, Stephen
Coward, Noël
Cox, Marcelene
Craig, Cal
Crates of Thebes
Creighton, Bishop Mandell
Crisp, Quentin
Cross, K. Patricia
Csikszentmihalyi, Mihaly
Cuban, Larry
Cummings, R. D.
Cuppy, Will
Curie, Marie

Cutright, Melitta J.

D

D'Alembert
D'Angelo, Anthony J.
da Vinci, Leonardo
Dahl, Roald
Daloz, Laurent A.
Dana, John Cotton
Dana, Jr., Richard Henry
Danforth, William
Danto, Arthur C.
Darling-Hammond, Linda
Darrow, Clarence
Darwin, Charles
Davies, Frank
Davies, Robertson
Davis, Elmer
Davis, Kathy
Day, Clarence
de Beauvoir, Simone
de Bono, Edward
De Bury, Richard
de Chasseboeuf, Constantin Francois
de Coubertin, Pierre
de la Bruyère, Jean
de La Place, Pierre Simon
de Gaulle, Charles
de Gues, Arie
de Mello, Anthony
de Montaigne, Michel
de Morgan
de Saint-Exupéry, Antoine
de Tocqueville, Alexis
de Unamuno, Miguel
De Vere, Sir Aubrey
De Vries, Peter
De Zouche, Dorothy
Decouvertes, Eugene Ionesco
Dellenbach, Robert K.
Demergue
Deming, W. Edwards
Democritus
DeRoberts, Suzie
Descartes, René
Dewey, John
Dickens, Charles
Dickenson, Emily
Dickey, John Sloan

Dimnet, Ernest
Dionysius Cato
Disney, Walt
Disraeli, Benjamin
Ditka, Mike
Dixon, Keith
Dodson, Dan W.
Doherty, Henry L.
Doisneau, Robert
Doman, Glenn
Domino, Fats
Donne, John
Donnell, S.
Doren, Mark Van
Dostoevsky, Fyodor
Douglas, Norman
Douglass, Frederick
Doyle, Sir Arthur Conan
Drouillard, Ray
Drucker, Peter
Dryden, John
Du Bois, W. E. B.
Duc de la Rouchefoucauld, François
Dumas, Alexandre
Duncan, Isadora
Duncan, Raymond
Durant, Will
Durrell, Lawrence
Dürrenmatt, Friedrich
Dylan, Bob

E

Ealy, C. Diane
Eckhart, Johannes
Eco, Umberto
Edelman, Marian Wright
Edison, Thomas
Edman, Irwin
Edmundon, Mark
Edward, Henry
Edwards, Bob
Edwards, Otis C.
Edwards, Tyron
Ehrenburg, Ilya
Ehrhard, Joseph
Ehrlich, Thomas
Eichbaum, Wilhelm Lange
Einstein, Albert
Eisenberg, Leon
Eisenberg, Rebecca L.

Halberstam, David
Hale, E. E.
Haley, Gail
Haley, Sir William
Haliburton, Thomas Chandler
Halmos, Paul
Halsey, Margaret
Hamerton, Philip G.
Hamilton, Edith
Hamilton, Jane
Hamilton, Robert M.
Hammerstein II, Oscar
Hampton, Judy
Hand, Learned
Hanks, Tom
Hannah, John A.
Hansen, Mark Victor
Hardwick, Elizabeth
Hardy, G. H.
Hardy, Thomas
Hargraves, Andy
Harper, Frances Ellen Watkins
Harrington, Sir John
Harris, Sidney J.
Harris, Townsend
Hart, B. H. Liddell
Haskins, Henry S.
Haughton, Rosemary
Hawking, Stephen
Hawthorne, Nathaniel
Hay, Ian
Hay, LeRoy E.
Hayes, Helen
Hayes, John R.
Hazlitt, William
Hegel, Georg
Hein, Piet
Heine, Heinrich
Heinlein, Robert
Helmers, Dane
Helps, Arthur
Helvetius, Claude Adrien
Hemingway, Ernest
Hena, Ibrahim
Hendrix, Jimi
Heraclitus
Herbert, Bob
Herbert, George
Herbert, Sir Alan
Herold, Don
Herrigel, Eugen

Hershey, Lenore
Hershey, Lewis B.
Herstein, I. N.
Herzog, Werner
Heschel, Abraham Joshua
Hesse, Hermann
Hibben, Dr. John G.
Hifler, Jane Sequichie
Highet, Gilbert
Hildebrand, Joel H.
Hill, Napoleon
Hitchcock, Alfred
Hitchcock, R. D.
Hoban, Russell
Hodge, A. A.
Hoffer, Eric
Hofstadter, Richard
Hogerson, Jeremy
Holder, Geoffrey
Holland, Josiah Gilbert
Holmes, J. A.
Holt, John
Holt, Henry
Holtby, Winifred
Holtz, Lou
Holzer, Madeline Fuchs
Homer
Hood, Paxton
Hooker, Michael K.
"hooks, bell"
Hoover, Herbert
Hope, Anthony
Hopkins, Tom
Hopper, Grace Murray
Horace
Horner, Martina
Horton, Miles
Houseman, A. E.
Houston, Sam
Howard, Alan
Howe, Edgar Watson
Howe II, Howard
Howell, James
Howells, William Dean
Huang-Po
Hubbard, Elbert
Hubbard, Kin
Hufstedler, Shirley
Hughes, Richard
Hugo, Victor
Hulbert, Harold S.

Huneker, James Gibbons
Hunter, Madeline
Hutchins, Robert
Huxley, Aldous
Huxley, Thomas

I

Iacocca, Lee
Illich, Ivan
Ingersoll, Robert Green
Inman, Reverend E.
Irving, John
Irving, Washington
Irwin, Steve
Ivins, Molly

J

Jackson, Andrew
Jackson, Holbrook
Jackson, Michael
Jackson, Wendy
Jacobi, Carl
James, Anna
James, William
Jefferson, Thomas
Jervis, Robert
Johannot, Louis
Johnson, Claudia Alta Taylor
"Lady Bird"
Johnson, David
Johnson, Earvin "Magic"
Johnson, John H.
Johnson, Lyndon B.
Johnson, Kenneth G.
Johnson, Samuel
Jones, Charles T.
Jones, Franklin P.
Jones, James Earl
Jonson, Ben
Jordan, Barbara
Jordan, David Starr
Joubert, Joseph
Jovanovich, William
Jowett, Benjamin
Joyce, Bruce
Joyce, James
Jung, Carl
Juster, Norman
Juvenal

MacMillan, Harold
Macaulay, Thomas B.
Macomber, Melissa
Macomber sisters
Madden, John
Madison, James
Madwed, Sidney
Maeterlinck, Maurice
Maher, Bill
Mai, Delissa L.
Malcolm X
Mallarmé, Stéphane
Malloy, Terry
Malone, Dudley Field
Mandela, Nelson
Mankiewicz, Frank
Mann, Horace
Mann, Thomas
Manske, Fred A.
Marissa, Agustin
Markham, Reed
Marquis, Don
Marquis of Halifax
Marriott, J. Willard
Marshall, Peter
Marshall, Sybil
Marshall, Thurgood
Martin, Everett Dean
Martin, Judith
Martineau, Harriet
Marx, Groucho
Maslow, Abraham
Massinger, Philip
Masterman, J. C.
Mathesis, Adrian
Matsushita, Konosuke
Matthew 15:14
Maugham, W. Somerset
Maurois, André
Max, D. T.
May, Lola
Mayor, Federico
Mays, Benjamin
McAdoo, William G.
McAuliffe, Christa
McCarty, Meladee
McColl Jr., Hugh
McCord, David
McEdelman, John
McGinnis, A.L.
McGranaghan, Mark
McGraw, Dr. Phil

McGuire, Al
McKay, David O.
McKenziem, E.C.
McLaughlin, Mignon
McLuhan, Marshall
McTamaney, Catherine
McWade, Meredith
McWilliams, Candia
McWilliams, Peter
Mead, Margaret
Mears, Henrietta
Medick, Jean
Meerloo, Joost A. M.
Meier, Deborah
Melby, Ernest
Melville, Herman
Mencken, H. L.
Menninger, Karl A.
Mercier, Louis
Merton, Paul
Michel, John
Michelangelo
Michener, James A.
Mill, John Stuart
Miller, Alice Duer
Miller, Henry
Millikan, Robert A.
Millman, Dan
Milne, A. A.
Milton, John
Mingus, Charles
Minsky, Marvin
Mistral, Gabriela
Mitchell, Maria
Mittenthal, Sue
Mizner, Wilson
Moats, Louisa
Molière
Montague, Ashley
Montaigne
Montapert, Alfred A.
Montesquieu
Montessori, Maria
Moore, Eliakim H.
Moore, Gordon
Moore, Thomas
Moravia, Alberto
Morgan, Arthur E.
Morgan, Barbara
Morgan, Brian
Morgan, Charles
Morgan, J. P.

Morley, Christopher
Morley, John
Morley, Robert
Morris, James W.
Morrison, Toni
Moser, Sir Claude
Moskowitz, Faye
Mother Teresa
Muhammad
Muhammad-Earl, Dr. Kimberly
Muir, John
Mumford, Lewis
Munro, H. H. (Saki)
Murphy, Patricia
Murrow, Edward R.
Myers, Joyce A.

N

Nabokov, Vladimir
Nader, Ralph
Nagel, Greta K.
Naipaul, V. S.
Namath, Joe
Nance, W. A.
Natanson, Maurice
Neal, Patricia
Neil, Humphrey B.
Neill, Rolfe
Neblette, C. B.
Nelson, Bob
Nelson, Jane
Nero, Howard
Neufeld, Barbara
Newman, John Henry Cardinal
Newman, Judith
Newman, Lewis I.
Newton, Isaac
Niemann, Scott D.
Niemeyer, John
Nietzsche, Friedrich
Nin, Anaïs
Noddings, Nel
Nolte, Dorothy Law
Norris, Kathleen
Northcote, James
Nyquist, Ewald B.

O

O'Connor, Flannery
O'Malley, Austin

S

Sa'Di
Sabato, Debbie
Safian, Louis A.
Sagan, Carl
Salinger, J. D.
Sampson, George
Samuel, Viscount Herbert
Sandwell, Barnard Keble
Sangster, Margaret E.
Santayana, George
Sapirstein, Milton
Saroyan, William
Satir, Virginia
Savile, George
Sayre, Wallace
Schelling, Felix E.
Schlesinger, Jr., Arthur
Schmidt-Nielsen, Knut
Schopenhauer, Arthur
Schostak, Rabbi Zev
Schulz, Charles
Schulz, Jim
Schumacher, E. F.
Schwab, Charles
Schweitzer, Albert
Schwint, Angela
Scorsese, Martin
Scott, Dana Stewart
Scott, Sir Walter
Sculley, John
Seeger, Pete
Selfridge. H. Gordon
Seneca, Lucius A.
Senge, Peter
Sergiovanni, Thomas J.
Serling, Rod
Shakespeare, William
Shalaway, Linda
Shanker, Albert
Shapiro, Svi
Shaw, George Bernard
Sheehan, Jaqui
Sheetz
Sheehy, Gail
Shelley, Mary
Shing, Li Ka
Shonkoff, Dr. Jack
Shostrom, Everett
Shula, Don
Sickert, Walter

Silverstein, Shel
Singer, Isaac Bashevis
Simmel, Georg
Simonides
Simpson, Alan
Singer, Ira
Sister Evangelist
Sizer, Theodore R.
Smith, Adam
Skinner, B. F.
Smith, Betty
Smith, Elinor Goulding
Smith, Frank
Smith, Logan Pearsall
Smith, Preserved
Smith, Sydney
Smith, W. B.
Smith, William Cooper
Smoller, Jordan W.
Smollett, Tobias
Snow, Dan
Sobol, Thomas
Sockman, Ralph M.
Socrates
Soichiro, Honda
Solís, Alicia
Solon
Sophocles
Southey, Robert
Southey, Robert
Spady, William G.
Spencer, Herbert
Spock, Benjamin
St. Ambrose
St. Augustine
St. John, George
St. Paul
St. Thomas Aquinas
Stack, Jack
Stafford, William
Stalin, Joseph
Standing, E. M.
Steadman, Edward C.
Steele, Sir Richard
Stein, Gertrude
Steinbeck, John
Steiner, Rudolf
Stellar, W. C.
Stendhal
Stephen, Leslie
Sterne, Laurence
Stevenson, Adlai E.

Stevenson, Robert Louis
Stockdale, James B.
Steoessinger, John G.
Stone, Joseph
Stone, W. Clement
Stoppard, Tom
Stovall, Jim
Stravinsky, Igor
Streightiff, Walt
Strujar, Margaret
Style, Lylee
Sufi Saint Kubir
Sugarman, Sidney
Sullivan, Anne
Sweetland, Ben
Swift, Jonathan
Swindoll, Charles
Swope, Herbert Bayard
Sydney Mith of Macaulay
Syrus, Publilius
Szasz, Thomas
Szent-Györgyi

T

Tabor, Mary B. W.
Tacitus
Tagore, Rabindranath
Taine, Hippolyte Adolphe
Talbert, Bob
Tauscher, Stacia
Taylor, Elizabeth
Taylor, Harold
Temple, William
Templeton, John
Tennyson, Alfred Lord
Terence
Theisman, Joe
Thomas, Dylan
Thomas, Lewis
Thomas, Lowell
Thompson, Dorothy
Thomson, James
Thoreau, Henry David
Thucydies
Thurber, James
Ting-Fang, Wu
Tiong, Ho Boon
Toffler, Alvin
Tolkien, J. R. R.
Tolstoy, Leo
Tomlin, Lily

Toomer, Jean
Toynbee, Arnold J.
Tracy, Brian
Traherne, Thomas
Traub, James
Treisman, Uri
Trench, R.C.
Trevelyan, G.M.
Trilling, Lionel
Trollope, Anthony
Troy, Frosty
Truman, Harry S.
Trump, Donald
Trump, J. Lloyd
Tse-Tung, Mao
Tsvetaeva, Marina
Tuchman, Barbara
Tupper, Martin
Twain, Mark
Tyger, Frank
Tzu, Sun

U

Upanishads
Updike, John
Usiskin, Zalman
Ustinov, Peter

V

Valvano, Jim
van Beethoven, Ludwig
Van Buren, Abigail "Dear Abby"
Van Doren, Mark
Van Dyke, Henry
van Gogh, Vincent
Vanderbilt, Cornelius
Vaughan, Bill
Vauvenargues, Marquis de
Venkatachalm, V.
Verdi, R.
Vespasianus, Titus
Victor, Jodie
Vidal, Gore
Viguers, Ruth Hill
Viorst, Judith
Virgil
Vivekananda, Swami
Volkart, Edmund H.
Voltaire

Von Goethe, Johann Wolfgang
von Hardenberg, Friedrich
Vonnegut, Kurt

W

Wagner, Victoria
Waitley, Denis
Walker, Lou Ann
Wallace, Lew
Walters, Barbara
Walton, Izaak
Walton, Sam
Ward, William Arthur
Warhol, Andy
Warner, Charles Dudley
Warren, Earl
Warren, John
Warren, Rick
Washburn, Lemuel K.
Washington, Booker T.
Washington, George
Watson, Sr., Thomas
Waugh, Evelyn
Waxman, Isabel
Wayne, John
Weatherford, Carl Warner
Weaver, Earl
Weber, Max
Webster, Daniel
Weierstrass, Karl
Weil, Simone
Wells, H. G.
Welles, Orson
Welty, Eudora
Welsh, Joan
Wendell Holmes, Oliver
Wenn, Jonathan
Wesley, John
West, Jessamyn
West, Nathanael
West, Walt
Wharton, Edith
Whipple, Edwin Perry
Whistler, James McNeil
White, E. B.
White, T. H.
White, W. J.
Whitehead, Alfred North
Whitman, Walt
Whitmore, Frank

Whyte, Lancelot Law
Wiesel, Elie
Wiggan, A. E.
Wilbur, Ray L.
Wilcox, Colleen
Wilde, Larry
Wilde, Oscar
Wilde, Stuart
Willard, Frances
Wilson, Eugene S.
Wilson, Sloan
Wilson, Tom
Wilson, Woodrow
Winchell, Walter
Winder, Barbara W.
Winfrey, Oprah
Winston, Alan Scott
Witherspoon, Reese
Wittgenstein, Ludwig
Wolfe, Thomas
Wollstonecraft, Mary
Wonder, Stevie
Wong, Harry
Wood, David
Wood, Sydney
Wooden, John
Woolf, Virginia
Wordsworth, William
Wright, Frank Lloyd
Wright, Steven
Wylie, Philip

Y

Yates, Richard
Yeatman, R. J.
Yeats, W. B.
Yeats-Brown, Francis
Yohe, Tom
Young, Brigham
Young, Neil
Yutang, Lin

Z

Zappa, Frank
Zeidner, M. A.
Ziglar, Zig
Zola, Émile